PUBLIC–PRIVATE PARTNERSHIP MONITOR
KAZAKHSTAN

DECEMBER 2022

ASIAN DEVELOPMENT BANK

ADB

Notes:
In this publication, $ refers to United States dollars and "T" refers to tenge.
ADB recognizes "China" as the People's Republic of China and "Korea" as the Republic of Korea.

On the cover: Vehicles crossing the Ishim River in Astana, elementary students from the Nazarbayev Intellectual School of Astana, Kazakh Eli Complex in Astana, windmills along the Almaty–Bishkek road, and a young girl playing near Almaty bridge (photos by Ariel Javellana and Andrey Tekekhov).
Cover design by Claudette Rodrigo.

Contents

Tables, Figures, and Box

Tables

Figures

Box

Foreword

Continuing our reports examining public–private partnership (PPP) environments in selected countries across Asia and the Pacific, we are pleased to present this *Public–Private Partnership Monitor—Kazakhstan*.

Availability of adequate infrastructure is a measure of a country's ability to sustain its economic growth. For economies across Asia and the Pacific, provision of basic infrastructure services, including water, sanitation, solid waste management, housing, health, energy, transportation, and communications, is an important public sector activity. As demand for infrastructure has increased faster than government budgets, the public sector has increasingly considered partnership with the private sector as an alternate modality for financing infrastructure.

The Asian Development Bank (ADB) estimates that Asia and the Pacific must spend $1.7 trillion a year on infrastructure until 2030 to maintain growth, meet social needs, and respond to the effects of climate change. That amount is expected to go up. The traditional sources of finance for infrastructure—the government's budgetary allocations—have not been enough to meet the demand. Prior to the coronavirus disease (COVID-19) pandemic, ADB estimated an annual infrastructure gap of $204 billion to be filled through private sector investment. That amount is also now expected to increase.

For the private sector, investment in infrastructure, whether through PPPs or otherwise, represents an investment avenue competing with various other investment options available. To compete and attract private capital into infrastructure, governments must provide conducive environments that establish and protect private investors' rights, with sufficient support to ensure every asset invested yields returns commensurate with risks.

The PPP Monitor provides the investor community with business intelligence on the enabling environment, policies, priority sectors, and deals to facilitate informed investment decisions. For ADB's developing member countries (DMCs), the PPP Monitor serves as a diagnostic tool to identify gaps in their legal, regulatory, and institutional frameworks. ADB and other international development agencies can also benefit from the PPP Monitor as it could be useful in initiating dialogues to assess a country's readiness to tap PPPs as a means to develop and sustain its infrastructure.

Building on the success of the previous editions of the PPP Monitor, the new PPP Monitor is now being brought online to widen its reach. More countries will be continually added in the PPP Monitor, and it is expected to become a primary knowledge base for assessing a country's PPP environment for the government and the business community. The PPP Monitor features an interactive online version which allows users to compare and contrast the key PPP parameters and features across the DMCs. The online version of the PPP Monitor may be accessed at http://www.pppmonitor.adb.org.

The PPP Monitor has been upgraded to provide a "one-stop" source of information, derived from a consolidation of (i) the previous PPP Monitor, (ii) leading PPP databases of multilateral development banks such as the World Bank and the International Finance Corporation, and organizations including the Economist Intelligence Unit and the Global Infrastructure Hub, (iii) reports from a national PPP unit, (iv) a country's legal framework, and (v) consultations with leading technical experts, legal firms, and financial institutions.

The PPP Monitor includes more than 500 qualitative and quantitative indicators to profile the national PPP environment, the sector-specific PPP landscape (for eight identified infrastructure sectors), and the PPP landscape for local government projects. The COVID-19 pandemic has pushed social infrastructure to the forefront of policy and planning; so wherever possible, this PPP Monitor takes a closer focus on social and municipal aspects such as healthcare, education, and affordable housing.

The PPP markets in most of ADB's DMCs are still at an emerging or developing stage, so continuous regulatory reforms and institutional reinforcements are required to facilitate private sector investment in infrastructure, and create sustainable bankable projects. Through the PPP Monitor, ADB continues to provide support for DMCs in addressing various infrastructure and PPP-related challenges, in developing sustainable infrastructure projects, and in delivering efficient and effective public services through PPPs. ADB also helps DMCs improve their investment climates, formulate sound market regulations, and build robust legal and institutional frameworks to encourage private sector participation in infrastructure through PPPs.

We hope that this PPP Monitor will pave the way for continued dialogue between the public and private sectors and stimulate the adoption of PPPs in the Asia and Pacific region.

F. Cleo Kawawaki
Head, Office of Public–Private Partnerships
Asian Development Bank

Acknowledgments

The Public–Private Partnership Monitor: Country Profile—Kazakhstan was prepared by the Asian Development Bank (ADB) Office of Public–Private Partnership (OPPP), in close coordination with the Kazakhstan Resident Mission.

This effort has been led by a team of public–private partnership (PPP) specialists in the PPP Thematic Group Secretariat, who developed, refined, and streamlined the analytical framework for capturing the national, subnational, and sectoral PPP-related landscape that has been utilized in this document.

The PPP Monitor uses data published by the governments of ADB developing member countries—on their official websites and in reports, publications, laws, and regulations—as well as data published by other multilateral development agencies and included in industry publications and databases such as those of the World Bank, European Bank for Reconstruction and Development, Organisation for Economic Co-operation and Development, World Economic Forum, International Monetary Fund (IMF), Inframation Group, IJGlobal, Economist Intelligence Unit (Infrascope Index), Global Infrastructure Hub, TheGlobalEconomy.com, Bloomberg, S&P Global, Trading Economics, and PPP Legal Resource Center.

ADB has partnered with Unicase Law, which shared its deep expertise on the Kazakhstan PPP market and provided inputs in developing the PPP Monitor for Kazakhstan.

Definition of Terms

Term	Definition
Public–private partnership (PPP)	Contractual arrangement between public (national, state, provincial, or local) and private entities through which the skills, assets, and/or financial resources of each of the public and private sectors are allocated in a complementary manner, thereby sharing the risks and rewards, to seek to provide optimal service delivery and good value to citizens. In a PPP, the public sector retains the ultimate responsibility for service delivery, although the private sector provides the service for an extended time. Within Asian Development Bank operations, all contracts such as performance-based contracts (management and service contracts), lease–operate–transfer, build–own–operate–transfer, design–build–finance–operate, variants, and concessions are considered as various forms of PPP. Excluded are • contracts involving turnkey design and construction as part of public procurement (engineering, procurement, and construction contracts); • simple service contracts that are not linked to performance standards (those that are more aligned with outsourcing to private contractor staff to operate public assets); • construction contracts with extended warranties and/or maintenance provisions of, for example, up to 5 years post completion (wherein performance risk-sharing is minimal as the assets are new and need only basic maintenance); and • all privatization and divestures.
Availability- or performance-based payments	Method of investment recovery in PPP projects, when payments to the private party are made by the government contracting agency over the lifetime of a PPP contract in return for making infrastructure or services available for use at acceptable and contractually agreed performance standards.
Build–own–operate	A PPP type whereby a private sector developer is authorized to finance, construct, own, operate, and maintain an infrastructure or development facility from which the private sector developer is allowed to recover its total investment and operating and maintenance costs, plus a reasonable return thereon, by collecting tolls, fees, rentals, or other charges from facility users.
Build–operate–transfer	Build–operate–transfer (BOT) and similar arrangements are a specialized concession in which a private firm or consortium finances and develops a new infrastructure project or a major component according to performance standards set by the government. Under BOTs, the private sector developer provides the capital required to build a new facility. Importantly, the private operator now owns the assets for a period set by the contract—sufficient to give the developer time to recover investment costs through user charges.

continued on next page

continued from previous page

Term	Definition
Commercial close	Indicates the signing of the PPP contract between the government contract agency and the identified private sector developer. Usually occurs after the terms and conditions of the draft PPP contract are negotiated and agreed between the government contracting agency and the identified private sector developer.
Competitive bidding	A process under which the bidders submit information detailing their qualifications and detailed technical and financial proposals, which are evaluated according to defined criteria—often in a multi-stage process—to select a preferred bidder. Competitive bidding may also include competitive negotiations and license schemes.
Concession	A PPP type which makes the concessionaire (established by the selected private sector developer) responsible for the full delivery of services in a specified area, including operation, maintenance, collection, management, and construction and rehabilitation of the system. Importantly, the private sector developer is responsible for all capital investment. Although the concessionaire is responsible for providing the assets, such assets are publicly owned even during the concession period. The public sector is responsible for establishing performance standards and ensuring that the concessionaire meets them. In essence, the public sector's role shifts from being the service provider to regulating the price and quality of service.
Currency conversion swap fee	A premium which is paid by the borrower to settle on a swap in which the parties sell currencies to each other subject to an agreement to repurchase the same currency in the same amount, at the same exchange rate, and on a fixed date in the future.
Design–build–operate	Design–build–operate (DBO) is a long-term contractual performance-based arrangement between an employer firm (usually the asset owner) and a contractor to design, build, operate, and maintain a facility; meet performance standards; carry out asset replacement over its life cycle, or most of it; and hand back the facility to the employer upon contract completion. DBO contracts are mostly used in water utilities.
Direct agreement	An agreement normally made between the concessionaire (established by the private sector developer), the government contracting agency, and the lenders. In Kazakhstan, direct agreements give the lenders step-in rights to propose replacement of the private partner. Direct agreements can be executed for PPP projects that meet certain criteria of "special importance."
Direct negotiations	A type of PPP procurement under which the PPP contract is awarded on the basis of a direct agreement with a private sector developer without going through the competitive bidding process.
Dispute resolution	A process to resolve any dispute between the government contracting agency and the private sector developer as agreed in the PPP contract. The possible dispute resolution mechanisms in a PPP contract could include resolution through • discussion between both parties, • dispute resolution board, • expert determination, • mediation or conciliation, or • arbitration.
Environmental impact assessment	A process of evaluating the likely environmental impacts of a proposed project or development, taking into account interrelated socioeconomic, cultural, and human health impacts, both beneficial and adverse.
Facilities management contract	A type of PPP contract where the private party operates, maintains, and repairs buildings and infrastructure. These contracts are common for the maintenance and operation of buildings such as hospitals, schools, prisons, sport complexes, convention centers, shopping malls, and hotels. In Kazakhstan, facilities management contracts are currently used for PPPs in healthcare.

continued on next page

continued from previous page

Term	Definition
Feed-in tariff (FIT)	A policy mechanism designed to accelerate investment in renewable energy technologies by offering long-term purchase agreements for the sale of renewable energy electricity.
Financial close	An event whereby (i) a legally binding commitment of equity holders and/or debt financiers exists to provide or mobilize funding for the full cost of the project, and (ii) the conditions for funding have been met and the first tranche of funding is mobilized. If this information is not available, construction start date is used as an estimated financial closure date.
Financial equilibrium	A mechanism in a PPP agreement for dealing with changes, when changes in specified conditions and circumstances trigger compensating changes to the terms of the agreement. Some civil law jurisdictions emphasize economic or financial equilibrium provisions that entitle a partner to changes in the key financial terms of the contract to compensate for certain types of exogenous events that may otherwise impact returns. The partner is protected as the economic balance of the contract must be maintained and adequate compensation paid for damages suffered. Unexpected changes that merit financial equilibrium may arise from force majeure (major disasters triggered by natural hazards or civil disturbances), government action, and unforeseen changes in economic conditions.
Force majeure	An event that is reasonably beyond the control of the affected party as a result of which such party's performance of its obligations under the PPP contract is prevented or rendered impossible. Force majeure events may include • war, civil war, armed conflict, or terrorism; • nuclear, chemical, or biological contamination unless the source or the cause of the contamination is the result of the actions of or breach by the concessionaire or its subcontractors; and • any other similar events that are beyond reasonable control of the affected party, and prevent or render impossible the performance by such party of its obligations under the PPP contract. In Kazakhstan, force majeure also dictates certain conditions for termination. For example, it limits payments to 100% of the total amount of all incurred and proven capital expenditures of the PPP project, minus payments that have already been paid by the public partner.
Government contracting agency	The ministry, department, or agency that enters into a PPP contract with the private sector and is responsible for ensuring that the relevant public assets or services are provided.
Government guarantee	Agreements under which the government agrees to bear some or all risks of a PPP project. It is a secondary obligation which legally binds the government to take on an obligation if a specified event occurs. A government guarantee constitutes a contingent liability, for which there is uncertainty as to whether the government may be required to make payments, and if so, how much and when it will be required to pay. In practice, government guarantees are used when debt providers are unwilling to lend to a private party in a PPP because of concerns over credit risk and potential loan losses. Government guarantees can also be used to benefit equity investors in a PPP company when they require protection against the investment risks they bear.

continued on next page

continued from previous page

Term	Definition
Government pay (Offtake)	Represents the payment made by the government contracting agency to the concessionaire (established by the private sector developer) for the infrastructure assets provided and services delivered through a PPP project. These payments could be • usage-based—for example, shadow tolls or output-based subsidies; or • based on availability—that is, conditional on the availability of an asset or service to the specified quality.
Gross-cost contract	A type of PPP contract arrangement in the railway sector under which all revenues (from fares and other sources) are transferred to the government contracting agency, and the risks absorbed by the developer are confined to those associated with the cost of operations.
Hybrid arrangement	A method of investment recovery in PPP projects when payments to the private party are made as a combination of user charges and availability payments over the lifetime of a PPP contract, in return for making infrastructure or services available for use at acceptable and contractually agreed performance standards.
Independent power producer (IPP) scheme	A scheme whereby a producer of electrical energy, which is not a public utility, makes electric energy available for sale to utilities or the general public. A scheme whereby a producer of electrical energy, which is a private entity, owns and/or operates facilities to generate electricity and then sells it to a utility, central government buyer, or end users. The IPP invests in generation technologies and recovers their cost from the sale of the electricity.
Institutional arbitration	An arbitration process in which a specialized institution intervenes and takes on the role of administering the arbitration process between the government contracting agency and the private sector developer for a PPP project-related dispute. This institution would have its own set of rules which would provide a framework for the arbitration, and its own form of administration to assist in the process.
Interest rate swap fee	A premium paid by the borrower for a hedging contract to convert a floating interest rate into a fixed rate. The two parties agree to exchange interest rate payments based on a notional principal amount, with typically one paying a fixed rate and the other generally paying a floating rate.
Joint venture	The infrastructure is co-owned and operated by the public sector and private operators. Under a joint venture, the public and private sector partners can either form a new company or assume joint ownership of an existing company through a sale of shares to one or several private investors. The company may also be listed on the stock exchange.
Lender's step-in rights	Lender's rights in project-financed arrangements to "step in" to the project company's position in the contract to take control of the infrastructure project where the project company is not performing.
Management contract	A PPP type which expands the services to be contracted out to include some or all of the management and operation of the public service (i.e., utility, hospital, port authority). Although the ultimate obligation for service provision remains in the public sector, daily management control and authority is assigned to the private partner or contractor. In most cases, the private partner provides working capital but no financing for investment.
Material adverse government action	An action by the government which directly and materially affects the private party of a PPP project in performing its obligations under the relevant PPP contract, and which would reasonably be expected to result in a material adverse effect.

continued on next page

continued from previous page

Term	Definition
National operator	A special legal status of "national operators" gives state-owned enterprises the right to become sole providers of services that the government deems important to protect from competition, and to receive direct support from the state budget. This status makes them more creditworthy from the financial point of view, thus enhancing the bankability of the projects they are part of.
Net-cost contract	A type of PPP contract arrangement in the railway sector under which all revenues (from fares and other sources) are retained by the developer, and traffic and revenue risks are absorbed either fully or as per a contractually agreed portion.
Nominal interest rate	The nominal interest rate is the interest rate applicable to a borrowing before taking inflation adjustment into account. In certain cases, nominal interest rate also refers to the advertised or stated interest rate on a borrowing, without taking into account any fees or compounding of interest. Nominal interest rate = Real interest rate + Inflation rate
Nonrecourse/ limited recourse project financing	The financing of the development or exploitation of a right, natural resource, or other assets where the bulk of the financing is to be provided by way of debt, and is to be repaid principally out of the assets being financed and their revenues.
Project bond financing	An alternative source of financing infrastructure project by placing bonds.
Project development	Indicates the stage of the PPP project life cycle including PPP project identification, selection, preparation, structuring, and procurement up to commercial close between the government contracting agency and the private sector developer.
Project development fund (PDF)	A fund dedicated to reimbursing the cost of feasibility studies, transaction advisers, and other costs of project development, to encourage contracting agencies to use high-quality transaction advisers and adopt best practices. PDFs provide the specialized resources needed to conduct studies, design and structure a PPP, and then procure the PPP.
Real interest rate	The real interest rate is the interest rate applicable to a borrowing that is adjusted to inflation. Real interest rate = Nominal interest rate – Inflation rate
PPP regulatory framework	A framework encompassing all laws, regulations, policies, binding guidelines or instructions, other legal texts of general application, judicial decisions, and administrative rulings governing or setting precedent in connection with PPPs. In this context, the term "policies" refers to other government-issued documents, which are binding on all stakeholders, are enforced in a manner similar to laws and regulations, and provide detailed instructions for the implementation of PPPs.
Regional PPP projects	Projects initiated and procured via regional authorities (*akimats*) are regarded as "regional," or "local." This distinction drives the procedural, contractual, and risk-related peculiarities in structuring, as described in Section 2 of this Monitor.
Rehabilitate–operate–transfer	A PPP type whereby an existing facility is handed over to the private sector developer to refurbish, operate, and maintain for a franchise period, at the expiry of which the legal title to the facility is turned over to the government contracting agency.
Republican PPP project	Projects initiated and procured via central government bodies (e.g., line ministries or national operators) are regarded as "republican," or "central." This distinction drives the procedural, contractual, and risk-related specifics in structuring, as described in Section 2 of this Monitor.

continued on next page

continued from previous page

Term	Definition
Risk allocation matrix	Matrix indicating the allocation of the consequences of each risk to one of the parties in the PPP contract, or agreeing to deal with the risk through a specified mechanism which may involve sharing the risk.
Service contract	A PPP type under which the government contracting agency hires a private company or entity to carry out one or more specified tasks or services for a period, typically up to 5 years. The government contracting agency remains the primary provider of the infrastructure service and contracts out only portions of its operation to the private partner. The private partner must perform the service at the agreed cost and must typically meet the performance standards set by the government contracting agency. Government contracting agencies generally use competitive bidding procedures to award service contracts, which tend to work well given the limited period and narrowly defined nature of these contracts.
Social impact assessment	Includes the processes of analyzing, monitoring, and managing the intended and unintended social consequences—both positive and negative—of planned interventions (policies, programs, plans, projects) and any social change processes invoked by those interventions. Its primary purpose is to bring about a more sustainable and equitable biophysical and human environment.
Social infrastructure	Covers social services, including hospitals, and other health facilities, schools and universities, prisons, housing, and courts.
State-owned enterprise (SOE)	A company or enterprise owned by the government or in which the government has a controlling stake. Some SOEs are regarded as quasi-state entities, a special legal status devised for some state-owned enterprises in Kazakhstan. A quasi-state status provides SOEs with exemptions from the state procurement rules and special recourse to the state budget in cases of financial distress, and creates a special corporate governance regime.
Swiss challenge	A process in public procurement when a government contracting agency that has received an unsolicited bid for a project publishes details of the bid and invites third parties to match or exceed it.
Tax holiday	A government incentive program that offers tax reduction or elimination to projects and/or businesses. In the context of a PPP project, tax holidays are provided to exempt the concessionaire from making any tax payments during the initial demand ramp up period to make the project financially viable.
Trust management contract	A type of contract which allows the private party to manage the public property or facility in the interests of the public party for a specified fee.
Unsolicited bid	A proposal made by a private party to undertake a PPP project. It is submitted at the initiative of the private party, rather than in response to a request from the government contracting agency.
User charges	A method of investment recovery in PPP projects when payments to the private party are fully derived from tariffs paid by users or offtakers over the lifetime of a PPP contract, in return for making infrastructure or services available for use at acceptable and contractually agreed performance standards.
Viability gap funding	A scheme wherein the projects with low financial viability are given grants (or other financial support from the government) up to a stipulated percentage of the project cost, making them financially viable as PPPs.

Abbreviations

ADB	–	Asian Development Bank
BAKAD	–	Big Almaty Ring Road PPP
COVID-19	–	coronavirus disease
CREM	–	Committee for Regulation of Natural Monopolies
EBRD	–	European Bank for Reconstruction and Development
EIA	–	environmental impact assessment
EIU	–	Economist Intelligence Unit
FSC	–	Financial Settlement Center of Renewable Energy LLP
GDP	–	gross domestic product
ICC	–	investment cost compensation
ICT	–	information and communication technology
IFC	–	International Finance Corporation
IMF	–	International Monetary Fund
JSC	–	joint stock company
KEGOC	–	Kazakhstan Electricity Grid Operating Company JSC
KOREM	–	Kazakhstan Electricity and Power Market Operator JSC
KTZ	–	Kazakhstan Temir Zholy JSC
LRT	–	light rail transit
MCI	–	monthly calculation index
MIID	–	Ministry of Industry and Infrastructure Development
MinEdu	–	Ministry of Education
MNE	–	Ministry of National Economy
MOE	–	Ministry of Energy
MOF	–	Ministry of Finance
MOH	–	Ministry of Healthcare
OCC	–	operational cost compensation

OECD	–	Organisation for Economic Co-operation and Development
PPA	–	power purchase agreement
PPI	–	Private Participation in Infrastructure
PPP	–	public–private partnership
PRC	–	People's Republic of China
RFP	–	request for proposal
RFQ	–	request for qualification
SOE	–	state-owned enterprise
VFM	–	value-for-money
VGF	–	viability gap funding

Currency Equivalents

(As of 1 September 2022)

Currency unit	–	tenge (T)
T1.00	=	$0.0021
$1.00	=	T469.6

Guide to Understanding the Public–Private Partnership Monitor

The *Public–Private Partnership Monitor* (PPP Monitor), a flagship publication of the Asian Development Bank (ADB), profiles PPP enabling environments in ADB's developing member countries (DMCs) across Asia and the Pacific. The PPP Monitor features, for the first time, a data-driven, interactive online version which allows users to compare and contrast the key PPP parameters and attributes across the featured DMCs. While the featured countries are a small sample, more countries will be continually added in the PPP Monitor, which is expected to become a knowledge base for assessing a country's PPP environment for the government and the business community. The new PPP Monitor builds on the success of the first and second editions of the PPP Monitor.

The PPP Monitor provides a snapshot of the overall PPP landscape in the country. This downloadable guide also assesses more than 500 qualitative and quantitative indicators that have been structured per topic—the national PPP landscape, the sector-specific PPP landscape (for eight identified infrastructure sectors and a separate section for other sectors), and the PPP landscape for local government projects. The PPP Monitor also captures the critical macroeconomic and infrastructure sector indicators (including the Ease of Doing Business scores) from globally accepted sources.

Each of the topics and associated subtopics presented below are characterized by qualitative and quantitative indicators. Qualitative indicators take the form of a question to which "Yes," "No," "Not Applicable," or "Unavailable" answers can be given. Quantitative indicators are represented in the form of numbers, ratios, investment value, and duration.

For each of the developing member countries covered, the information and data are organized along the following topic clusters:

Overview

Topic	Subtopics
Overview	• Overview of the PPP legal and regulatory framework • Number of PPP projects reaching financial close from 1990 till end of 2021 across sectors • Total investment made in PPPs from 1990 to 2021 across sectors • Features of past PPP projects including the number of PPPs procured through various modes • Number of PPP projects under preparation and procurement • Number of PPP projects supported by the government • Payment mechanism for PPPs • Foreign sponsor participation in PPPs from 1990 to 2021 • Challenges associated with the PPP landscape in the country

National Public–Private Partnership Landscape Indicators

To profile the national PPP landscape, the indicators are grouped into three major categories: national PPP enabling framework, government support for PPP projects, and maturity of the PPP market.

Topic	Subtopics
National PPP legal and regulatory framework	Details on the legal and regulatory framework applicable to PPPs and its evolution since the introduction of PPPs in the country Details on the other supporting laws and regulations governing PPPs in the country
PPP types	Details on the PPP types allowed to be used according to the PPP legal and regulatory framework. In case the PPP legal and regulatory framework doesn't specify the PPP types, this section provides the details on the specific PPP types which have been adopted for various PPP projects at various stages of the PPP life cycle
Eligible sectors	Details on various infrastructure sectors for which projects could be procured through the PPP route according to the PPP legal and regulatory framework
Public–private partnership institutional framework **Entities responsible for PPP project identification, approval, and oversight** **Entities responsible for PPP project monitoring**	Details on the PPP institutional framework including the availability of a PPP unit, the functions of the PPP unit, the principal public entities associated with PPPs and their respective functions, and the details of the public entities responsible for PPP project identification, appraisal, approval, oversight, and monitoring
The public–private partnership process	Details on the various stages of the PPP process including PPP project identification, preparation, structuring, procurement, and management according to the PPP legal and regulatory framework in the country
PPP standard operating procedures, tool kits, templates, and model bid documents	Details on the standard operating procedures, and standard templates or model bidding documents available for PPPs (if any) Details on the key clauses in a PPP agreement based on the review of select PPP agreements already executed, and/ or the review of the PPP legal and regulatory framework
Lender's security rights	Rights of lenders including the charge of project assets
Termination and compensation	Definition on whether the private player is eligible for compensation in case of PPP project termination due to various reasons
Unsolicited PPP proposals	Details on the possibility of submission of unsolicited PPP proposals, and their treatment, including potential advantages provided to the unsolicited PPP proposal proponent at the PPP procurement stage
Foreign investor participation restrictions	Definition on whether there are any statutory restrictions on foreign equity investments and ownership in PPP projects
Dispute resolution	Definition of the dispute resolution process and the mechanisms available in the country
Environmental and social issues	Details on whether the legal and regulatory framework governing PPPs stipulates a mechanism for managing the environmental and social impact of a PPP project, including the potential environmental and social issues which could be caused by a PPP project

continued on next page

continued from previous page

Topic	Subtopics
Land rights	Definition of the various mechanisms through which landownership and/or land use rights could be provided to the private partner in respect of the project site for a PPP project Details on land records and registration which could be provided to the private partner
Project development funding support	Details on the various sources through which funding could be availed for the development activities (preparation, structuring, and procurement) of a PPP project Details on stages of the PPP project development during which such funding could be availed and utilized, including payments to transaction advisors
Government financial support for PPP projects	Details on the various mechanisms of government financial support available to make PPP projects financially viable, including funding and revenue support Salient features of government financial support mechanisms available
PPP project statistics	Details on the key PPP statistics in the country such as the availability of (i) a PPP database showing distribution of PPP projects across sectors and across various stages of the PPP life cycle, and (ii) a national PPP project pipeline and its alignment with the National Infrastructure Plan for the country
Sources of PPP financing	Details on the sources of financing for PPP projects in the country Details on typical key financing terms for various sources of financing, banks active in project finance for the last 24 months, active PPP project sponsors in the country for the last 24 months, availability of derivatives market, and availability of credit rating agencies in the country

Sector-Specific Public–Private Partnership Landscape Indicators

To profile the sector-specific PPP landscape, the indicators are grouped into five major categories: (i) sector-specific PPP contracting agencies, (ii) sector laws and regulations, (iii) sector master plan (including sector-specific PPP pipeline), (iv) features of the past PPP projects in the sector, and (v) sector-specific challenges for PPPs. Sectors that do not appear consistently across the featured countries are covered under the "Other Sectors" category in the sector-specific PPP landscape.

Topic	Subtopics
Contracting agencies in the sector	Details on which government agencies could act as the contracting agencies for a PPP project
Sector laws and regulations	Details on the applicable sector laws and regulations for PPP projects, including the sector regulators and their respective functions.
Foreign investment restrictions in the sector	Details on the maximum allowed foreign equity investment in greenfield PPP projects in the sector
Standard contracts in the sector	Specification on whether standard contracts are available for PPP projects in the sector

continued on next page

continued from previous page

Topic	Subtopics
Sector master plan	Details on the master plan and/or road map adopted for infrastructure development in the sector by the national government and the corresponding line ministry Details on the pipeline of PPP projects for the sector aligned with this sector master plan and/or road map Details on the PPP projects under preparation and procurement in the sector
Features of past PPP projects	Features of the past PPP projects based on supporting indicators in terms of the number and value (where applicable) of PPP projects for each supporting indicator
Tariffs applicable to the sector	Details on the indicative tariffs applicable in the sector based on the examples of select PPP or other projects operational in the sector
Typical risk allocation for PPP projects in the sector	Details on the typical risk allocation between the government contracting agency and the private partner based on the examples of select PPP projects which have achieved commercial close
Financing details for PPP projects in the sector	Typical financing details based on past PPP projects on the lines of the supporting indicators
Challenges associated with PPPs in the sector	Details on the PPP-related and sector-specific challenges faced by PPP projects in the sector
Typical sector-specific infrastructure indicators for the country	Details on select sector-specific infrastructure indicators for the country

Local Government Public–Private Partnership Landscape

To profile the PPP landscape for local government projects, the indicators are grouped into seven major categories: (i) local governance system, (ii) infrastructure development plans for local governments, (iii) sectors in which local governments can implement PPPs, (iv) revenue sources for local governments, (v) borrowings by local governments, (vi) budgetary allocation to local governments, and (vii) credit rating of local governments.

Topic	Subtopics
Key indicators related to local governments in the country	Details on the local governments using select key indicators on (i) the number and levels of local governments, (ii) the typical expenditure profile and heads, (iii) the typical revenue profile and heads, (iv) the typical debt profile and heads, and (v) grants and transfers from the higher levels of government
Local governance system	Details on the local governance system in the country, including the various levels of local governments; their roles, responsibilities, and functions; and the devolution of powers from the higher levels of government to the various levels of local governments
Infrastructure development plan for local governments	Details on the infrastructure development plans prepared by the local governments based on their capital investment projects in the pipeline, and the coverage of such infrastructure development plans
PPP enabling framework for local governments	Details on the PPP enabling framework applicable to local government PPP projects, including PPP legal and regulatory framework, PPP policy framework, and PPP institutional framework

continued on next page

continued from previous page

Topic	Subtopics
Eligible sectors for PPPs for local governments	Details on the eligible sectors in which PPPs could be undertaken by the local government as government contracting agency
Revenues for local governments	Details on the typical sources of revenue for local governments
Borrowings by local governments	Details on the typical sources of debt financing available for local governments, the purpose for which borrowed funds could be used, the terms of such borrowings, and the borrowing exposure of select local governments
Budgetary allocation to local governments	Details on the budgetary allocations and transfers to the local governments from the higher levels of government
Credit rating of local governments	Details on the precedence of local governments being rated by credit rating agencies in the country, and the details of credit ratings obtained by select local governments in the past

Time Periods

The research was carried out in 2022 with the aim of reflecting the status as of the end of 2021. Therefore, some indicator data may have changed between the said period and the publication date of this report.

In country-level and sector-level sections, quantitative data in relation to the number of projects reflect the cumulative number of projects over the periods 1990–2019, 1990–2020, and 1990–2021. Otherwise, the data represent the status in each individual year.

I. Overview

Kazakhstan is the largest landlocked country in the world with one of the lowest population densities. It is strategically located in the middle of the Eurasian continent at the crossroads between the People's Republic of China (PRC) and Western Europe, connected by road, rail, and a port on the Caspian Sea. Kazakhstan is a middle-income developing country with high economic dependence on energy resources. The country possesses the ninth largest oil reserves in the world, which constituted 21% of its gross domestic product (GDP) in 2020 and about 73% of its exports in 2022.[1] As a result of the coronavirus disease (COVID-19) pandemic, the country's GDP fell for the first time in 2 decades, down by 2.5% in 2020. It bounced back by 4.3% in 2021 and is estimated, according to the Asian Development Bank (ADB), to register a GDP growth of around 3.0% in 2022 as a result of improved domestic activity, recovery of the global oil demand, continued fiscal support measures, and a successful vaccination program tackling the COVID-19 pandemic.[2]

In February 2021, Kazakhstan updated its National Development Plan to 2025, which elaborates its medium-term vision of economic diversification through reforms of the agro-industrial and transport sectors, promotion of small and medium-sized enterprises (SMEs), plus development of tourism and other sectors. This plan's key objectives are to raise productivity as a driver, and help the country become one of the 30 richest economies by 2030, through increasing private investments post-COVID. The government finalized its New Economic Policy (NEP), which was approved in September 2022 following the President's address to the nation. Its main principles stipulate (i) private property guarantees, (ii) a favorable investment climate, (iii) fair competition, (iv) public finance management, (v) lower administrative barriers, (vi) a smaller state role in the economy, and (vii) social protection. The NEP's implementation measures are being developed by the Agency for Strategic Planning and Reforms of Kazakhstan. Estimates show annual investments are now at about 20% of GDP, compared with the 30 richest countries' average of 28%. Sustained government effort is therefore expected to improve the enabling environment for private investments.

However, productivity growth will depend on the extent to which upstream measures liberalize the economy, improve fiscal and debt management, enforce the new Environmental Code of 2021, and align with downstream coordination of private and public investments.

The Economist Intelligence Unit's (EIU's) Infrascope report of 2019 ranks Kazakhstan's public–private partnership enabling environment at 11th among 21 Asian countries, 7th in terms of overall investment and business climate, 8th in terms of institutions, 11th in terms of financing environment, 13th in terms of regulations, and 15th in terms of market maturity.[3]

---

[1] Trading Economics. https://tradingeconomics.com/kazakhstan/exports (accessed October 2022).
[2] Asian Development Bank. Economic Indicators for Kazakhstan. https://www.adb.org/countries/kazakhstan/economy (accessed October 2022).
[3] Economist Impact. The Infrascope Archives 2009–19. https://infrascope.eiu.com/.

Infrastructure Investment Needs in Kazakhstan

In 2012, the government adopted its *Kazakhstan 2050 Strategy*—a comprehensive state plan, aiming to secure the country's place among the world's 30 most developed economies by 2050. The three sectors prioritized under the 2050 Strategy are healthcare, education, and infrastructure (with emphasis on transport). The Ministry of National Economy (MNE), the Ministry for Industry and Infrastructure Development (MIID), the Ministry of Healthcare (MOH), the Ministry of Education (MinEdu), and the *akimats* (local governments) of regions and major cities are the main government players in achieving these goals. Further, in 2013, Kazakhstan adopted the *Concept for the Transition Towards a Green Economy*, with a commitment to meet 50% of the country's energy needs from alternative and renewable sources by 2050. In December 2020, during the Climate Ambition Summit, the President of Kazakhstan announced the ambitious target of carbon neutrality by 2060; a strategy to achieve this target was to be approved in the fourth quarter of 2022. The net investment in low-carbon technologies is estimated at $666.5 billion, which is 24% of gross fixed capital or 38% of investments in new technologies and fixed assets according to estimates presented by the government.[4]

The infrastructure needs of Kazakhstan are increasing in line with its expanding economy and growing population. A 2019 Organisation for Economic Co-operation and Development (OECD) report notes that if Kazakhstan's GDP grows at 4.3% per year, the country will need to spend $292 billion (or 3.93% of GDP) on average in infrastructure until 2040 which, when compared with the current levels of spending, translates into an investment gap of $84 billion (1.11% of GDP). While this gap is generally observed across all sectors, it is more evident in cross-border infrastructure, energy, and road transport; it also affects the construction of new infrastructure, as well as the operations and maintenance of existing infrastructure. It is estimated that approximately 75% of existing infrastructure requires replacement or rehabilitation.[5]

Climate change also affects the amount of infrastructure investment required, in three ways. First, Kazakhstan's commitments to significantly reduce greenhouse gas emissions under the Paris Agreement will require massive investments in the decarbonization of power, transport, construction, and waste infrastructure, among other sectors. Second, Kazakhstan's projected 2°C increase in average temperatures by 2030 will require significant investments in adaptation, especially in water conservation, energy efficiency, and greening of urban infrastructure.[6] Third, the increased climate change-related risks of disasters triggered by natural hazards (e.g., floods, droughts, fires) will inevitably affect the projects' capital and operational expenditures, costs of financing, and insurance costs.

Figure 1 indicates the value of infrastructure projects in Kazakhstan that are planned and under implementation. Out of the $195.6 billion investments tracked between 2000 and 2019, energy projects account for just more than half of Kazakhstan's planned and under construction infrastructure projects at around $112.5 billion (58%), while transport projects make up 20%, manufacturing 14%, and mining and quarrying 7%. Water projects, which include water supply, irrigation, and water resources management projects, are limited to only $471 million. Investments in irrigation are still very limited. Between 2006 and 2010, investment in the sector was less than $20 million annually, which was inadequate to maintain millions of hectares of irrigation facilities. Although investment resumed in 2014 and 2015, reaching $250 million, water demand is rising in Kazakhstan, with projections that by 2030, demand will outstrip all possible water supplies.[7]

---

4   Government of Kazakhstan, Ministry of National Economy, Institute of Economic Research. 2022. *Draft Strategy to Achieve Carbon Neutrality by 2060*. Astana.

5   OECD. 2019. *Trends in Kazakhstan's Sustainable Infrastructure Investments*. Paris. https://www.oecd-ilibrary.org/sites/a8bff43d-en/index.html?itemId=/content/component/a8bff43d-en.

6   UNDP. 2021. *IPCC Alarm Report: Global Climate Trends and Forecasts for Kazakhstan*. Astana.

7   ADB. 2018. *Kazakhstan: Accelerating Economic Diversification*. Manila.

Figure 1: Value of Planned and Under-Construction Infrastructure Projects by Sector, 2000–2019
($ million)

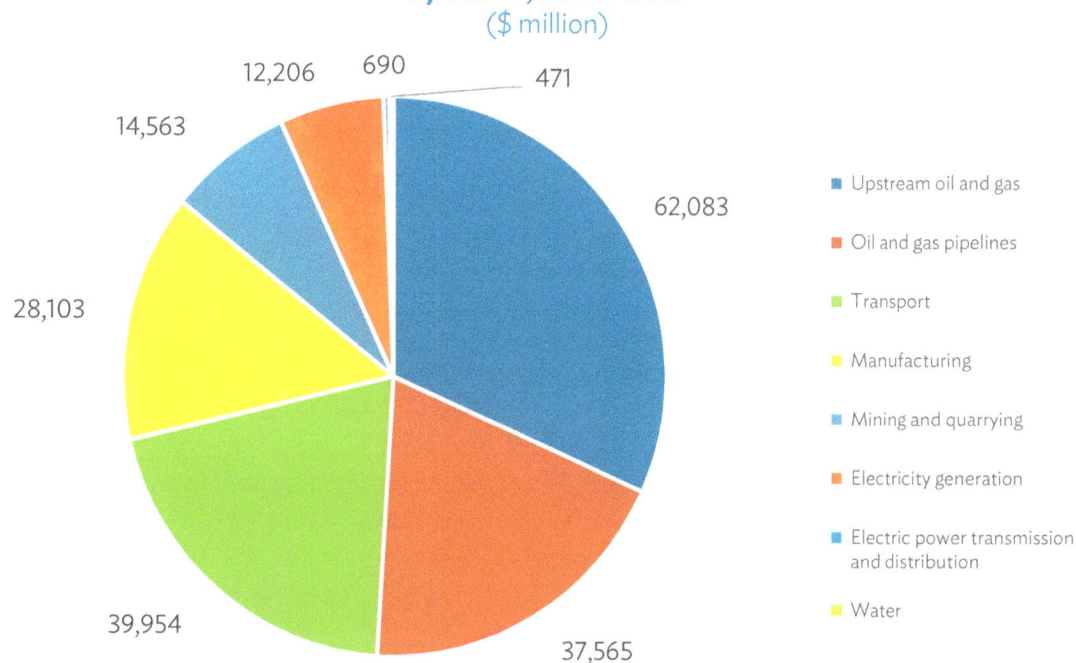

Legend:
- Upstream oil and gas
- Oil and gas pipelines
- Transport
- Manufacturing
- Mining and quarrying
- Electricity generation
- Electric power transmission and distribution
- Water

Values shown: 12,206 · 690 · 471 · 14,563 · 62,083 · 28,103 · 39,954 · 37,565

Note: Electricity generation projects include natural gas-fired electric power plants, wind farms, solar plants, hydroelectric power plants, and coal-fired electric power plants. Upstream oil and gas projects include oil and gas field development projects. Manufacturing projects include petrochemical plants, cement plants, plants for the production of ferrosilicon, aluminum plants, polypropylene plants, metallurgical complexes, production of motor fuels, acid plants, steel plants, and bioethanol plants. Source: OECD. 2019. Trends in Kazakhstan's Sustainable Infrastructure Investments. https://www.oecd-ilibrary.org/sites/a8bff43d-en/index.html?itemId=/content/component/a8bff43d-en.

Overview of the Public–Private Partnership Legal and Regulatory Framework

The government considers PPP as an important source of infrastructure funding and service delivery. Much effort has been put into the development of PPPs in the last decades, by continuously improving the legal mechanisms of PPP, developing the institutional setup, and structuring pilot projects.

The concept of public–private partnership as a procurement method was not used in Kazakhstan prior to 2006.[8] When Parliament adopted the *Concessions Law* defining the concept of PPP, this marked the birth of legal and institutional frameworks to support it. A further *PPP Law* was adopted in 2015.

The government has also established several institutions to support the deployment of PPPs. The Center for Public–Private Partnerships (the PPP Center) is a research and expertise center acting as PPP adviser for the Government of Kazakhstan. The joint stock company (JSC) Financial Center under MinEdu, and the JSC Turar Healthcare under the MOH, are the national operators mandated to promote PPP development in social infrastructure. *Akimats* also established regional PPP centers to promote local PPPs.

---

[8]   Prior to 2006, the notion of "concession" was used only in relation to subsoil use rights.

Kazakhstan has used PPP to deliver economic and social infrastructure including education, healthcare, transport, power, housing and public utilities, on both republican (central) and regional (local) levels. At the republican level, only a handful of PPP projects have reached financial close, mostly due to bankability issues.

Kazakhstan's main experience in implementing PPP projects is in transport, information and communication technology (ICT), and public services. It has developed a regulatory and institutional framework that reflects the government's commitment to PPPs as a procurement modality. However, despite considerable progress establishing this enabling environment, only one project, the Big Almaty Ring Road (commonly known as "BAKAD" by its local abbreviation), is regarded as an internationally tendered long-term PPP that has reached financial close with the participation of foreign banks. This fact concurs with Infrascope's 2019 ranking of Kazakhstan as "low" on the "PPP Maturity" dimension. While the country scores in the top tier for political will to pursue PPPs, the low maturity score indicates a mismatch between intention and execution, as well as possible systemic impediments, which limit private appetite for infrastructure PPPs.[9]

Public–Private Partnership Projects Reaching Financial Close From 1990 to 2021

The World Bank Private Participation in Infrastructure (PPI) database has been the basis for evaluating the past PPP projects at the national level and across each sector. The World Bank database has been used across all 15 countries covered as part of the PPP Monitor for the purpose of consistency and to enable cross-country and cross-sector comparisons. The charts below are elaborations from the World Bank PPI database. However, the PPP Center of Kazakhstan maintains a database of all PPP projects under its purview which includes projects taken up across republican (central) and regional (local) government levels. From this list, updated by the PPP Center on 1 September 2022, an assessment of projects under procurement and preparation is provided, under the respective sectors. The number of projects and investment amounts vary between the two databases, due to different definitions of PPP used by the World Bank and the PPP Center, and diverse methods estimating project values. Projects related to privatization and divestitures have been excluded from the analysis.

From 1990 to 2021, according to the World Bank database, 23 PPP projects from different sectors such as transport (including roads, railways, and airports), energy, ICT, and municipal solid waste (MSW) achieved financial close. The total investment in these projects was approximately $2.6 billion (based on the World Bank PPP database estimate). During this period, one PPP project was canceled (Astana airport management contract), which accounts for 4% of the total number of projects. The energy sector has been most active, accounting for 73% of the total projects that achieved financial close. Figure 2 and Figure 3 depict the number of PPP projects that achieved financial close and the status of projects across various sectors.

---

9   The Economist Intelligence Unit. 2019. *Infrascope: Kazakhstan Country Report.* https://infrascope.eiu.com/.

Figure 2: Public–Private Partnerships Financially Closed and Canceled, 1990–2021

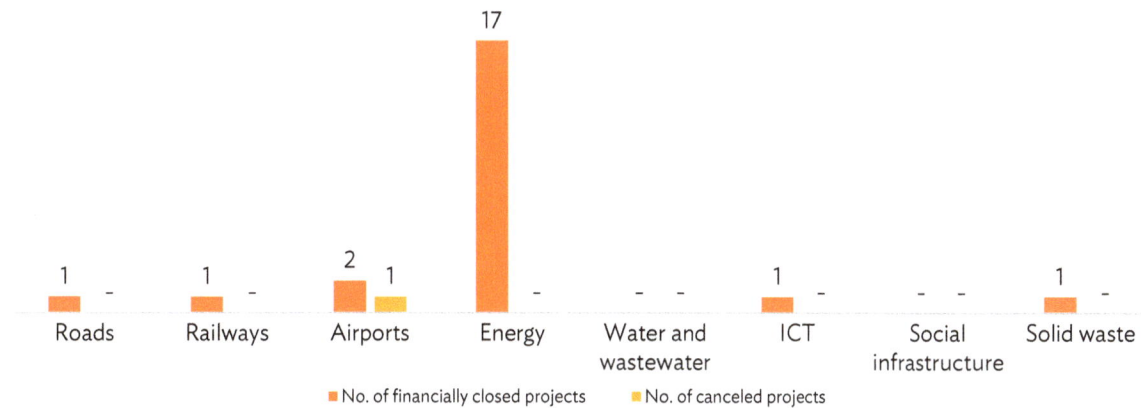

ICT = information and communication technology.
Note: Total projects include projects that are active, canceled, distressed, and concluded. "-" means there are no projects in the sector, and/or information is not available or not applicable according to the Private Participation in Infrastructure (PPI) database.
Source: World Bank. Infrastructure Finance, PPPs and Guarantees. Country Snapshots. Kazakhstan. https://ppi.worldbank.org/en/snapshots/country/kazakhstan (accessed 18 October 2022).

Figure 3: Status of Public–Private Partnership Projects Across Sectors

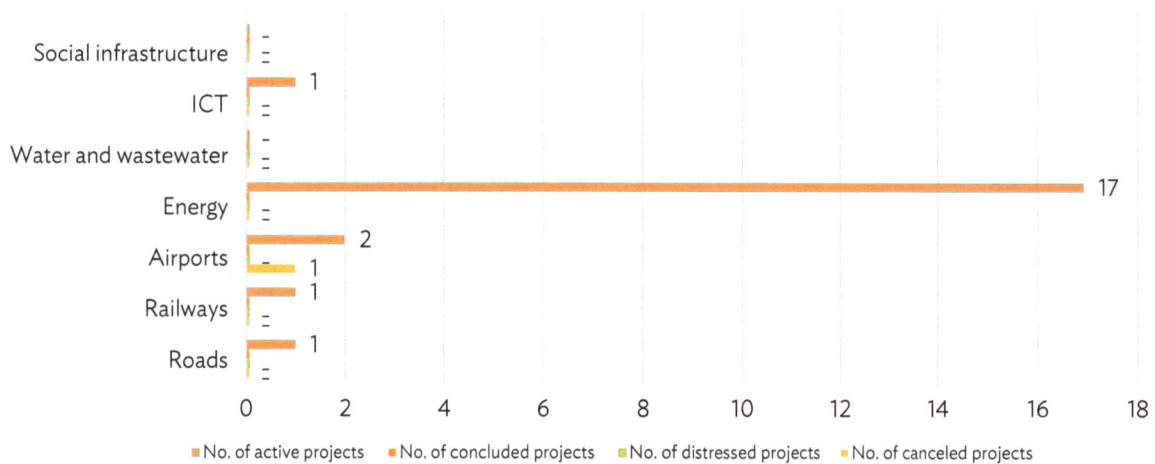

ICT = information and communication technology.
Note: Total projects include projects that are active, canceled, distressed, and concluded. "-" means there are no projects in the sector, and/or information is not available or not applicable according to the Private Participation in Infrastructure (PPI) database.
Sources: World Bank. Infrastructure Finance, PPPs and Guarantees. Country Snapshots. Kazakhstan. https://ppi.worldbank.org/en/snapshots/country/kazakhstan (accessed 18 October 2022).

The average size of a project reaching financial close was $65 million in the energy sector. Although roads were the largest average project size, followed by railways, there was only one project in each of these sectors. On aggregate, across all sectors, the average size of a project reaching financial closure was $108 million. Figure 4 shows the total investment in each sector from 1990 to 2021, and the average size of a PPP project in each of the sectors.

Figure 4: Investments in Public–Private Partnerships by Sector, 1990–2021
($ million)

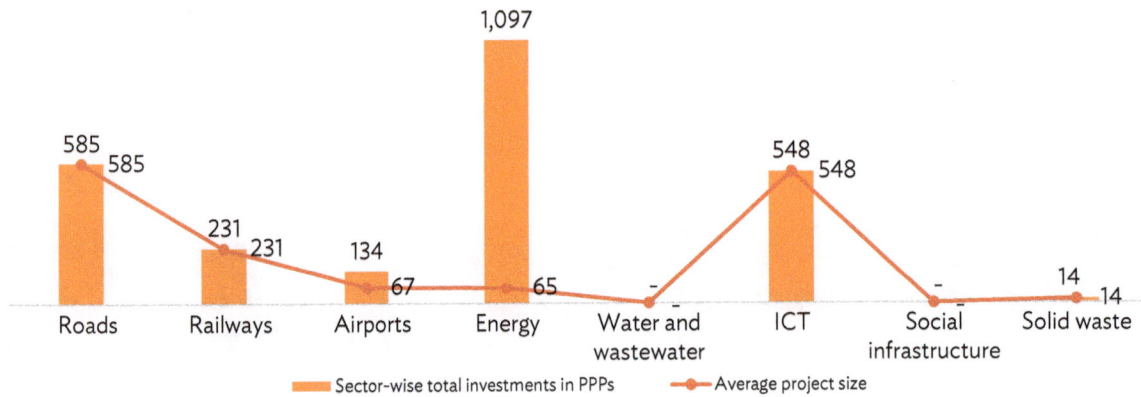

ICT = information and communication technology.
Note: Total projects include projects that are active, canceled, distressed, and concluded. "-" means there are no projects in the sector, and/or information is not available or not applicable according to the Private Participation in Infrastructure (PPI) database.
Source: World Bank. Infrastructure Finance, PPPs and Guarantees. Country Snapshots. Kazakhstan. https://ppi.worldbank.org/en/snapshots/country/kazakhstan (accessed 18 October 2022).

From 1990 to 2021, across infrastructure sectors seven projects were procured through unsolicited proposals, and 12 projects through competitive bids. Figure 5 indicates the number of projects that were procured through different modes.

Figure 5: Various Modes of Procuring Public–Private Partnership Projects, 1990–2021

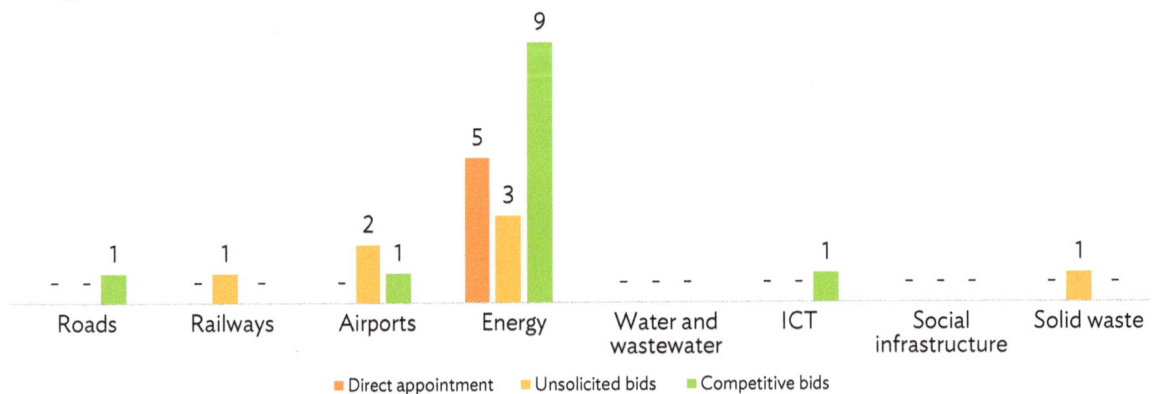

ICT = information and communication technology.
Note: Total projects include projects that are active, canceled, distressed, and concluded. "-" means there are no projects in the sector, and/or information is not available or not applicable, according to the Private Participation in Infrastructure (PPI) database.
Sources: World Bank. Infrastructure Finance, PPPs and Guarantees. Country Snapshots. Kazakhstan. https://ppi.worldbank.org/en/snapshots/country/kazakhstan (accessed 18 October 2022); Unicase Law, Limited Liability Partnership (LLP).

Figure 6: Public–Private Partnership Projects under Preparation and Procurement, 2021

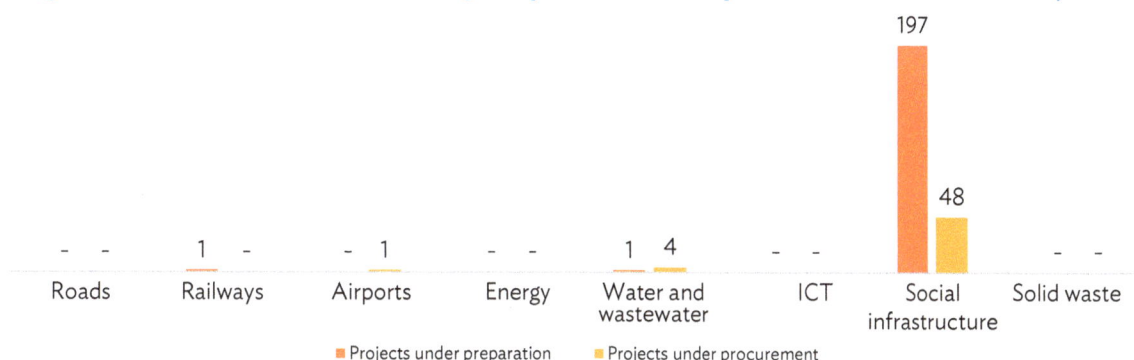

ICT = information and communication technology.
Note: The data presented above is an elaboration of the data from the PPP Center's project database. "-" means that there are no projects in that sector and stage.
Sources: Kazakhstan Public–Private Partnership Center. PPP Project Database. http://www.kzppp.kz/projects (accessed 18 October 2022); Unicase Law, Limited Liability Partnership (LLP).

Figure 6 shows the PPP projects at various stages of preparation and under procurement across various infrastructure sectors as of 2021. These data are drawn from the PPP Center database.

Government Support for Infrastructure Development

The most recent state programs for infrastructure development were Nurly Zhol, followed by Nurly Zher. In the first stage of Nurly Zhol, this program committed $19.2 billion to develop and modernize the country's infrastructure between 2015 and 2019. The second stage of Nurly Zhol for 2020–2025 was approved in 2019 and the program committed $12.1 billion for this stage to promote economic growth and improve the living standards of the country's population by creating an efficient and competitive transport infrastructure, developing transit and transport services, and improving the technological and institutional environment. Of the total investment requirements, 12.9% is to be contributed through PPP and private sector investments.

Launched in 2017, the first stage of Nurly Zher aimed to stimulate the construction of more affordable houses. It also included budget-funded investments in the construction and expansion of urban utilities infrastructure. While the main source of financing was the state budget, it was designed to blend in the investments from local construction companies, state-owned enterprises (SOEs), municipal bonds, and loans from international development institutions. The second stage of Nurly Zher includes investments in heat and water supply and sanitation, modernization of the communal sector, and development of housing infrastructure. The scope has also been expanded to include legal and institutional improvements, strengthening of regulatory capacity, improvements in the financial standing of utilities, and transfer of technologies. The total program budget is around $11.9 billion.

From 1990 to 2021, only one project received a government guarantee. No viability gap funding (VGF) has been provided. Figure 7 shows this finding.

Figure 7: Public–Private Partnership Projects with Government Support, 1990–2021

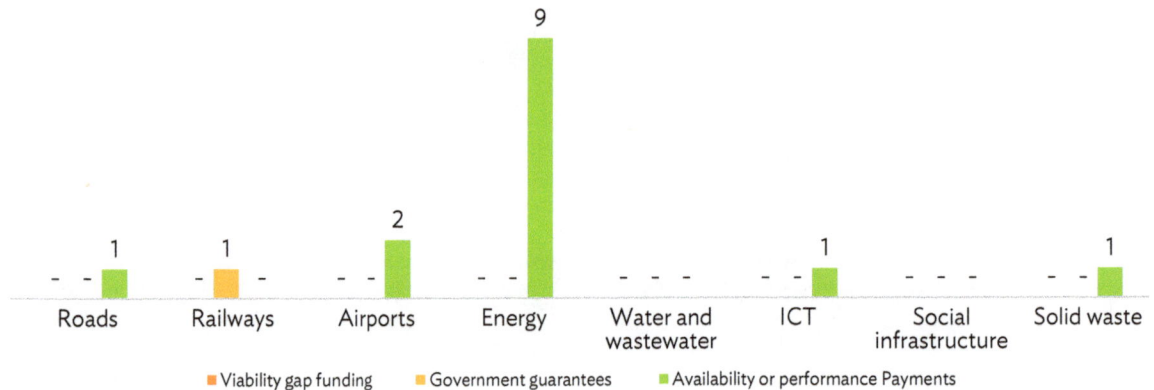

ICT = information and communication technology.
Notes: Total projects include projects that are active, canceled, distressed, and concluded. "-" means there are no projects in the sector, and/or data are unavailable or not applicable according to the database. The graph reflects the author's elaboration of the database.
Sources: World Bank. Infrastructure Finance, PPPs and Guarantees. Country Snapshots. Kazakhstan. https://ppi.worldbank.org/en/snapshots/country/kazakhstan (accessed 18 October 2022); Unicase Law LLP.

In terms of funding or payment mechanism, during the same period, 11 projects were awarded on a user-charge basis, while 13 projects were on government pay (offtake). Figure 8 shows the sectoral breakdown of these projects and their payment mechanisms.

Figure 8: Payment Mechanism for Public–Private Partnership Projects, 1990–2021

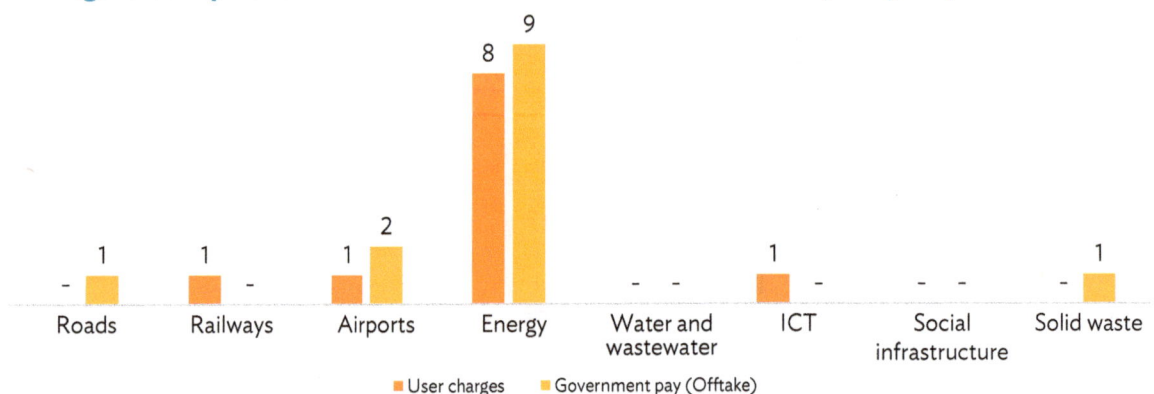

ICT = information and communication technology.
Note: Total projects include projects that are active, canceled, distressed, and concluded. "-" means there are no projects in the sector, and/or data are unavailable or not applicable according to the database.
Sources: World Bank. Infrastructure Finance, PPPs and Guarantees. Country Snapshots. Kazakhstan. https://ppi.worldbank.org/en/snapshots/country/kazakhstan (accessed 18 October 2022); Unicase Law LLP.

Foreign Sponsor Participation

Over the two decades, some 21 projects in Kazakhstan attracted foreign sponsors' participation. Figure 9 shows the distribution of PPP projects across various infrastructure sectors.

Figure 9: Foreign Sponsor Participation, 1990–2021
(No. of Projects, % of Total)

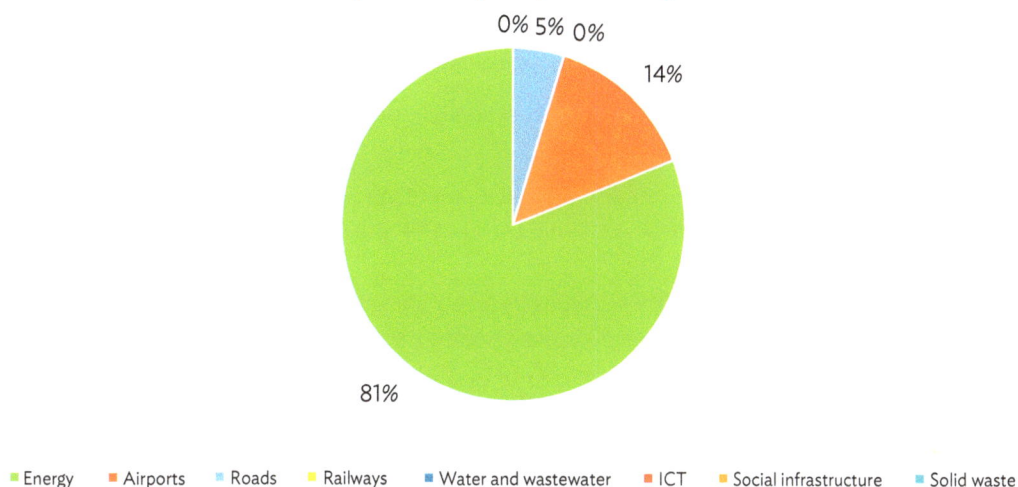

0% 5% 0%

14%

81%

Energy   Airports   Roads   Railways   Water and wastewater   ICT   Social infrastructure   Solid waste

ICT = information and communication technology.
Note: Total projects include projects that are active, canceled, distressed, and concluded. Foreign sponsors were seen only in roads, airports, energy, and ICT sectors.
Sources: World Bank. Infrastructure Finance, PPPs and Guarantees. Country Snapshots. Kazakhstan. https://ppi.worldbank.org/en/snapshots/country/kazakhstan (accessed 18 October 2022); Unicase Law LLP.

Challenges in the Public–Private Partnership Landscape

Despite progress in the last decade, shortcomings must be resolved to ensure that Kazakhstan's PPP environment sets a leading standard in Central Asia. Conducting separate investigations into PPP practice in 2019, the General Prosecutor's Office, the Ministry of Finance Accounts Committee, and the Atameken National Chamber of Entrepreneurs, all confirmed a lack of transparency and misuse of PPP mechanisms.[10]

---

[10]   The American Chamber of Commerce in Kazakhstan and Grata International. 2020. *IV Investors' Voice: Kazakhstan's Economic Recovery—Obstacles to Public–Private Partnership Development in Kazakhstan.*

Legal and regulatory frameworks must address the following major issues:

- The existence of two laws and the overlaps within them create ambiguity from the investor's perspective. The PPP Law is younger and covers all forms of PPP, including concessions. The Concessions Law applies "to the matters not regulated by PPP Law."
- The lack of a PPP champion undermines the development and implementation of the entire PPP process.
- Unclear responsibilities among public stakeholders create ambiguities in the long-term planning of government liabilities.
- The lengthy approval process results in projects being canceled or procured as unsolicited proposals.
- The lack of formal requirements to conduct any cost–benefit or value-for-money analysis affects the ability to account for contingent liabilities.
- The PPP Center is responsible for methodology development, and provision of expert opinions on PPP projects, which creates conflicts of interest within the key PPP stakeholder.

It is critical that the government addresses these issues by establishing robust frameworks to ensure transparency, and by adopting a programmatic approach to balance large and small projects, as well as those initiated centrally and locally. Improvements in policy guidance and clarity of purpose between the Concessions Law and the PPP Law will also inspire greater confidence among investors and long-term financiers.

II. National Public–Private Partnership Landscape

During the two decades since Kazakhstan's independence, its PPP landscape has evolved—so this can be divided into five stages (Table 1).

Table 1: The Evolution of Public–Private Partnerships in Kazakhstan

Stage	Years	Description
1	1991–1993	PPP legal framework for foreign investors only, in the form of Law of Concessions, which included provision for awarding a concession only to foreign entities or citizens. This law was abolished in 1993 after which the country did not have any PPP-specific legislation until 2006.[a]
2	1994–2005	Absence of PPP-specific legal framework and a series of "pilot" projects. Many projects and a number of agreements concluded during this period despite the lack of a legal framework. They were based on the principles of PPP and relied on the general principle of freedom of contract according to the Civil Code of Kazakhstan.
3	2006–2015	New Concessions Law adopted, formation of legal and institutional frameworks.
4	2015–2018	PPP Law adopted. Active deployment of PPPs as a result of the key performance indicators on a number of PPP projects imposed on republican and regional government agencies. Many of these projects were small in scale and were based on unsolicited proposals.
5	2019–present	Adjustments to the PPP framework with stricter requirements attempting to push back on unsolicited proposals (the key incentive is to control budget obligations).[b]

PPP = Public–Private Partnership.

[a] According to local legal experts, the law has "unbalanced" distribution of risks and rewards between the government and the private sector and focuses on subsoil use rights rather than on infrastructure. See https://online.zakon.kz/Document/?doc_id=30060703&pos=4;-106#pos=4;-106 (in Russian).

[b] Prime Minister's Official Information Site. 2021. *Interview with Talgat Matayev, Head of Kazakhstan's PPP Center*. Astana. See https://primeminister.kz/ru/news/interviews/intervyu-o-razvitie-gchp-v-kazahstane-sostoyanie-tendencii-i-perspektivy-1053646 (in Russian).

Source: Unicase Law, 2022.

In 2006, Kazakhstan adopted a new Concessions Law, which allowed the government to award several major concession projects, including the operation of the passenger terminal at the Aktau International Airport, construction and operation of the Yeraliyevo–Kuryk railway line, electrification of the Makat–Kandyagash railway line, construction and operation of the Kandyagash gas turbine power plant, and the BAKAD. For details on these projects, see the Sectors section.

At the end of 2015, the government enacted the Law on Public–Private Partnership (the "PPP Law") along with the necessary by-laws to support it. The new law did not replace the Concessions Law of 2006, which now intends to support "large-scale complex concessions," but aims to function in parallel as a more flexible framework to implement small-scale and simpler projects at the regional level. From 2006, the legal term "concession agreement" could not be applied to any type of subsoil use contracts, whereas the PPP Law covers contracts involving subsoil use but only in conjunction with the provisions of the Subsoil Use Code. The government pushed for decentralized preparation, approval, and implementation of PPP projects, so that the regional and local authorities would have more power and could implement the regional-level PPP projects faster, without getting any approvals from the PPP Center or the line ministries.

The new amendments of the PPP Law and the Concessions Law passed in 2021 have introduced provisions that allow a concessionaire or a private partner to be selected based on the results of an auction. However, the necessary by-laws, including details and procedures for such auctions, have not yet been approved. Therefore, it is not yet clear how exactly the PPP and concession auctions will be conducted.[11]

National Public–Private Partnership Enabling Framework

1. PPP Legal and Regulatory Framework

Parameter	
Does the country have	
– National PPP law and PPP regulations?	✓
– Public financial management laws and regulations	✓
– Sector-specific laws and regulations	✓
– Procurement laws and regulations	✓
– Environmental laws and regulations	✓
– Laws and regulations for social compliance	✓
– Laws and regulations governing land acquisition and ownership	✓
– Taxation laws and regulations	✓
– Employment laws and regulations	✓
– Licensing requirements	✓
What are the other components of the PPP legal and regulatory framework?	Key legal acts clarifying the concession and PPP legislation are Order 157 dated 22 December 2014 (regulation of concessions), and Order 725 dated 25 November 2015 (regulation of PPP).

✓ = yes, ✗ = no, NA = not applicable, PPP = public–private partnership, UA = unavailable.

Kazakhstan has two separate laws governing PPP:

- Law No. 167-III ZRK on Concessions, dated 7 July 2006 (the "Concessions law"); and
- Law No. 379-V ZRK on Public–Private Partnership, dated 31 October 2015 (the "PPP law"), along with the amendments thereto.

This duality has evolved from the initial absence in the PPP landscape of the build–transfer–operate (BTO) model, which has been first introduced in the Concessions Law and subsequently, with a wider range of available

---

[11] Unicase Law. 2021. *PPP Law Version 2.1: Must-know Latest Amendments to the PPP Legislation*. Almaty. https://unicaselaw.com/ppp-law-version-21-must-know-latest-amendments-ppp-legislation.

models, in the PPP law (e.g., use of unsolicited proposals, equity participation via "institutional PPP," three-party agreements). The current PPP landscape does not provide clear guidance on the choice between the two laws and specific instances or cases where one is preferred over the other.

The current legal framework and key acts that affect the PPPs in Kazakhstan include the following:[12]

- Constitution of Kazakhstan
- Civil Code of Kazakhstan
- PPP Law
- Concessions Law
- Commercial Code of Kazakhstan
- Law of Kazakhstan on State Property
- Tax Code of Kazakhstan
- Land Code of Kazakhstan
- Budget Code of Kazakhstan
- Law of Kazakhstan on Securities Market
- Law of Kazakhstan on Project Finance and Securitization
- Law of Kazakhstan on Special Economic Zones
- Law of Kazakhstan on Natural Monopolies.

From a legal perspective, concession agreements are governed by the general provisions of the PPP Law (since they are also mentioned in the PPP Law) and in specific cases by the Concessions Law. The interaction between these two laws remains to be clarified, as this creates a legal ambiguity. In practice, the government perceives the Concessions Law as specific to only "complex concession projects."[13]

There remain some strong legal uncertainties in both laws (e.g., regulation of the termination payments; accounting for, and treatment of, concession/PPP obligations from the state budget perspective). Two legal acts issued by MNE attempt to address some of them:

- Order 157 dated 22 December 2014 (regulation of concessions), and
- Order 725 dated 25 November 2015 (regulation of PPPs and concessions, since the concessions are legally part of PPPs).

The key differences between the Concessions Law and the PPP Law (including the two Orders by MNE) from bankability perspective are summarized in Table 2.

---

[12] Grata International. 2021. *PPP in Kazakhstan*. Almaty. http://www.gratanet.com/up_files/%5BGRATA%5D%20PPP%20in%20Kazakhstan.pdf.
[13] Large-scale, capital-intensive projects with long-term nature (similar to BAKAD).

Table 2: Comparison of the Concessions Law and the Public–Private Partnership Law

Element	Concessions Law	PPP Law
Process	Full package of tender documentation should be approved and shared with the market (no limitations) before the request for qualifications (RFQs) stage.	RFQ stage may be announced with the limited amount of information. Tender documentation may be prepared and approved between RFQ and request for proposals (RFPs) stages.
Documentation	Local feasibility study may be done by the government or prequalified bidders.	Local feasibility study may be done by the government or the winning bidder.
Forms	Only contractual PPP (no joint ventures with private investors). Concession agreement may have only two parties.	More than one government agency/quasi-state agency can be a party to the PPP contract. Joint ventures with private partners are envisaged.
Models	Only the build–transfer–operate model is available.	Several models of PPP are envisaged (according to Article 7 of the Law).
Arbitration	Only "special importance" projects can benefit from international arbitration.	International arbitration is applicable if one of the private partner shareholders (share is greater than 25%) is a foreign legal entity and the project itself is larger than a certain amount in terms of construction value.[a]
Unsolicited proposals	Unsolicited proposals are not allowed.	Use of unsolicited proposals is allowed.
Funding support	– Availability payments – Land grants – Government guarantees	– Availability payments – Viability gap funding – Equity contribution – Land grants – Government guarantees

[a] The total construction value should not be less than 4 million of monthly calculation index (monthly calculation index is T3,180 as of September 2022. The total value should be about $27 million).
Source: Unicase Law LLP.

Projects of Special Importance

Schedule 4 of Order 725 stipulates that for a project to be recognized as one of "special importance," it should meet the following criteria:

- High technical complexity of the project. The project should be attributed Category I of technical complexity, defined by the Law of the Republic of Kazakhstan dated 16 July 2001 "On architectural, urban planning and construction activities in the Republic of Kazakhstan."

- It is socially important.[14]

---

[14]   A public authority promoting a concession project can categorize its project as "socially important" in its tender documentation, if the project relates to social welfare, public service and protection, healthcare, secondary schools, preschool or nursery education, municipal infrastructure, or transport spheres and will result in increasing the number of facilities in said spheres.

- Its economic benefits are spread across several regions of Kazakhstan (excluding light rail transit [LRT] projects in Astana, Almaty, and Shymkent).[15]

- Its estimated total construction value is not less than 4 million of monthly calculation index (monthly calculation index [MCI] is T3,180 as of 2022, that is, a total value of about $27 million).

- Evaluation and selection applications are carried out by a special commission created by the Government of Kazakhstan in relation to republican concession projects and the local executive body in relation to local concession projects (see Concessions Law, Article 19, para. 4).

- Evaluation and selection of competitive applications of potential private partners is carried out by a special commission created by the organizer (see Order No. 725, Appendix 1, clause 75).

According to both the Concessions Law and the PPP Law, the Government of Kazakhstan approves the list of projects of special importance.

Small Public–Private Partnerships

The main goal for introducing small forms of PPPs was the implementation of PPP projects at the lowest level of governance (district level). Small PPPs have the following criteria:

- The PPP project does not belong to the sector of natural monopolies.

- The cost of the PPP project does not exceed $27 million, or about T13 billion (projects implemented at the local level).

- The selection of a private partner is carried out by using the standard tender documentation.[16]

- The PPP contract is signed in accordance with the standard draft.

Both laws require improvements in terms of bankability (Table 3).

Table 3: Outstanding Bankability Issues of Public–Private Partnership Legal and Regulatory Framework

Issue	Status Quo	International Best Practice
Lenders direct agreement (LDA)	The concept of "direct agreement" is available only for PPP/concession projects of "special importance" (see section on Projects of Special Importance).	Allow LDAs for all PPPs and concessions.
International arbitration	International arbitration is available only to the "special importance" concession projects and to PPPs with foreign shareholders.	Allow international arbitration for all PPPs and concessions.
Calculation of termination payment	The calculation of termination payments in both laws is linked to capital expenditure estimates, not to outstanding senior debt and equity. This creates ambiguities in numbers and requires legal drafting, in order to align with international practice. Swap breakage costs should be directly stipulated in the concession agreement.	Link the termination payment to senior debt and equity.

continued on next page

---

[15] LRT projects are not required to meet this criterion.
[16] See answers in the table under Section 6 of this chapter – "Public–Private Partnership Standard Operating Procedures, Toolkits, Templates, and Model Bid Documents."

Table 3 *continued*

Issue	Status Quo	International Best Practice
Budgeting of termination payments	The budget legislation does not provide for a clear procedure for budgeting long-term obligations under PPP/concession agreements or a procedure for budgeting termination payments. Calling for termination payment is untested as of 2021.	Provide a clear procedure for the budgeting of termination payments.
PPP budget limits	The PPP/concession budget limits set for regional *akimats* are restrictive (maximum of one to two large-scale projects).	Link the concession/PPP limits to the net present value of annual payments under PPPs.
Tender process	The tender process for PPPs/concessions is not in line with international best practices (e.g., request for qualification and request for proposal documentations are not separated for concessions, requirement to submit technical pre-feasibility study, use of only financial criteria for pre-qualification).	Clearly separate request for qualification stage from request for proposal stage. Allow to use technical and nontechnical qualification criteria.
Acquisition of land plots	Resettlement compensation is provided on market value basis.	Provide resettlement compensation based on the replacement cost.
Approval process for concessions	The approval process of a project concept and tender documentation under the Concessions Law is too complicated and rigid (e.g., the need for a detailed local feasibility study in practice, and detailed capital expenditures and operational expenditures calculations should be based on local benchmarks).	Provide more flexibility for the project with the tender procedures as only the market can indicate true costs of the project.
Limited use of facility management model	Due to the limitations of the Concessions Law and the PPP Law, the separation of operations (e.g., medical, education, water) from the facility management services are limited only to healthcare projects.	Allow facility management model for all infrastructure sectors.

Source: Unicase Law LLP.

2. Types of Public–Private Partnerships

The Concessions Law is specifically designed to accommodate the build–transfer–operate (BTO) model. The PPP Law expanded the list of PPP types:

- concession contract
- property rental (lease) of state property
- trust management of state-owned property
- leasing
- contracts for the development of technology, prototyping, pilot testing, and small-scale production
- life cycle contract
- service contracts
- joint venture with the private partner ("institutional PPP")
- other contracts corresponding to the features of public–private partnership

The PPP Law also expanded the list of PPP arrangements. There are now two ways to formalize a PPP:

- institutional basis (with the creation of a special purpose vehicle as a joint venture), or
- contractual basis (with or without the creation of a special purpose vehicle).

The objectives of the projects proposed on institutional basis are

- to create an alternative to state entrepreneurship;
- for the public and private partners to form equity to attract funding, thereby increasing the ability to take up more projects; and
- to adopt a mechanism for the state's exit from the project over time.[17]

In terms of models, the PPP legal landscape allows for the use of a wide range of structures, including

- build–transfer–operate (BTO);
- build–operate–transfer (BOT), build–own–operate–transfer (BOOT), or design–build–finance–operate–maintain (DBFOM); and
- build–own–operate (BOO).

As was mentioned above, the Concessions Law focuses on BTO model only.

The use of facility management model is only applicable for healthcare projects. As for the projects in all other sectors, the concessionaire/private partner would have to be responsible for the primary service provision along with the operations of the facility, according to the amendments to the Healthcare Code introduced specifically to allow it. Other industry-specific laws do not contain such caveats.

Payment mechanisms are also to be structured out of several separate payments, each designated to compensate for capital expenditures, operation and maintenance costs, and financing costs, among others (Section 2.3). This requirement potentially creates gaps in understanding what is covered between the expectations of the sponsors and senior lenders from one side, and the government from the other side.

3. Eligible Sectors for Public–Private Partnerships

PPP has been utilized in a wide range of infrastructure sectors and subsectors in Kazakhstan across the republican and regional levels and across various economic and social infrastructure sectors.

Both laws state that the PPP procurement method can be used for projects in any sector of the economy. Social infrastructure has been identified as a key priority, including education, healthcare, housing, and public utilities. Transport and power are also prioritized by these laws.

However, Government Resolution No. 710 dated 6 November 2017 "On list of objects which cannot be transferred for implementation of public–private projects, including concession," defines some limits, wherein

---

[17]   Nurlan Shokbarbayev, Director, Investment Policy, Department of the Ministry of National Economy. 2021. *Law as the Basis for the Development of PPP in Kazakhstan.* Presentation at the PPP Forum. https://forum.kzppp.kz/en/ (in Russian).

certain types of property may not be PPP or concession assets, such as land, water, property of national bodies, military equipment, or backbone railway network.

According to the legal act, among other things,

- water sources and water supply facilities cannot be transferred into concession, unless they are inseparable from the land use rights related to, or for the purposes of realization of a concession project; and
- health organizations engaged in blood supply service and prevention of HIV/AIDS and organizations of emergency medicine cannot be transferred through PPP.

This legal act applies to both the PPP Law and the Concessions Law.

Table 4 provides the details on the eligible sectors for PPP in Kazakhstan.

Table 4: Eligible Sectors and Subsectors for Public–Private Partnerships

Eligible Sectors		
Level 1	Level 2	Level 3
Transport and logistics	Roads	Roads, expressways, highways, bridges
	Railways	Metro rail, monorail, LRT, and trams
	Airports	Passenger terminal, cargo terminal, other airport facilities
	Transmission pipelines	
	Multimodal logistics parks	
	Dry Ports	
Energy	Power generation	Renewables and non-renewables
	Power transmission	
	Power distribution	
	Natural resources	
	Oil and gas	
	Energy conservation and street lighting	
Water and sanitation[a]	Water supply	Integrated water supply system, raw water transmission and treatment, water treatment plants, water treatment and distribution, bulk water supply
	Water resources and irrigation	Irrigation network, dams, weir, reservoirs, water storage infrastructure
	Wastewater	Sewerage/wastewater treatment plants, sewerage/wastewater treatment, and distribution of treated water
	Solid waste management	Integrated solid waste management system, waste collection, segregation and transfer, waste treatment and disposal

continued on next page

Table 4 *continued*

Eligible Sectors		
Level 1	**Level 2**	**Level 3**
Social infrastructure	Education	Primary education, international schools, student dormitories
	Healthcare	Hospitals (primary, secondary, tertiary), diagnostic centers
	Public housing	
	Government buildings	
	Industrial zones and special economic zones	
	Exhibition and convention centers	
	Sports, arts, and cultural facilities	Stadiums, cultural buildings
	Public markets	
Other infrastructure sectors	Information and communication technology (ICT)	Telecommunication infrastructure, broadcasting infrastructure, e-governance infrastructure, techno parks, other ICT infrastructure

LRT = light rail transit.
a Water sources and water supply facilities cannot be transferred into a concession, unless they are inseparable from the land use rights related to, or for the purposes of realization of a concession project.
Source: Government Resolution No. 710 dated 6 November 2017.

4. Public–Private Partnership Institutional Framework

Parameter	
Does the country have a national PPP unit?	✓
What are the functions of the national PPP unit?	
Supporting the design and operationalization of the national PPP enabling framework?	✓
Helping develop a national PPP pipeline?	✗
Supporting the arrangement of funding for project preparation (budgetary allocations, technical assistance funding from multilateral development agencies, operating a dedicated project preparation/project development fund)?	✓ Turar Healthcare (healthcare PPPs); Financial Center (education PPPs)
Guidance for project preparation to and coordination with the government agencies responsible for sponsoring the projects?	✓ Turar Healthcare (healthcare PPPs); Financial Center (education PPPs)
Making recommendations to the PPP Committee and/or other approving authorities to provide approvals associated with various stages of the PPP process?	✓

✓ = yes, ✗ = no, NA = not applicable, PPP = public–private partnership, UA = unavailable.

MNE is the authorized ministry for leading the PPPs in the country and is assisted by the PPP Center which plays the role of a PPP unit for the country. MNE plays an overarching monitoring role for the PPPs and is responsible for drafting PPP legislations and issuing guidelines. The other entities that play an important role in the development of the PPP policy in the country include the MOF, line ministries, local authorities, Turar Healthcare (for healthcare PPPs only), JSC Financial Center (for education PPPs only), and the Atameken National Chamber of Entrepreneurs (Table 5).

Table 5: Key Institutions Responsible for Public–Private Partnership

Institution	Role in Promoting PPP
Government of Kazakhstan	Approves the list of "PPP projects of special importance" and the list of PPP facilities that require closed competitive bidding process. Approves the concession/PPP obligations for each republican project (via State Budget Commission).
Ministry of National Economy (MNE)	Responsible for the state policy and framework for implementation of PPP projects and coordination of the PPP activities within the country. Provides the regulations for setting limits of total concession/PPP obligations at the republican and local budget level. Approves (via PPP Center) tender documentation packages for the republican projects.
Ministry of Finance (MOF)	Executes state guarantee agreements and state surety agreements on behalf of the state. Approves the tender documentation packages for the republican PPPs.
Each central government authority (line ministry)	Responsible for national PPP projects within its sectors of responsibility. The sector ministry prepares and approves tender documentation packages related to the national state property project, taking into account private initiative proposals, and organizes the tender.
Akimats (regional governments)	Responsible for regional PPP projects in their respective regions. It prepares proposals related to projects that are municipal property and acts as organizer of the tender process or of direct negotiations in the case of unsolicited proposals. The list of PPP projects has to be approved by the local representative body (*Maslikhat*). The local PPP centers under the *akimats* act as a center of expertise and approval body for local PPPs.
Center for Public–Private Partnership (the PPP Center)	The PPP Center is a research and expertise center acting as an adviser on PPPs for the Government of Kazakhstan. The key role of the PPP Center is to approve tender documentation packages for the republican PPPs on behalf of MNE and provide PPP-related capacity building training.
Turar Healthcare and Financial Center	JSC Turar Healthcare is the national operator of projects in the healthcare sectors responsible for the promotion of PPP and investment projects in the sector. JSC Financial Center is the operator of PPP in the education sector. Both are mandated to engage in the development and implementation of PPP projects in their respective sectors and be parties to PPP agreements.
National Chamber of Entrepreneurs "Atameken"	The main functions of the National Chamber of Entrepreneurs include participation in the tender commission to determine a private partner and participation in monitoring the implementation of PPP projects.

JSC = joint stock company, PPP = public–private partnership.
Sources: ADB. 2019. *Public–Private Partnership Monitor*. Second Edition. Manila. https://www.adb.org/sites/default/files/publication/509426/ppp-monitor-second-edition.pdf; Unicase Law LLP.

Entities Responsible for PPP Project Identification, Approval, and Oversight

Parameter	
Who is responsible for identifying, preparing, and procuring the PPP projects?	Identification and preparation – line ministries for republican projects; regional *akimats* for regional projects. Approval – line ministry, MNE (via PPP Center) and MOF for republican projects; local *akimats* for regional projects. Procurement – line ministries (Republic of Kazakhstan) on a republican level, local *akimats* on a regional level.
Is there a PPP Committee for providing approvals at various stages of the PPP projects?	✗

continued on next page

continued from previous page

Parameter	
Who are the approving authorities other than the PPP Committee for PPP Projects?	Project identification – approval from the line ministry; Feasibility study – Gosexpertiza (construction inspection and approval under MIID); Tender documentation – line ministry, MNE (via PPP Center), MOF. Tender evaluation – tender committee (representatives from the line ministry, MNE, MOF, Atameken, and other relevant government agencies and bodies on a case-by-case basis.) State Budget Commission approves limits on concession/PPP commitments. Variations during project implementation – line ministry, MNE, MOF, State Budget Commission). State Budget Commission approves limits on concession/PPP commitments for both national and local budgets
Does the country have an independent think tank for various PPP planning, budgeting, and policy decisions?	✗
Is there a legislature for the PPP program oversight?	✗

✓ = yes, ✗ = no, MIID = Ministry of Industry and Infrastructure Development, MNE = Ministry of National Economy, MOF = Ministry of Finance, NA = not applicable, PPP = public–private partnership, UA = unavailable.

Figure 10 depicts the overall process of project identification, preparation, approval, and procurement. For the regional PPPs, the process is almost identical, with *akimats'* respective departments (economic, financial department, regional PPP center, etc.) instead of the ministries.

Figure 10: Concession and Public–Private Partnerships Preparation and Procurement Process

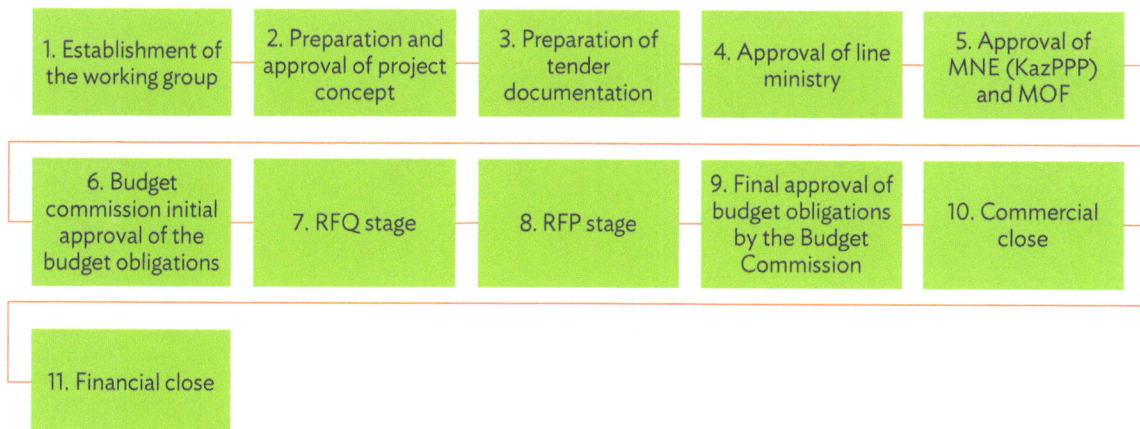

KazPPP = Kazakhstan PPP Center, MNE = Ministry of National Economy, MOF = Ministry of Finance, PPP = public–private partnership, RFP = request for proposal, RFQ = request for qualification.
Source: Unicase Law LLP.

In the case of concessions, full tender documentation pack (including RFQ and RFP information, and concession agreement draft) should be prepared and approved before the tender launch. The tender documentation should be disclosed to prospective bidders without limitations. Detailed approved shadow-bid financial models should be part of the tender documentation, which is somewhat unusual from the market perspective.

As for the PPPs, in contrast, the two-stage tenders may be announced with the terms of reference only, without requiring complex approvals, and the tender documentation itself should be prepared and approved between RFQ and RFP stages.

In the absence of a VFM methodology, and with the emergence of unsolicited proposals, for some projects, stages 1 and 2 are often skipped, and the line ministries and *akimats* proceed straight to preparing the tender documentation.

Entities Responsible for Public–Private Partnership Project Monitoring

Parameter	
Monitoring of PPP projects post commercial close?	MOF and line ministries via the PPP Center for republican projects *Akimats* for regional projects
Supporting the monitoring and management of fiscal risks and liabilities from PPP projects for the Ministry of Finance (MOF)?	MNE and line ministries via the PPP Center for republican projects *Akimats* for regional projects

MNE = Ministry of National Economy, MOF = Ministry of Finance, PPP = public–private partnership.

The process of monitoring project performance for concessions (regulated by Order 157) and PPPs (regulated by Order 725) is under both the line ministries (e.g., MOH for healthcare projects, and the MNE via the PPP Center). For regional projects, project monitoring is under the responsibility of the *akimats*. The PPP Center has no monitoring role for regional projects.

The day-to-day contract management is usually done by the relevant line ministry or the *akimat* (the contracting authority).

5. The Public–Private Partnership Process

Parameter	
Does the PPP legal and regulatory framework provide for a PPP implementation process covering the entire PPP lifecycle?	✓
Feasibility assessment stage	
– Technical feasibility?	✓
– Socioeconomic feasibility?	✓
– Environmental sustainability?	✓
– Financial feasibility?	✓
– Fiscal affordability assessment?	✓

continued on next page

continued from previous page

Parameter	
– Legal assessment?	✓
– Risk assessment and PPP project structuring?	✓
– Value-for-money assessment?	✗ᵃ
– Market sounding with stakeholders?	✗ᵃ
Is the PPP procurement plan required to be prepared?	✗
Is there a need to set up a separate PPP Procurement Committee?	✗ᵇ
Is competitive bidding the only method for selecting a PPP private developer?	✗
– Is the pre-qualification stage necessary? Or does the PPP legal and regulatory framework allow flexibility to skip the pre-qualification stage?	✗
– Does the PPP legal and regulatory process provide the option to the preferred bidder for contract negotiations?	✓
– Does the PPP legal and regulatory framework allow unsuccessful bidders to challenge the award or submit complaints?	UA
– What is the maximum time allowed for submitting a complaint or challenging the award by unsuccessful bidders from the announcement of the preferred bidder?	UA
– Does the PPP legal and regulatory framework provide for transparency?	✓ (for open tenders)
Which of the following are required to be published?	
– Findings from the feasibility assessment?	✓
– Procurement notice?	✓
– Outcome of stakeholder consultations from market sounding?	✗
– Clarifications to pre-qualification queries?	✓
– Pre-qualification results?	✓
– Clarifications to pre-bid queries?	✓
– Results for the bid stage and selection of preferred bidder?	✓
– Final concession agreement to be entered between the government agency and the preferred bidder? And other PPP project agreements executed between government agency and preferred bidder?	✗
– Confidentiality	✓

✓ = yes, ✗ = no, NA = not applicable, PPP = public–private partnership, UA = unavailable.
ᵃ World Bank Group. 2020. Benchmarking Infrastructure Development 2020 in Kazakhstan. https://bpp.worldbank.org/economy/KAZ.
ᵇ Points 74 and 75 of Order 725 define tender commission setting procedures, composition, representatives, and functions in the tender process.
Sources: ADB. 2019. *Public–Private Partnership Monitor*. Second Edition. Manila. https://www.adb.org/sites/default/files/publication/509426/ppp-monitor-second-edition.pdf; Unicase Law LLP.

The Concessions Law provides the opportunity to select concessionaire via a competitive process only:

- in an open tender (one-stage, two-stage); and
- via an auction (not specified in the legal acts and not used in practice as it was introduced recently).

Figure 11 depicts the tender process.

Figure 11: Tender Process (Concessions Law)

1. Tender announcement	2. RFQ stage	3. Competitive dialogue	4. RFP stage	5. State expertise of submitted bids
6. Announcement of preferred bidder	7. Negotiations stage	8. Commercial close	9. Negotiations stage	10. Financial close

RFP = request for proposal, RFQ = request for qualification.
Source: Unicase Law LLP.

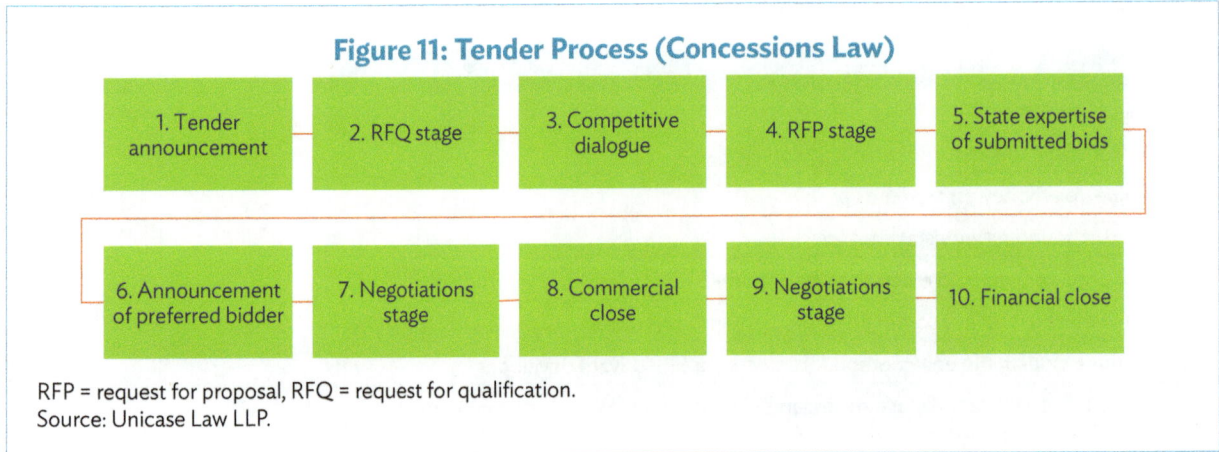

For the single stage tenders, only RFP stage is used without RFQ.

Unlike the Concessions Law, the PPP Law provides for the possibility to select a private partner through various processes:

- Open tender (one-stage, two-stage, simplified – for local project only)
- Auction (not specified in the legal acts and not used in practice)
- Direct negotiations (for unsolicited proposals).

The simplified tender procedure can be held only for the regional projects whose construction costs do not exceed 4 million times the monthly calculated index,[18] using standard tender documentation and standard contract,[19] and the project is not subject to natural monopoly regulation.

The tender procedure for a two-stage process under the PPP Law is described in Figure 12.

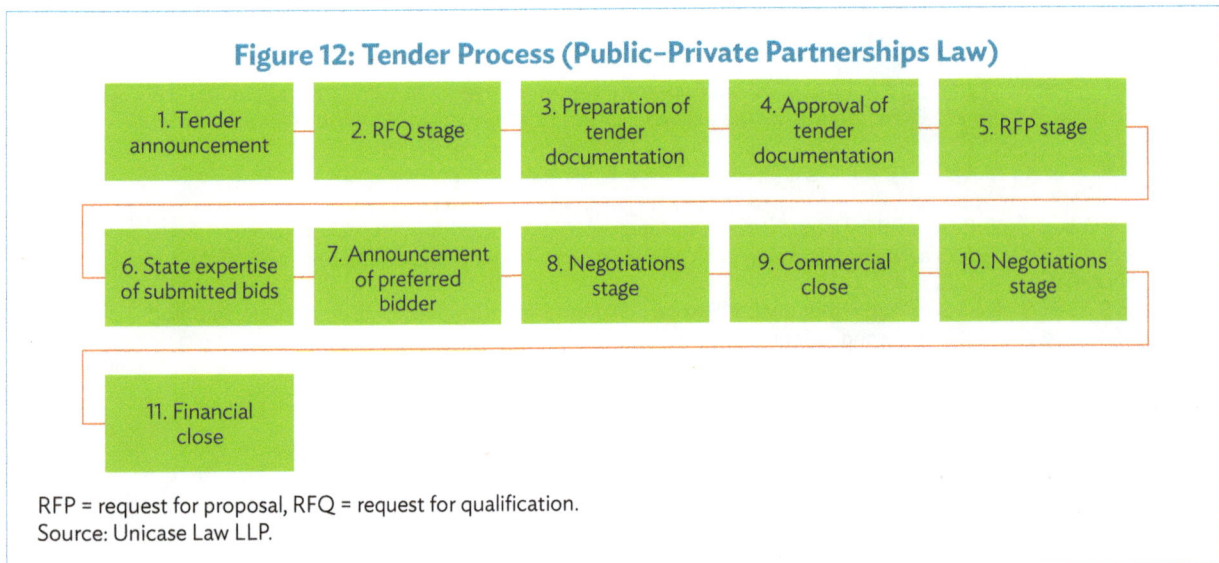

Figure 12: Tender Process (Public–Private Partnerships Law)

1. Tender announcement	2. RFQ stage	3. Preparation of tender documentation	4. Approval of tender documentation	5. RFP stage
6. State expertise of submitted bids	7. Announcement of preferred bidder	8. Negotiations stage	9. Commercial close	10. Negotiations stage
11. Financial close				

RFP = request for proposal, RFQ = request for qualification.
Source: Unicase Law LLP.

---

[18] MCI is T3,180 as of September 2022, i.e., total value should be about $27 million.

[19] Mostly social infrastructure. See Section 3 for details of the sectors where templates of contracts are available.

Single-stage tenders only require an RFP, without the RFQ. No state approval is required in the simplified procedure.

6. Public–Private Partnership Standard Operating Procedures, Toolkits, Templates, and Model Bid Documents

Parameter	
Does the country have PPP guidelines/PPP guidance manual?	✓
Does the PPP guidelines/PPP guidance manual adequately cover the process, entities involved, roles and responsibilities of various entities, approvals required at various stages, and the timelines for the various stages of the PPP project lifecycle?	✓
What are the templates and checklists available in the PPP guidelines/PPP guidance manual? – Project needs assessment and options analysis checklist? – Project due diligence checklist? – Technical assessment checklist? – Environmental assessment checklist? – PPP procurement plan template?	 ✗ ✗ ✗ ✗ ✗
Does the country have standardized/model bidding documents for PPPs? – Model request for qualification document? – Model request for proposal document? – Model PPP/concession agreement? – State support agreement? – Viability gap funding agreement? – Guarantee agreement? – Power purchase agreement? – Capacity take-or-pay contract? – Fuel supply agreement? – Transmission and use of system agreement? – Performance-based operations and maintenance contract? – Engineering, procurement, and construction contract?	 ✓ ✓ ✓ ✗ ✗ ✗ ✓ ✗ ✗ ✓ ✗ ✗
Does the country have standardized PPP agreement terms?	✓
Does the country have standardized/model toolkits to facilitate identification, preparation, procurement, and management of PPP projects? – PPP family indicator? – PPP mode validity indicator? – PPP suitability filter? – PPP screening tool? – Financial viability indicator model? – Economic viability indicator model? – Value-for-money indicator tool? – Readiness filter?	 ✗ ✗ ✗ ✗ ✗ ✗ ✗ ✗
Is there a framework for monitoring fiscal risks from PPPs? – Process for assessing fiscal commitments? – Process for approving fiscal commitments? – Process for monitoring fiscal commitments? – Process for reporting fiscal commitments? – Process for budgeting fiscal commitments?	 ✓ ✓ ✓ ✓ ✓
Are there fiscal prudence norms/thresholds to limit fiscal exposure to PPPs?	✓
Is there a process for assessing and budgeting contingent liabilities from PPPs?	✓

✓ = yes, ✗ = no, NA = not applicable, PPP = public–private partnership, UA = unavailable.

Order No. 277 dated 27 March 2015 provides the concession agreement template, while Order No. 724 dated 25 November 2015 approves the PPP agreement template as well as the standard tender documentation pack for PPP projects.

The PPP Center has also prepared a White Book which summarizes the required procedures for concession and PPP projects.[20]

Key Clauses Related to Public–Private Partnership Agreements

Both the Concessions Law (Article 21) and the PPP Law (Article 46) prescribe the key elements of agreements between the public and parties in Kazakhstan. The key differences between the Concessions Law and the PPP Law from a bankability perspective are summarized in Table 6.

Table 6: Differences Between the Concessions Law and the Public–Private Partnership Law

Element	Concessions Law	PPP Law
Parties	Only two parties can be sides to the agreement.	Both public and private sides can have multiple parties to the agreement, including financing organizations.
Forms	Only contractual public–private partnership (PPP) (no joint ventures with private investors). Concession agreement may have only two parties.	More than one government agency/quasi-state agency can be a party to the PPP contract. Joint ventures with private partners are envisaged.
Models	Only the build–transfer–operate model is available.	Several models of PPP are envisaged, according to Article 7 of the Law.
Available funding support	– Availability payments – Land grants – Government guarantees	– Availability payments – Viability gap funding – Equity contribution – Land grants – Government guarantees
Arbitration	Only "special importance" projects can benefit from international arbitration.	International arbitration is applicable if one of the private partner shareholders (share is greater than 25%) is a foreign legal entity and the project itself is larger than certain amount in terms of construction value.[a]
Foreign exchange cover	Only "special importance" projects can benefit from indexation of payments to foreign exchange.	The PPP Law allows the inclusion of clauses to mitigate foreign exchange risks regardless of the project's status.

[a] Total construction value should not be less than 4 million of monthly calculated index (MCI is T3,180 as of September 2022, total value should be about $27 million).
Source: Unicase Law LLP.

20   Yvision.kz. 2016. *White Book: Practical Recommendations for Implementing PPP*. Almaty. https://yvision.kz/post/690174 (in Russian).

Other Critical Contractual Provisions and PPP Enabling Considerations

Parameter	
Does the law specifically enable lenders the following rights?	
– Security over the project assets	× for Concessions Law ✓ for PPP Law
– Security over the land on which they are built (land use right)	×
– Security over the shares of a PPP project company	×
– Can there be a direct agreement between the government and lenders?	✓ (For special importance projects only)
– Do lenders get priority in the case of insolvency?	✓
– Can lenders be given step-in rights?	✓ [a] (For special importance projects only)

✓ = yes, × = no, NA = not applicable, PPP = public–private partnership, UA = unavailable.
[a] The regulations provide for substitution rights, and does not explicitly indicate the step-in rights, by the lenders in consultation with the granting authority.
Sources: ADB. 2019. *Public–Private Partnership Monitor*. Second Edition. Manila. https://www.adb.org/sites/default/files/publication/509426/ppp-monitor-second-edition.pdf; Unicase Law LLP.

The Civil Code of Kazakhstan provides for the following types of security interests: penalty, pledge, retention of the debtor's property, suretyship, guarantee, deposit, and guarantee deposit. Pledges and guarantees are the most used forms of security in Kazakhstan.

Though the assignment is not strictly indicating a type of security under Kazakhtan's law, it is quite often a part of a standard security package in international finance transactions. It should be noted that both the Concessions Law and the PPP Law stipulate the right of concessionaire/private partner to transfer its rights to third parties with the consent from the grantor (security clauses are not stipulated directly).

Furthermore, in a typical project finance deal, creditors require "step-in" rights that enable them to appoint a nominee to undertake the project company rights together with the project company itself (with the project company remaining liable for all the obligations) or appoint a new obligor in place of the project company to repay the amounts due to the lenders. These "step-in" rights enable the lenders to take over control of the project. The concept of "step-in" rights is recognized in the Concessions Law and the PPP Law for projects with "special importance" status only.

Termination and Compensation

Parameter	
Does the law specifically enable compensation payment to the private partner in case of early termination due to:	
– Public sector default or termination for reasons of public interest	✓
– Private sector default	✓
– Force majeure	✓

continued on next page

continued from previous page

Parameter	
Does the law enable the concept of economic/financial equilibrium?	✗
Does the law enable compensation payment to the private partner due to:	
– Material adverse government action	✓
– Force majeure	✓
– Change in law	✓

✓ = yes, ✗ = no, NA = not applicable, UA = unavailable.
Sources: ADB. 2019. *Public–Private Partnership Monitor*. Second Edition. Manila. https://www.adb.org/sites/default/files/publication/509426/ppp-monitor-second-edition.pdf; Unicase Law LLP.

The regulatory framework expressly regulates the modification allowed or renegotiation of a concession/PPP agreement, in particular:

- when there is a change in the investment plan or contract duration,

- in case of a force majeure event, and

- when there is a material adverse action from the government.

According to the Concessions Law and the PPP Law, the public partner can terminate the concession/PPP agreement:

- in case of material breach of the agreement by the private partner;

- if the private partner is in bankruptcy; and

- in the interest of society and the state (effectively an expropriation opportunity).

For projects under the PPP Law, a court order may be required.

The private partner can only terminate the agreement by the court's order, but only in case of material breach of the agreement by the public partner.

The termination compensation formula is rather unusual. Instead of the widely accepted "senior debt plus some equity" approach, Order 725 stipulates (both for PPPs and concessions) that the state would only compensate for "incurred and verifiable capital costs associated with the construction/reconstruction of the PPP facility minus the payments already provided by the public partner." Calculation of capital costs is usually based on local feasibility study,[21] which in turn, may be based on outdated local cost norms and estimates. This creates ambiguity and additional complexity from the lenders' point of view.

---

[21]   A local feasibility study is the document prepared in accordance with the legislation of the Republic of Kazakhstan. The calculations should be based on the local norms and benchmarks which are outdated. The local feasibility study is approved by the government (Gosexpertiza, a construction permitting agency under MIID).

7. Unsolicited Public–Private Partnership Proposals

Parameter	
Does the PPP legal and regulatory framework allow submission and acceptance of unsolicited proposals?	✓
What are the advantages provided to the project proponent for an unsolicited bid?	
Competitive advantage at bid evaluation?	✗
– Swiss challenge?	✗
– Compensation of the project development costs?	✗
Government support for land acquisition and resettlement cost?	✗
Government support in the form of viability gap funding and guarantees?	✗

✓ = yes, ✗ = no, NA = not applicable, PPP = public–private partnership, UA = unavailable.
Sources: ADB. 2019. *Public–Private Partnership Monitor*. Second Edition. Manila. https://www.adb.org/sites/default/files/publication/509426/ppp-monitor-second-edition.pdf; Unicase Law LLP.

Article 44 of the PPP law stipulates a possibility for unsolicited proposals ("direct negotiations") if the PPP project is initiated by a private partner that possesses the land plot/PPP facility (ownership or long-term lease) or the private partner has the intellectual property rights which are linked inextricably to the PPP facility.

Regarding the intellectual property rights, this clause was intended to be used for ICT projects. However, the vague wording of Article 44 has invited broader application of unsolicited proposal practices as well as attempts to use it in social infrastructure sector.

The procurement authority may initiate a competitive PPP procurement procedure if there are several unsolicited proposals for the same PPP project.

It is, however, noted that provisions regulating the evaluation of unsolicited proposals do not address the need to ensure that the project is consistent with government priorities.

The conduct of accepting unsolicited proposals follows a step-by-step process:

- initiation of a PPP project by a potential private partner;
- general notification of the market of the initiation of a PPP project indicating the key technical and economic parameters of the PPP project and requested payments from the budget and/or measures of state support (If no alternative proposals have been received, parties move to the approval of a business plan);
- approval of a business plan (developed by the potential private partner) for a PPP project (similar to the feasibility study);
- negotiations between potential parties to a PPP agreement on the terms of the PPP agreement; and
- conclusion of a PPP agreement.

Unsolicited proposals are not allowed under the Concessions Law.

8. Foreign Investor Participation Restrictions

Parameter	
Is there any restriction for foreign investors on:	
– Land use/ownership rights as opposed to similar rights of local investors	✓[a]
– Currency conversion	✗[b]
PPP projects with foreign sponsor participation (number)	21

✓ = yes, ✗ = no, NA = not applicable, PPP = public–private partnership, UA = unavailable.
[a] Foreign ownership on land is allowed except for agricultural lands, where foreigners and legal entities with foreign ownership of 50% and more cannot own land.
[b] There are no currency conversion restrictions. Foreign exchange comfort may be provided via payment mechanism in concession/PPP agreements.
Sources: World Bank. Infrastructure Finance, PPPs and Guarantees. Country Snapshots. Kazakhstan. (accessed 18 October 2022); Unicase Law LLP.

9. Dispute Resolution

Parameter	
Does the country have a dispute resolution tribunal?	✓
Does the country have an institutional arbitration mechanism?	✓
Can a foreign law be chosen to govern PPP contracts?	✓ Only for PPPs when the private partner (a special purpose vehicle) is a foreign entity
What dispute resolution mechanisms are available for PPP agreements?	
– Court litigation	✓
– Local arbitration	✓
– International arbitration	✓ Concessions – for the special importance projects only and if one of the shareholders of the concessionaire is a foreign entity; PPP – only if one of the shareholders of the private partner is a foreign entity (share is more than 25%) and the size of the project is more than 4 million times the monthly calculated index[a]
Has the country signed the New York Convention on the Recognition and Enforcement of Foreign Arbitral Awards?	✓

✓ = yes, ✗ = no, PPP = public–private partnership.
[a] MCI is T3,180 as of September 2022, that is, the total value should be about $27 million.
Source: Unicase Law LLP.

The PPP law explicitly confirms that if a private sector partner under a PPP agreement is a nonresident, the parties shall have the discretion to choose the applicable law of the PPP agreement.

When the dispute cannot be resolved, the parties to the PPP contract have the right to settle the dispute in accordance with the requirements of the Republic of Kazakhstan legislation in the courts or in arbitration (with limitations, table in section 9).

Schedule 8 of Order 157 stipulates the special importance criteria for the concession projects which are identical to the criteria in Order 725 with one exception—Order 157 does not introduce a special regime for LRT projects.

10. Environmental and Social Issues

Parameter	
Is there a local regulation establishing a process for environmental impact assessment?	✓
Is there a legal mechanism for the private partner to limit environmental liability for what is outside of its control or caused by third parties?	✗
Is there a local regulation establishing a process for social impact assessment?	✗
Is there involuntary land clearance for PPP projects?	✗

✓ = yes, ✗ = no, PPP = public–private partnership.
Sources: World Bank Group. 2020. Benchmarking Infrastructure Development 2020 in Kazakhstan. https://bpp.worldbank.org/economy/KAZ; Unicase Law LLP.

In Kazakhstan, the environmental legislation falls under the Environmental Code.[22] The environmental impact assessment (EIA) is mandatory for facilities that can have an impact on the environment or human health. The Code is based on the experience of OECD countries. The Code provides a detailed procedure for conducting an environmental impact assessment. The Code defines the nature and detail of the environmental permits required based on the industry's category.

Chapter 7 of the Environmental Code provides a section on EIA, cases for which they have to be done, and the procedure for conducting the EIA.

Since all major PPPs in the country are usually supported by international financial institutions, the Equator principles and the environmental, social, and governance (ESG) safeguards are of critical importance for bankability. The key concern for such bankability in the local regulation is the resettlement compensation for which the market value for expropriated property should be applied instead of the "replacement cost." The issue is normally resolved through the preparation of Land Acquisition and Resettlement Frameworks (or similar documents) which stipulate who will be responsible for the differences between the local regulations and the requirements of the Equator principles.[23]

11. Land Rights

Parameter	
Which of the following is permitted to the private partner:	
– Transfer land lease/use/ownership rights to third party	✗
– Use leased/owned land as collateral	✓
– Mortgage leased/owned land	✓
Is there a legal mechanism for granting wayleave rights, for example, laying water pipes or fiber cables over land occupied by persons other than the government or the private partner?	✓

continued on next page

---

[22]   Environmental Code of the Republic of Kazakhstan No. 400-VI 3PK dated 2 January 2021.
[23]   The preparation of such frameworks is customary for transport PPPs where the number of affected land plots/buildings may be significant.

continued from previous page

Parameter	
Is there a land registry/cadastre with public information on land plots?	✓
Which of the following information on land plots is available to the private partner:	
– Appraisal of land value	✓
– Landowners	✓
– Land boundaries	✓
– Utility connections	✓
– Immovable property on land	✓
– Plots classification	✓

✓ = yes, ✗ = no.
Sources: ADB. 2019. *Public–Private Partnership Monitor*. Second Edition. Manila. https://www.adb.org/sites/default/files/publication/509426/ppp-monitor-second-edition.pdf; Unicase Law LLP.

The provision of land plots for concession and PPP projects is directly stipulated in the Land Code of Kazakhstan.[24] There are direct links in the Concessions Law and the PPP Law to the land legislation. The details on the provision of land plots are also provided in Order 157 (for concessions) and Order 725 (for PPPs).

Under current PPP practice, the land plots are usually allocated by the government or local *akimats* before the start of the approval procedures, and to be provided after the tender to the winning bidder. As a result, most risks related to the land (e.g., access roads and utilities) are borne and mitigated by the government.

Government Support for Public–Private Partnership Projects

Parameter	
Project funding support	
Is there a dedicated government financial support mechanism for PPP projects?	✓
What are the instruments of government financial support available under this government financial support mechanism?	
– Capital grant	✓
– Operations grant	✓
– Annuity/availability payments	✓

– Guarantees to cover
  – Currency inconvertibility and transfer risk
  – Foreign exchange risk
	✗
	✓ for projects of special importance only

– War and civil disturbance risk	✓
– Breach of contract risk	✗
– Regulatory risk	✗
– Expropriation risk	✓
– Government payment obligation risk	✓
– Credit risk	✓
– Minimum demand/revenue risk	✓
– Risk of making annuity/availability payments in a timely manner	✓

continued on next page

---

24   Land Code, Article 36, Point 1.

continued from previous page

Parameter	
What are the caps/ceilings for the government financial support under each of the abovementioned government financial support instruments?	Total investment in the project
– Is there a minimum PPP project size (investment) for a PPP project to be eligible for receiving government financial support?	✗
Are there minimum equity investment requirements that the private developer should meet for availing of any of the above government support mechanisms?	✓ 10% of total project cost under the Concessions Law 20% under the PPP Law
Are there minimum financial commitment requirements for the private developer equity before the government support could be drawn?	✗
Is the government financial support required, usually the bid parameter for PPP projects?	UA
Are unsolicited PPP proposals eligible to receive government financial support?	✓
Are there standard operating procedures for providing government financial support to PPP projects? – Appraisal and approval process – Budgeting process – Disbursement process – Monitoring process – Accounting, auditing, and reporting process	 ✓ ✓ ✓ ✓ UA
Who are the signatories to the Government Financial Support Agreement?	Public partner and private partner as a general rule. The Ministry of Finance signs state guarantee and surety agreements.
Who is responsible for monitoring the performance of PPP projects availing government financial support? – Independent engineer? – Government agency? – Ministry of Finance?	 ✗ ✓ Line ministry or relevant *akimat* ✗ Ministry of National Economy
What are the other forms of government support available for PPP projects?	
– Land acquisition funding support?	✗
– Funding support for resettlement and rehabilitation of affected parties?	✗
– Tax holidays/exemptions?	✓
– Real estate development rights?	✓
– Advertising and marketing rights?	✗
– Interest rate/cost of debt subventions?	✗
– Other subsidies and subventions?	✓
Can the other forms of government support be availed over and above the government financial support through various instruments listed above?	✓

✓ = yes, ✗ = no, PPP = public–private partnership, UA = unavailable.
Sources: ADB. 2019. *Public–Private Partnership Monitor*. Second Edition. Manila. https://www.adb.org/sites/default/files/publication/509426/ppp-monitor-second-edition.pdf; Unicase Law LLP.

The legislation in general and the Budget Code in particular allow for three types of state support to PPP projects: (i) funding support, in the form of cofinancing; (ii) revenue support, mainly availability-type payments post completion and during operation; and (iii) credit enhancement instruments in the form of sureties and guarantees. However, the level of support, guarantees, and rights provided to concessionaires and private partners varies depending on the level of the project (republican vs. regional) and its specifics (e.g., social importance, special significance).

The amounts of state support committed by the state for PPP/concession projects are bound by the limits of acceptance of PPP/concession obligations which are set each year for 3 years within the standard budget process. The limits (accrued and new) are calculated in accordance with formulae adopted by the Ministry of National Economy in its Order No.731 (last amended in December 2020).[25] The PPP/concession limits depend on the annual revenues of each subnational budget, and the level of its obligations and liabilities to creditors, including banks and bonds. In most cases, they are prohibitively low to accommodate for large-scale, long-term regional projects.

In April 2021, the Ministry of National Economy amended its Order No. 129 of 5 December 2014 to add a new compulsory prerequisite (criterion) for the implementation of PPP projects (including concession projects). The amendment provides that the state obligations under the PPP projects, including state concession obligations (if necessary), should not exceed the amount of money spent or involved by the private partner (concessionaire) in the PPP (concession) project, including the private partner's own funds. At the same time, the private partner shall involve its own funds into the project in the amount not less than 10% (for concession) and 20% (for PPP) of the value of the object. The effectiveness of this change was suspended until 1 April 2022; this suspension has now expired.[26] This revision can potentially disrupt all future PPP projects as the state will not be able to provide availability payments and structure availability payment-based PPPs.

Funding Support

Cofinancing from state budget is currently the only method of providing viability gap funding for PPP projects that can be committed directly from the republican and/or regional budgets at the implementation stage, as reflected in Article 27, point 5 of the PPP Law and Concessions Law (Article 14, para. 1, sub-para 5). A more detailed mechanism for assuming and implementing the commitments on cofinancing is prescribed in Article 11 of the Budget Rules.[27] It is unclear if they also apply to the projects structured in accordance with the Concessions Law. The implementing entities (i.e., line ministries or *akimats*) can cofinance the capital expenditures of the PPP projects within the budget limits of their respective budgets and programs, as calculated in accordance with the PPP Limits Methodology (footnote 25).

Equity contributions have become available with the adoption of the PPP Law and its concept of "institutional PPPs" (Chapter 6 of the PPP Law). It envisages the participation of the state-owned enterprises and quasi-state companies as an alternative to the cumbersome budget process of receiving state support as part of the contractual PPP. Approved according to the participating companies' internal procedures, such involvement enhances the creditworthiness of the special purpose vehicle and may positively impact the financing cost.

---

[25]   Order of the Minister of National Economy of the Republic of Kazakhstan dated 26 November 2015 No. 731 "On the Methodology of Determining the Limits of State Obligations on Concession/PPP Projects of the Government of the Republic of Kazakhstan and Local Executive Authorities" (the PPP Limits Methodology).

[26]   Unicase Law Firm. 2021. *Kazakhstan – PPP Criteria "1 To 1" Postponed for a Year*. Almaty. https://www.conventuslaw.com/report/kazakhstan-ppp-criteria-1-to-1-postponed-for-a/.

[27]   Order of the Minister of Finance of the Republic of Kazakhstan dated 4 December 2014 No. 540 "On approval of the rules of budget execution and its cash service" (the Budget Rules).

Provision of land grants is administered in accordance with the relevant clauses of the Land Code (for instance, gratuitous provision of plot for use).[28] The law allows for the risk allocation on the land plot-related risks, such as access roads, communications, and resettlement, to be borne by the public party. Land expropriation and resettlement risks should be carefully assessed and managed as the provisions of the Land Code may be insufficient to ensure compliance with ESG and Equator principles. In terms of expropriation and resettlement, a decree needs to be published by the government or the relevant *akimat* on the planned alienation of land, indicating the purpose, location, owner, and date of the property.

Revenue Support

The bulk of the PPP-specific state support measures relate to the project's post-construction operations stage. The government provides revenue support through the following:

Investment cost compensation (ICC) is payable at the commencement of the project's operation stage in accordance with the agreed payment schedule.[29] It is limited to the following justifiable costs:[30]

- preparation of design documentation, cost estimates, surveys, assessments, evaluation of project feasibility, and obtaining licenses and receiving permits prior to project implementation required by Kazakhtan's legislation
- raw materials and materials, works, and services used in the creation (construction) of the object
- project implementation and management expenses during the construction and implementation period, including technical and administrative expenses
- accrued interest on short- and long-term debt (at market interest rates) and other debt service related expenses
- all types of insurance costs required during the creation and/or reconstruction of the PPP object
- depreciation accrued on the fixed and intangible assets used directly in the creation (construction) of the object
- other project implementation related expenses.

Operational cost compensation (OCC) is paid out of the state budget (republican or regional) aimed at reimbursing the expenses of the private partner related to the operation of the PPP object in accordance with a PPP agreement.[31] OCC can be used to compensate the following operational costs:[32]

- costs related to the operation and maintenance of engineering and technological equipment
- maintenance costs of buildings (structures) and territories
- administrative costs (e.g., remuneration of administrative and managerial personnel, insurance costs, banking fees, communication and security services)
- tax expenses

---

[28] Article 27 of the PPP Law; Article 6 of the Concessions Law.
[29] Order of the Minister of Finance of the Republic of Kazakhstan dated 4 December 2014 No. 540 "On approval of the rules of budget execution and its cash service" (the Budget Rules), para. 546.
[30] Rules No. 725, Appendix No. 7, para. 8.
[31] The Budget Rules, para. 564-1.
[32] Rules No. 725, Appendix No. 7, para. 23.

- insurance costs

- debt service

- other operating costs, which may include routine repairs, average repairs, and material costs (e.g., raw materials necessary for the operation of the PPP object, fuel, spare parts)

- costs of keeping stocks, inventory, and reserves necessary for the operation of the PPP object (e.g., work clothes, food).

Management fee has been specifically introduced to reimburse for cases where the private partner is mandated with the responsibility of operating a state-owned asset (for concession projects, management fee description also includes the rent payable from the state budget to the concessionaire). Management fee effectively includes return on equity, foreign exchange related payments, debt service not covered by ICC, and other project-related costs (Box).

Box: BAKAD's Payment Structure

The Big Almaty Ring Road public–private partnership, commonly referred to as "BAKAD" for its Russian abbreviation, had its payment mechanism structured in accordance with the provisions of the Concessions Law and Order 157. It consists of the following:

Fixed part (A)

- ICC, based on the investment costs of the local feasibility study (commonly referred to as "TEO"), not on the estimates of the winning bidder

- OCC, also based on the estimates of the TEO (also based on local feasibility study)

- Management fee, consisting of

  - cost of equity,

  - compensation for expenses during service period,

  - additional expenses for construction (construction costs of the winning bid minus the construction costs according to the TEO), and

  - additional expenses for operation (operating costs of the winning bid minus the operating costs according to the TEO).

Variable, or contingent, part (B)

- The foreign exchange compensation (legally part of the management fee)

- Adjustments for deductions

The foreign exchange compensation part should be calculated in accordance with the following formula:

$$\left(\frac{FX_n}{FX_o}\right) \times B, \text{ where}$$

FX_o –   initial exchange rate

FX_n –   exchange rate at the moment of payment of availability payment in period n

B   –   fixed component of availability payment in period n

continued on next page

Box 1 *continued*

The toll payments are collected by the government and are not part of the concessionaire's revenue structure.

The BAKAD experience has demonstrated to the investor community the willingness of the public entity to accommodate the requirement for a robust payment that includes essential contingent obligations, such as the foreign exchange adjustment component.

The project is expected to generate tax revenue for the Government of Kazakhstan, and contribute to the national budget. Tax revenues will be generated through income taxes and corporate taxes on expenditures, operational and corporate revenues, and incomes of employees.

———————————
BAKAD = Big Almaty Ring Road, ICC = investment cost compensation, OCC = operation cost compensation, PPP = public–private partnership, TEO = local feasibility study.
Source: Unicase Law LLP.

While the maximum amounts of management fee are set by the PPP/concession agreement, the actual amounts can be reduced if the private partner is in violation of the agreement terms related to service quality.[33]

Availability payments can be included in the PPP/concession agreement as payable out of the state budget, where availability is to be specified as operational and qualitative characteristics as well as individual, technical, and economic parameters of the PPP/concession object.[34] According to the Concessions Law, they can be the sum of ICC, OCC, and the management fee while in the PPP Law, they are a sum of OCC and the management fee (ICC is a separate component). Availability payments can be combined with other means of state support payable from the state budget.[35] However, unlike the Concessions Law, the PPP Law does not provide a requirement for the PPP project to be "socially important" to qualify for the availability payment.

Credit Enhancement Measures

The PPP Law contemplates various measures of state support aimed at enhancing the ability of the private partner to raise affordable long-term debt and encourage the participation of institutional investors. Among such measures are the following:

- state sureties for infrastructure bonds (not necessarily placed on the Kazakhstan stock exchange)
- state guarantees for loans, aimed at financing PPP projects
- demand-related guarantees (e.g., offtakes by the state entities, shadow tolls)
- rent fee for use of the object owned by the private partner.

The guarantees are applicable for the projects initiated by the government entity as well as those initiated by the private player under the direct negotiation model defined in the PPP Law, subject to the receipt of various approvals listed in the Budget Rules on the provision of government guarantees.[36]

Typically, a fee of 2% of the guarantee amount is charged from the private player seeking guarantees.

———————————
[33] The Budget Rules, para. 574.
[34] The PPP Law, Article 1 (4).
[35] Rules No. 725, Appendix 7, para. 23.
[36] The Budget Rules No. 674 on the provision of sovereign guarantees dated 2 June 2019.

According to the PPP Law, the budget execution central authorized body shall

- enter into contracts of state guarantees and sureties under contracts of PPP,
- keep a register of state guarantees and sureties provided by the state under PPP agreements, and
- record the acceptance and fulfillment of the state's financial obligations under a PPP agreement.

The Concessions Law also mentions the following credit enhancement instruments:

- state guarantees for infrastructure bonds under concession agreements
- state guarantees for loans attracted to finance concession projects
- guaranteed offtake of a certain volume of goods (works, services) by the state.

Project Development Funding

Project Development Funding	
What are the various sources of funds for PPP project preparation?	
– Budgetary allocations	✓
– Dedicated project preparation/project development fund	✓
– Technical assistance from multilateral, bilateral, and donor agencies?	✓
– Recovery of project preparation funding from the preferred bidder?	✓
At what stage of the PPP project can the project preparation/development funding be availed by the government agency?	
– Pre-feasibility stage	✓
– Detailed feasibility stage	✓
– Transaction stage	✓
Is there a threshold size (investment) for a PPP project to avail project development funding?	✗
Is there a list of project preparation/project development activities toward which the project development funding can be utilized?	✓
Can the project development funding be utilized to appoint transaction advisors for PPP projects?	✓
Is there a specific process to be followed by government agencies to appoint transaction advisors?	✓
What are the payment mechanisms for making payments to transaction advisors?	
– Timesheet based	✗
– Milestone based	✓
Are there standard agreements and documents to avail project development funding?	✗
Who are the signatories to the project development funding agreements?	Respective line ministry or *akimat*

✓ = yes, ✗ = no, PPP = public–private partnership.

The function of project preparation for PPP projects is scattered among many entities both at the republican and regional levels. At the republican level, the most prominent entities are Turar Healthcare under the MOH, JSC Financial Center under the MinEdu, and KazCenter ZhKH under the MIID, a national operator for state programs in housing and utilities. At the regional level, each *akimat* has established its own PPP center whose functions sometimes overlap with project preparation and approval. The financing of project preparation (if initiated by the public entity) is mostly provided from the state budget (republican and/or regional) and quasi-state-owned enterprises. There is also significant support from the IFIs (ADB, European Bank for Reconstruction and Development [EBRD], and the International Finance Corporation [IFC]) in providing technical assistance for project preparation. Where projects are initiated by the private entity, the project preparation is financed by the prospective concessionaires themselves.

PPP Center

The joint stock company "Kazakhstan Center for Public–Private Partnership" (the PPP Center) was set up in 2008 in accordance with Government Resolution No. 693 dated 17 July 2008. Its sole shareholder is the Ministry of National Economy (via the Ministry of Finance's State Assets and Privatization Committee). Its main purpose is the provision of expert opinions and advisory to the government. It mainly provides support during tenders, assists with the coordination of project monitoring, keeps the PPP project register, and renders methodological advice and training to regional PPP centers.

The PPP Center is financed out of the republican budget via the payments for provision of expert opinions on projects, training, and project marketing activities.

Turar Healthcare and Financial Center

JSC Turar Healthcare has been established in 2020 with the aim to address healthcare infrastructure gap and attract investments in the sector. It acts as the national healthcare sector operator under the MOH, with government being its sole stakeholder. Turar Healthcare's main role with regard to PPP is to attract investors, act as the medical operator in facility management PPPs, and provide advisory support for healthcare projects during project structuring.[37]

JSC Financial Center is the national operator for PPP allowing educational facilities to build or reconstruct student dormitories with the assistance from developers, construction firms and provides financing for private schools and dormitories on a per-capita basis. The government, via the MinEdu, guarantees the reimbursement of the developers' investments. As an operator for this program, the Financial Center is also responsible for the provision of standards, calculations, and assistance in contracting. It is also a party to PPP agreements.[38]

Regional PPP Centers and Social Entrepreneurial Corporations

Regional governments have been strongly encouraged to use PPPs to deliver infrastructure and public services. The regional PPP centers have emerged from social-entrepreneurial corporations (SECs), which had been created in each regional/republican city in 2006, to promote regional economic development through social corporate responsibility. Initially, the SECs have been responsible for promoting public–private partnerships in their respective regions. In 2013, the government created a PPP Coordination Council which instructed all *akimats* to set up regional PPP centers to take over the function of promoting PPP from the SECs.

There are currently 16 regional entities involved in PPP, fully owned by their respective *akimats*. These centers are mostly developing small-scale PPPs in social infrastructure and urban utilities. They provide services for

---

[37]   Government Resolution No. 723 "On the Creation of Non-profit Joint Stock Company Turar Healthcare" dated 30 October 2020.
[38]   Government Resolution No. 281 "On Determining the Operator for State Educational Accumulation System" dated 27 March 2013.

preparation, assessment, and ex-post evaluation of PPP projects to their respective regional governments. They are funded by the regional governments themselves, while project preparation costs can be recovered out of the winning bids.

International Financial Institutions

The three most active players supporting PPP among the international financial institutions (IFIs) are ADB, EBRD, and IFC. Each have PPP as a priority in their country programs and operational strategies, supporting a pipeline of PPP projects, such as in healthcare, transport, urban infrastructure, and water supply. Table 7 depicts a pipeline of selected projects supported by the IFIs.

Table 7: International Financial Institutions' Support to Public–Private Partnership Project Preparation

Project	Project Cost, Status	Supporting IFI	Comment
BAKAD	$585 million, closed	IFC – as lead financial and technical consultant. EBRD – provided grant for legal advisor.	It took 11 years for project preparation, tendering, and reaching financial close.
Almaty LRT	$270 million–$320 million, tender announced	EBRD – provided grants for feasibility study, financial consultant, and legal consultant (between 2009 and 2018). UNDP – provided grant for technical and financial consultant (2016–2018).	The project was structured as a regional PPP according to the PPP Law. The RFQ was announced in 2018 and attracted the attention of reputable international bidders. The *Akimat* of Almaty City has not yet announced the second stage.
Asfendiyarov Hospital	$100 million–$120 million, under approval	EBRD – provided grant for financial, technical, and legal consultant.	The project is structured as a republican facility-management PPP in accordance with the provisions of the PPP Law. The grantor is the MOH and the primary service provider is the Almaty Medical University.

BAKAD = Big Almaty Ring Road, EBRD = European Bank for Reconstruction and Development, IFC = International Finance Corporation, LRT = light rail transit, MOH = Ministry of Healthcare, PPP = public–private partnership, RFQ = request for qualification, UNDP = United Nations Development Programme.
Source: Unicase Law LLP.

C. Maturity of the Public–Private Partnership Market

Parameter	
PPP project statistics	
Is there a national PPP database for the country?	✓
Is the distribution of PPP projects across infrastructure sectors available?	✓
Is the distribution of PPP projects across various stages of the PPP lifecycle available?	✓

✓ = yes, ✗ = no, PPP = public–private partnership.
Sources: ADB. 2019. *Public–Private Partnership Monitor*. Second Edition. Manila. https://www.adb.org/sites/default/files/publication/509426/ppp-monitor-second-edition.pdf; Unicase Law LLP.

The Kazakhstan PPP Center regularly updates the PPP Project Database in their website. The database provides a list of projects that are undertaken on PPP. The latest statistics from the database, updated by the PPP Center on 1 September 2022, are reflected in Table 8.

Table 8: Public–Private Partnership Projects Database

Description	Units
Total number of projects	1,362
At the bidding stage	62
Signed contracts	1,054
Terminated contracts	72
Total amount of attracted and planned investments	$2,289 million

Source: Government of Kazakhstan, Kazakhstan Public–Private Partnership Center. PPP Project Database. http://www.kzppp.kz/projects (accessed 18 October 2022).

The project database provides various details such as the contracting agency, project type, stage of development, estimated cost, final cost, sector, dates, project capacity, form of PPP, and name of the private player.

The database is also collated and maintained at different levels. For example, the PPP Law states that

- the local executive bodies shall keep a register of concluded PPP agreements on local PPP projects, and
- access to the register is provided by the state assets record keeper to the authorized representatives of state bodies.

The World Bank PPP Reference guide defines PPP as "a long-term contract between a private party and a government entity, for providing a public asset or service, in which the private party bears significant risk and management responsibility, and remuneration is linked to performance."[39]

The PPP Law, however, provides a different definition as mentioned above (PPP Law, Article 4):[40]

- conclusion of PPP agreement
- mid- or long-term project life (from 5 to 30 years)
- joint participation of the grantor and the private partner in the PPP project
- combination of resources of the grantor and the private partner to develop the PPP project
- investments from the private partner side.

Consequently, quite a few of the projects listed in the database are too short in duration (5 years), and do not involve risk transfer (mostly regional primary education PPPs), and management responsibility and remuneration may not be linked to performance.

---

[39] PPP Legal Resource Center. What is a PPP: Defining "Public–Private Partnership." https://ppp.worldbank.org/public-private-partnership/what-ppp-defining-public-private-partnership.

[40] The Concessions Law does not contain an explicit description of concession distinctive features.

This is the main reason behind the vast discrepancies in the number of PPP projects among the various databases (e.g., 24 in the PPP Legal Resource Center[41] vs. 1,362 in Kazakhstan's PPP Center database).

Parameter	
Does the country publish a national PPP project pipeline?	✓
At what frequency is the national PPP project pipeline published?	UA
Is the national PPP project pipeline based on the National Infrastructure Plan for the country?	✓

✓ = yes, ✗ = no, PPP = public–private partnership, UA = unavailable.

The republican PPP project pipeline is published from time-to-time as a government order issued by the Ministry of National Economy. Before approval, the regional pipelines are published by the regional *Maslikhats* (local representative bodies).

Parameter	
Sources of PPP financing	
Who are the typical entities financing PPP projects in the country?	
– Private developers	✓
– Construction contractors	✓
– Institutional/financial/private equity investors	✓
– Pension funds	✗
– Insurance companies	✗
– Banks	✓
– Non-banking finance companies/financial institutions	✗
– Donor agencies	✓
– Government agencies and state-owned enterprises	✓
What is the distribution of financing among these entities financing PPP projects?	UA
Does the country have the history/track record of issuing bonds by infrastructure projects?	✓
How many infrastructure projects/private developers for infrastructure projects have raised funding through bond issuances?	2
What is the value of funding raised through capital markets by PPPs?	UA
Does the country have a matured derivatives market to hedge certain risks associated with PPPs?	✗
Does the country have a National Development Bank?	✓
Does the country have credit rating agencies to rate infrastructure projects?	✗
Typically, what are the credit ratings achieved/received by infrastructure projects?	UA
Is there a threshold credit rating for infrastructure PPPs below which institutional investors, pension funds, and insurance companies would not invest in infrastructure PPPs?	UA
What is the typical funding model for infrastructure PPPs – corporate finance or project finance?	UA
Are there regulatory limits/restrictions for the maximum exposure that can be taken by banks to infrastructure projects?	UA

✓ = yes, ✗ = no, PPP = public–private partnership, UA = unavailable.
Sources: ADB. 2019. *Public–Private Partnership Monitor*. Second Edition. Manila. https://www.adb.org/sites/default/files/publication/509426/ppp-monitor-second-edition.pdf; Unicase Law LLP.

---

41   PPP Legal Resource Center. Country Profile: Kazakhstan. https://ppp.worldbank.org/public-private-partnership/country-profile-kazakhstan.

Typical Contours of Infrastructure Financing

Table 9 reflects the key parameters and contours of the infrastructure financing in Kazakhstan.

Table 9: Key Infrastructure Financing Sources in Kazakhstan

	Non/ Limited Recourse Loan	Non/ Limited Recourse Local Currency Loan	Project Financing, Local Public Sector Banks	Interest Rate Swaps	Currency Swaps	Project Financing through Project Bond Issuance
Maximum Tenor, in years	15	No data	15 years	Only for hard currency loans (data unavailable) $	Forward duration of currency rate swap – 1 to 2 years for $	
Upfront arrangement fee, bps	Up to 100 bps	Up to 100 bps				
Floor rate	LIBOR	KIBOR or current official inflation rate				
Margin rate, bps	150–800 bps	150–800 bps				
Political risk cover premium	10–50 bps					
Percentage of foreign debt out of total debt for project financing						NA
Percentage of project bonds out of total debt for project financing			<30%			
Typical debt–to–equity ratio			No data			
Timeline to financial close (month)			6–12 months			
Minimum DSCR covenant levels, x			1.1x–1.5x			

bps = basis point, DSCR = debt service cover ratio, KIBOR = Kazakhstan interbank offered rate, LIBOR = London inter-bank offered rate.
✓ = yes, ✕ = No, NA = not applicable.
Source: Unicase Law LLP.

The principal sources of financing in Kazakhstan are as follows:

- **Debt from multilateral development institutions**. The key banks lending to the PPP projects on a limited recourse basis are ADB, EBRD, and the Islamic Development Bank (IsDB). Eurasian Development Bank (EDB) and Development Bank of Kazakhstan (DBK) have recently joined the peers.

- **Debt from state-owned institutions.** Baiterek Holding and its affiliates offer a wide range of financing from equity to debt to guarantees.

- **Bond finance.** PPP project entities can issue infrastructure Tenge-denominated bonds, supported by government guarantees. Listing on Kazakhstan's stock exchange might be attractive due to an exemption from withholding tax for listed bonds. Batys Transit, a PPP project on the construction of a high-voltage transmission line in West Kazakhstan, issued such bonds in 2006.

- **Local bank debt.** Local commercial banks could not provide financing to PPP projects due to strict prudential requirements on loans secured by take-or-pay contracts and future receivables (provisions are up to 50% of exposure). The Agency for Regulation of Financial Markets of Kazakhstan has recently issued a regulation lifting this requirement, which should make local bank financing more available for future PPP projects.

The overwhelming majority of the more than 1,300 PPP projects signed in Kazakhstan to date and registered in the PPP Center's database are small by amount (for instance, as small as T1,200, or approximately $28, for management of a school canteen in Jambyl Region) and short-term in duration (e.g., 2 years for management of a stadium café in North Kazakhstan). The private parties in such PPP are predominantly individual entrepreneurs or SMEs with limited borrowing capacity, if any.

Against this trend, there have been four large-scale concession/PPP projects in the past 36 months, which have been sponsored and financed on a limited recourse basis. Two of them were based on unsolicited proposals; only BAKAD has been tendered out internationally. Table 10 lists the sponsors of these four projects.

Table 10: Active Project Sponsors in 36 Months Preceding March 2021

Name of Sponsor (Project)	Financing Raised ($ million)	No. of Transactions
Alsim Alarco, Türkiye (BAKAD)	585	1
Makyol, Türkiye (BAKAD)	585	1
SK Ecoplant, Republic of Korea (BAKAD)	585	1
Korea Expressway Corp (BAKAD)	585	1
YDA (Turkestan Airport)	277	1
ADFD, UAE (Turkestan Airport)	277	1
Kazakhtelecom, Kazakhstan (rural broadband internet)	546	1
Transtelecom, Kazakhstan (rural broadband internet)	546	1
Eurotransit, Kazakhstan (automobile border crossing point with the PRC)	205	1

ADFD = Abu Dhabi Fund for Development, BAKAD = Big Almaty Ring Road, PRC = People's Republic of China, UAE = United Arab Emirates.
Source: Unicase Law LLP.

Table 11 shows the most active lenders during 2019–2021 for PPP projects in Kazakhstan.

Table 11: Active Lenders to Public–Private Partnership Projects in 36 Months Preceding March 2021

Name	Debt Provided ($ million)	No. of Transactions
ADB (renewables)[a]	>40	2
EBRD (BAKAD)	225	1
EBRD (renewables)[a]	>200	11

continued on next page

Table 11 *continued*

Name	Debt Provided ($ million)	No. of Transactions
EDB	315	3
Bank of China	100	1
IsDB	100	1
DBK	90	1
PGGM	25	1

ADB = Asian Development Bank, BAKAD = Big Almaty Ring Road, DBK = Development Bank of Kazakhstan, EBRD = European Bank for Reconstruction and Development, EDB = Eurasian Development Bank, IsDB = Islamic Development Bank, PGGM = Pensioenfonds Voor De Gezondheid Geestelijke en Maatschappelijke.
Note: The list of active lenders includes banks and non-banking financial institutions.
[a] While renewable energy projects supported by state-sponsored power purchase agreements are not considered as PPP in Kazakhstan, most banks treat them as such.
Source: Unicase Law LLP.

Credit Rating Agencies in Kazakhstan

A new state body, the Agency for Regulation and Development of the Financial Market of the Republic of Kazakhstan, was formed based on the Decree No. 203 dated 11 November 2019 to further improve the "state administration system of the Republic of Kazakhstan." The agency is a state body responsible for protecting the rights and legitimate interests of consumers of financial services. It also contributes to the stability of the financial system and the development of the financial market, carries out state regulation, controls the financial market, and supervises financial organizations and people within their competence.

The new state body provides information on credit bureaus operating in the country which include JSC "The State Credit Bureau" and the "First Credit Bureau" LLP. They provide personal credit and corporate credit reports.

- **First Credit Bureau LLP.** The First Credit Bureau is one of the largest technology companies in Kazakhstan with the most up-to-date database of credit histories and more than 40 services in the field of providing data for credit and non-credit processes, statistics, and predictive analytics for the financial market. The first credit bureau is a leader in the field of credit analytics and scoring models used in different segments of the financial market.[42]

- **The State Credit Bureau.** The State Credit Bureau was established as a joint stock company by the Resolution of the Board of the National Bank of Kazakhstan "On approval of the joint-stock company," State Credit Bureau No. 213 dated 4 July 2012. The State Credit Bureau is a specialized nonprofit organization whose main activities are the formation of credit histories and the provision of credit reports and credit scoring services.

There are local rating agencies in the country including Rating Agency of Regional Financial Center of Almaty, Expert RA Kazakhstan, and KZ-rating Agency. However, specific information related to full-fledged credit rating agencies operating in Kazakhstan is not available.

[42] First Credit Bureau. 2022. https://www.1cb.kz/about.

III. Sectors

As a civil law country, Kazakhstan's infrastructure sectors are governed by general codes and laws, which share common features in institutional design, commercial regulation, and strategic planning. To support the analysis of each sector in this Monitor, this section describes these commonalities and defines common terminologies and approaches. Where relevant, sector-specific differences are described.

Contracting Agencies

The PPP Law and the Concessions Law allow for three types of public-side contracting agencies across the infrastructure sectors covered in this Monitor:

- At the republican level, the line ministries can assume the public party obligations in concession/PPP agreements on behalf of the Republic of Kazakhstan.
- At the regional level, the relevant *akimats* can sign concession/PPP agreements within the boundaries of financial capabilities provided to them by the Budget Code.
- For both republican and regional projects, national operators and/or state-owned, quasi-state enterprises can become parties of the concession/PPP agreements which require creation of joint ventures (according to the provisions of the PPP Law's institutional PPPs), or which rely on take-or-pay and demand guarantee commitments.

Sector Laws and Regulations

Each sector is governed by an industry-specific law that sets the regulatory and institutional design; technical regulations; and roles, rights, and obligations of various stakeholders, among others. These laws define a sector-specific "competent body"—a line ministry and/or its committee, department, or agency—with the functions of strategic planning, policy coordination, regulation, and monitoring. In some sectors, there are also quasi-state enterprises with the special legal status of "national operators" (for PPP legislation only) which gives them the right to become sole providers of services that the government deems to protect from competition; and they receive support from the state budget.

Environmental Impact Assessment

According to the new Environmental Code adopted in January 2021, all activities that have a significant impact on the environment are subject to mandatory environmental impact assessment (EIA). The assessments should be conducted in six stages, from project initiation to ex-ante analysis of actual impacts, and must include 30-day public consultations. Conducting EIAs is a licensed activity and entails responsibility for the accuracy, completeness, and timeliness of the data, information, analysis, and conclusions of the assessments. The regional departments of the Committee on Environmental Regulation and Control under the Ministry of Ecology, Geology and Natural Resources are the authorities that grant permits and approvals based on the findings of EIAs.

Tariffs and Commercial Regulation

Commercial regulation is governed by laws and sublegal acts common to all infrastructure sectors. Depending on the nature of services, tariff setting is based on one, or a combination of, the following three approaches:

- If the activity is regarded as **a natural monopoly**—tariffs are regulated by the Law of the Republic of Kazakhstan "On Natural Monopolies" No. 272-I dated 9 July 1998 (the NML). Certain sectors may have separate sector-specific tariff setting procedures, methodologies, or instructions that detail the clauses of the NML.

- If the activity is **an oligopoly**, or if the service provider enjoys a dominant market position—tariffs are subject to the provisions of the Entrepreneurial Code of the Republic of Kazakhstan No. 375-V ZRK dated 29 October 2015 (the Protection of Competition regulation).

- If the activity is **not regulated**—tariffs can be regulated by the conditions agreed in the contract between the public and private party.

The key commercial regulating entities are listed in Table 12.

Table 12: Key Entities Responsible for Commercial Regulation in Kazakhstan

Agency	Description and functions
Committee for Regulation of Natural Monopolies (CREM)	The Committee is under the Ministry of National Economy and is responsible for commercial regulation by setting tariffs for services that are deemed as natural monopolies.
Agency for Protection and Development of Competition (AZK)	The Agency for Protection and Development of Competition is a state executive body of the Ministry of National Economy and ensures competition protection and restriction of monopolistic activities in relevant commodity markets. It enforces control and regulation of activities related to the sectors defined as state monopoly.

Source: Unicase Law LLP.

Tariffs for natural monopoly and dominant services are approved separately for each entity subject to regulation.

Table 13 provides an overview of the regulatory regimes for the sectors covered in this Monitor.

Table 13: Tariff Setting Approach for Selected Sectors

Sector	Tariff setting
Roads	The tolls are set by MIID.[a]
Railways	Track operation and maintenance tariffs are subject to natural monopoly regulation by CREM. Locomotive traction services are either non-regulated or dominant market participant, depending on the region.[b] Rolling stock operations are either non-regulated or dominant market participant, depending on the region.
Airports	Tariffs are set for each legal entity either as natural monopoly (airport/terminal) by MIID or as dominant market participant (e.g., ground handling, fuel supply, passenger services) by AZK.
Energy	Generation – The MOE sets price caps by type of generation. High-voltage transmission, distribution, system operation and dispatch – tariffs are subject to natural monopoly regulation by CREM. Trading and energy supply – tariffs are subject to the regulation on protection of competition.

continued on next page

Table 13 *continued*

Sector	Tariff setting
Water and wastewater	CREM sets the tariffs for each legal entity (water utility) and separately for water and wastewater activities.
ICT	The tariffs are not regulated.
Social	Healthcare – unified tariff system for all state-owned hospitals is set by the MOH. Education – per-capita spending amounts for each public school is set by the Ministry of Education. Housing – unregulated.
Solid waste	Tariffs are determined by *akimats* for city and the region.

AZK = Agency for Protection and Development of Competition, CREM = Committee for Regulation of Natural Monopolies, ICT = information and communication technology, MIID = Ministry for Industry and Infrastructure Development, MOE = Ministry of Energy, MOH =Ministry of Healthcare.
[a] KazAvtoZhol's official website. https://ru.qaj.kz/motorists/ (in Russian).
[b] KTZ official website. https://www.railways.kz/articles/infrastruktura/tarify (in Russian).
Source: Unicase Law LLP.

Standard Contracts

MNE Order No. 277 dated 27 March 2015 provides a general concession agreement template for all sectors, while Order No. 724 dated 25 November 2015 approves the PPP agreement templates for some sectors, mostly in social infrastructure. These templates may be used as a starting point for project structuring and can be changed to fit the purposes of individual projects. There are no approved standard engineering, procurement, and construction (EPC) and performance-based management (PBM) contracts for any sector yet.

Master Plans

Kazakhstan's strategic planning is conducted in three levels:

- Overarching strategic documents (e.g., National Plan 2025) which set the direction of social and economic development of the country
- Multisectoral government programs, most notable of them are the following:
  - **Nurly Zhol** is the main state program on infrastructure development covering 2020–2025 (approved by Decree No. 1053 dated 31 December 2019).
  - **Nurly Zher** is the main state program on the development of housing and utilities sector, covering 2020–2025 (approved by Decree No. 1054 dated 31 December 2019).
- Sector-specific programs, such as the following:
  - **Digital Kazakhstan** is the state program which aims to promote digitalization of the country's economy (approved by Decree No. 827 dated 12 December 2017).
  - **Regional Development Program** for 2020–2025 aims to address regional development disparities (approved by Decree No. 990 dated 27 December 2019).
  - **Innovation and Industrial Development Program** for 2020–2025 aims to promote investment in innovation and industrial development (approved by Decree No. 1050 dated 31 December 2019).

In 2021, the state programs have been replaced by 10 national projects.

PPP Projects Data

For the sake of consistency and comparability, the evaluation of past PPP projects uses the World Bank PPI database in each sector. Additional data used in the analysis refers to the information retrieved from the database maintained by the PPP Center. As mentioned in Section 2, the number of PPP projects may be different between the databases of international sources and the PPP Center because of their differences in the definitions of PPP between local legislation and the international practice. In addition, the PPP Center uses the sum of nominal government payments denominated in local currency for the entire contract period as a proxy for PPP project value, which can further create discrepancies in PPP project amounts, while international sources use total capital expenditures for PPP project value.

A. Roads

Parameter	Value	Unit
Length of the total road network	96,846	Kilometers
Quality of road infrastructure	3.60	1(low) – 7(high)

Sources: MIID. 2022. Roads. Astana. https://www.gov.kz/memleket/entities/roads/activities/252?lang=en; World Bank. Data Bank 2022. https://data.worldbank.org/indicator/IS.RRS.TOTL.KM?locations=KZ.

The roads in Kazakhstan are classified by three types, each under the responsibility of different levels of government and their respective road organizations:

- Roads of republican importance are under the responsibility of MIID and managed by the Committee of Roads.
- Regional (rural) roads are under the oblasts/*akimats* and their respective transport departments.
- Urban roads and streets are under town/city municipalities.

1. Contracting Agencies in the Road Sector

The Roads Committee under MIID is the competent body that performs regulatory, implementation, and control functions in the road sector. It is in charge of planning, preparation, development, procurement, and monitoring of construction, and the operation and maintenance of the national road network. It is authorized to decide on which road passages can be subject to toll payments. It also decides on the procurement mode for the new/existing roads and then executes that procurement.

The national operator for the roads of republican importance is KazAvtoZhol, a joint stock company under the full ownership and coordination of MIID. KazAvtozhol is responsible for the operation of toll roads and the development and operation of roadside services.[43]

For regional projects, each oblast/large city *akimat* would have a transport and roads department responsible for their respective peripheral road network.

---

[43]   As of April 2022, KazAvtoZhol is to be merged with KazakhAvtoDor, a state-owned road construction and maintenance company.

2. Road Sector Laws and Regulations

The industry-specific legal acts for the road sector are the following:

- The Law of the Republic of Kazakhstan No. 156 dated 21 September 1994 "On Transport in the Republic of Kazakhstan" (the Transport Law) defines the basis for legal, economic, and organizational activities of transport in general.
- The Law of the Republic of Kazakhstan No. 245 dated 17 July 2001 "On Automobile Roads" (the Law on Roads) regulates the legal, organizational, and economic basis of automobile roads, their construction, operation, and development, including the provisions on toll roads.

2.1 Foreign Investment Restrictions in the Road Sector

Parameter	2019	2020	2021
Maximum allowed foreign ownership of equity in greenfield projects	100%	100%	100%

Sources: ADB. 2019. *Public–Private Partnership Monitor*. Second Edition. Manila. https://www.adb.org/sites/default/files/publication/509426/ppp-monitor-second-edition.pdf; Unicase Law LLP.

The maximum equity investment allowed for foreign investors is 100%.

2.2 Standard Contracts in the Road Sector

Type of Contract	Availability
PPP/concession agreement	✗
Performance-based operation and maintenance contract	✗
Engineering procurement and construction contract	✗

✗ = no, PPP = public–private partnership.
Source: Unicase Law LLP.

There are no standard contracts specific to the road sector yet. ADB is currently assisting the Roads Committee and KazAvtoZhol with piloting of performance-based maintenance (PBM) contracts to support road maintenance reforms. Non-standard EPC contracts are implemented under sovereign-guaranteed loans from Exim Bank of China to KazAvtoZhol.

3. Road Sector Master Plan

The state plans for road sector development are reflected in the Nurly Zhol program, which highlights the need for an extensive network of roads both for transit and for national traffic. Over 2020–2025, the government plans to implement 18 projects on new construction and reconstruction of 10,000 km of roads. To implement these projects, the government plans to raise around T3.5 trillion (approximately $7.4 billion) of budget funds and sovereign loans.

The only mention of PPP procurement mode in the program relates to the plans of investigating the possibilities of rolling out electrical charging stations along the roads in and around the major cities of Kazakhstan.

3.1 Projects under Preparation and Procurement in the Road Sector

Figure 13 shows the details on the PPP projects that are under preparation and procurement in the road sector of Kazakhstan.

Figure 13: Public–Private Partnership Road Projects under Preparation and Procurement

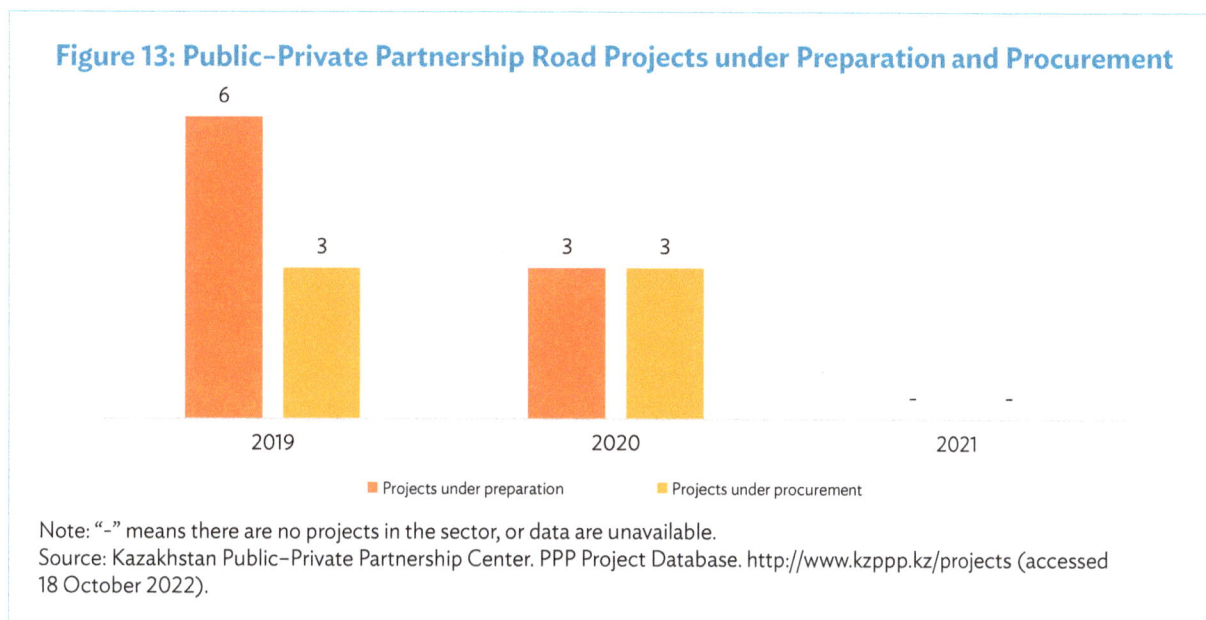

Note: "-" means there are no projects in the sector, or data are unavailable.
Source: Kazakhstan Public–Private Partnership Center. PPP Project Database. http://www.kzppp.kz/projects (accessed 18 October 2022).

4. Features of Past Public–Private Partnership Projects in the Road Sector

Figure 14 shows the number of PPP projects procured through various modes, including direct appointment, unsolicited bids, and competitive bids, in the road sector of Kazakhstan.

Figure 14: Modes of Procurement for Public–Private Partnership Roads

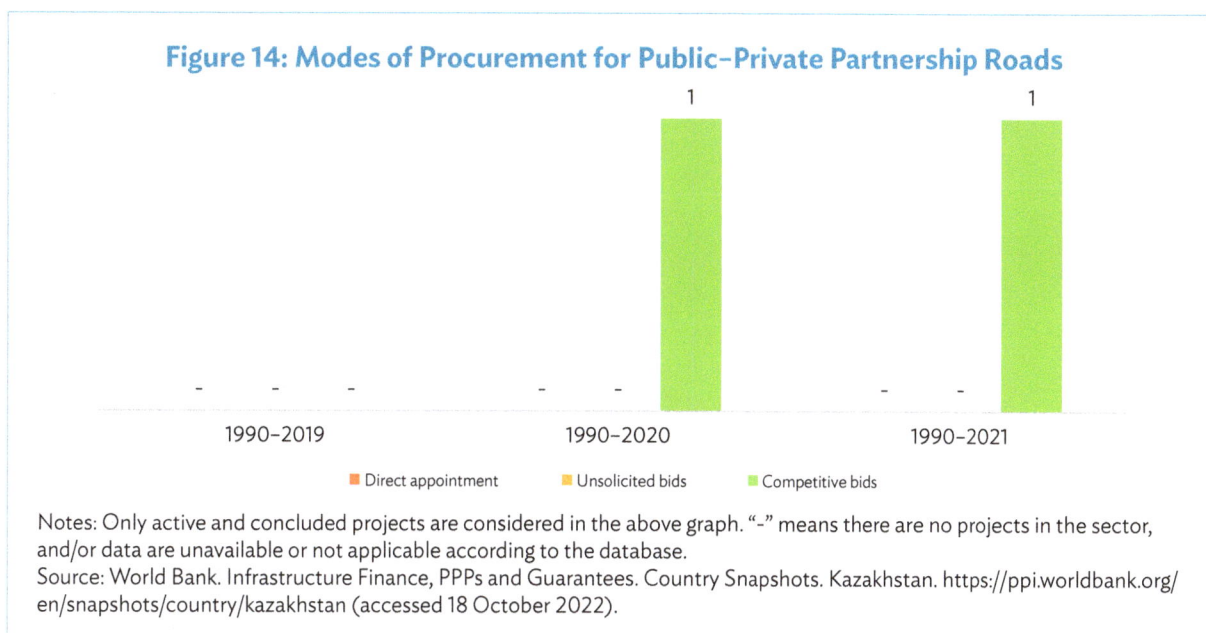

Notes: Only active and concluded projects are considered in the above graph. "-" means there are no projects in the sector, and/or data are unavailable or not applicable according to the database.
Source: World Bank. Infrastructure Finance, PPPs and Guarantees. Country Snapshots. Kazakhstan. https://ppi.worldbank.org/en/snapshots/country/kazakhstan (accessed 18 October 2022).

The Government of Kazakhstan awarded the 66-kilometer BAKAD concession project through a competitive bid, which reached a financial close in August 2020. BAKAD is the largest PPP project in Central Asia, supported by the EBRD, the Bank of China, PGGM, the Eurasian Development Bank, and the Islamic Development Bank.

Figure 15 shows the number of PPP projects that have reached financial close and the total value of those projects in the road sector of Kazakhstan.

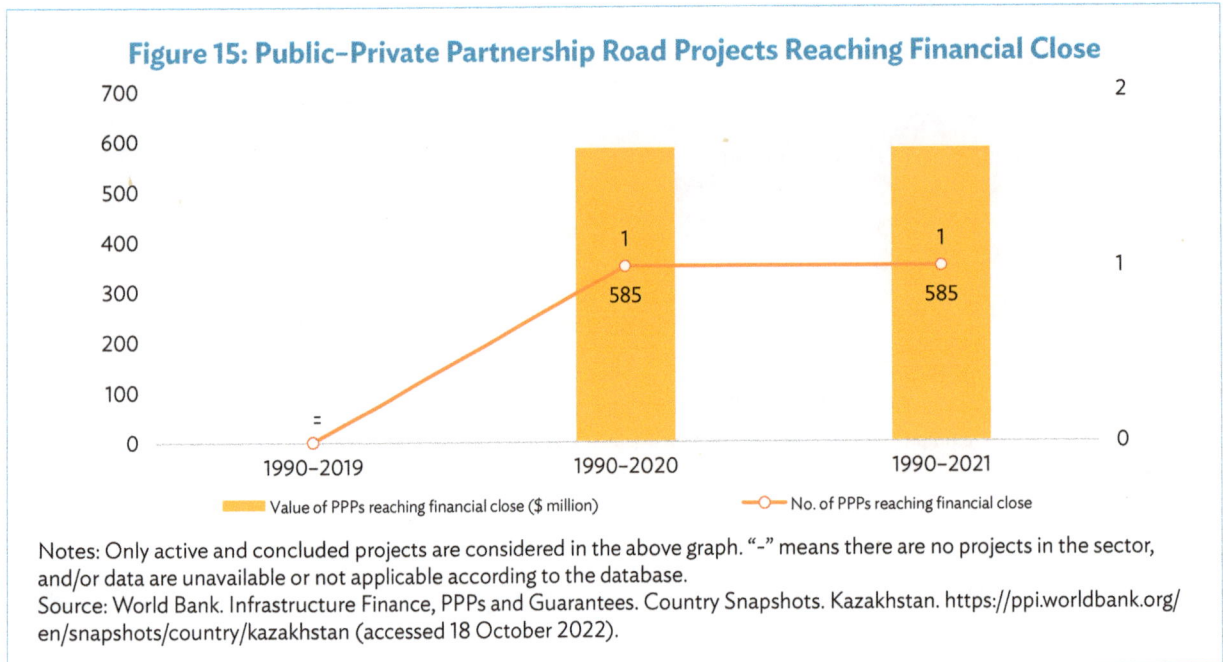

Figure 15: Public–Private Partnership Road Projects Reaching Financial Close

Value of PPPs reaching financial close ($ million)
No. of PPPs reaching financial close

Notes: Only active and concluded projects are considered in the above graph. "-" means there are no projects in the sector, and/or data are unavailable or not applicable according to the database.
Source: World Bank. Infrastructure Finance, PPPs and Guarantees. Country Snapshots. Kazakhstan. https://ppi.worldbank.org/en/snapshots/country/kazakhstan (accessed 18 October 2022).

Figure 16 shows the number of PPP projects that have received foreign sponsor participation in the road sector of Kazakhstan.

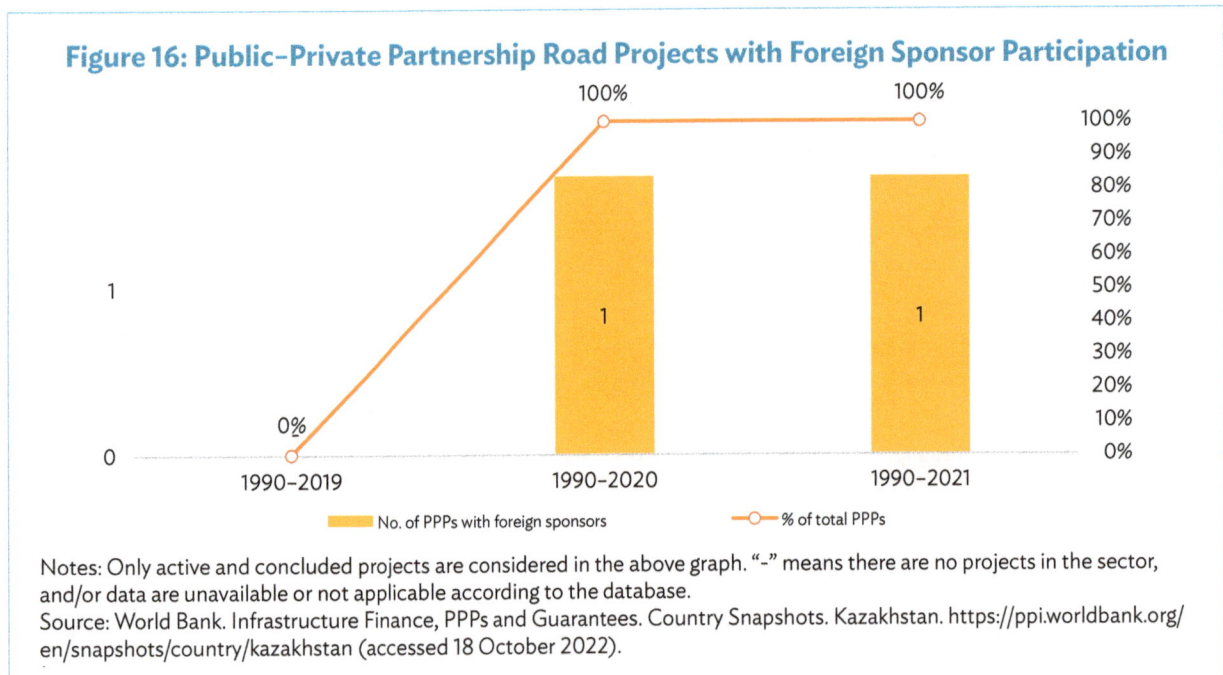

Figure 16: Public–Private Partnership Road Projects with Foreign Sponsor Participation

No. of PPPs with foreign sponsors
% of total PPPs

Notes: Only active and concluded projects are considered in the above graph. "-" means there are no projects in the sector, and/or data are unavailable or not applicable according to the database.
Source: World Bank. Infrastructure Finance, PPPs and Guarantees. Country Snapshots. Kazakhstan. https://ppi.worldbank.org/en/snapshots/country/kazakhstan (accessed 18 October 2022).

Figure 17 shows the number of PPP projects that have received government support including viability gap funding (VGF) mechanism, government guarantees, and availability or performance payment in the road sector of Kazakhstan.

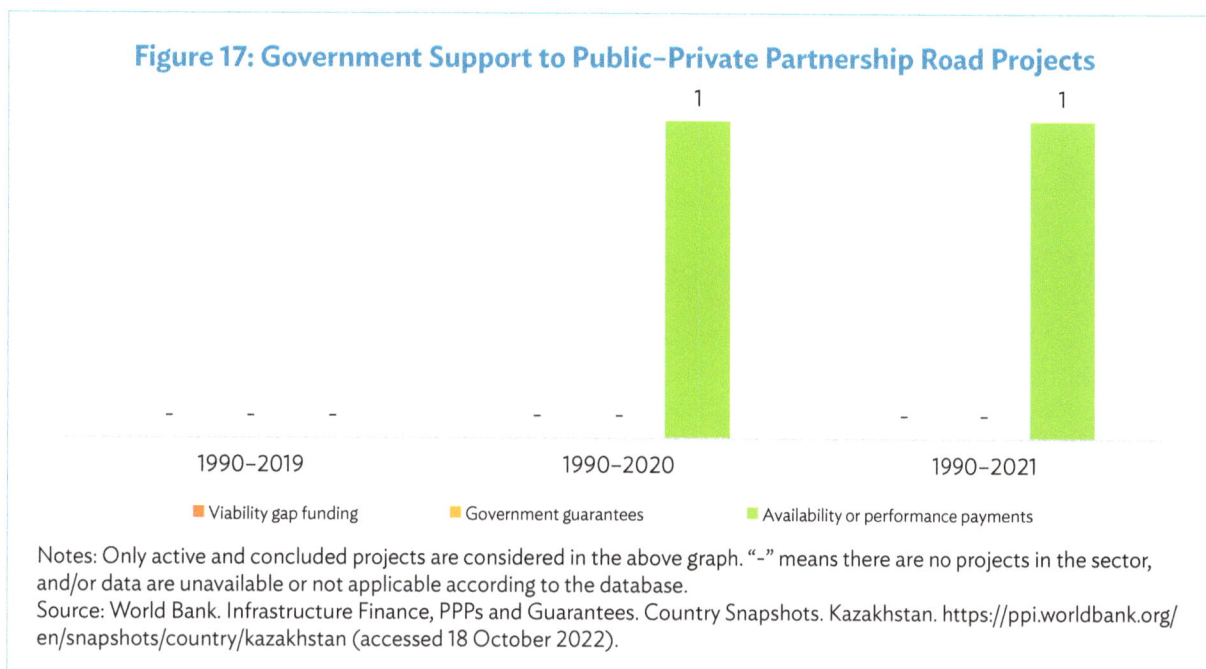

Figure 17: Government Support to Public–Private Partnership Road Projects

Legend: Viability gap funding · Government guarantees · Availability or performance payments

Notes: Only active and concluded projects are considered in the above graph. "-" means there are no projects in the sector, and/or data are unavailable or not applicable according to the database.
Source: World Bank. Infrastructure Finance, PPPs and Guarantees. Country Snapshots. Kazakhstan. https://ppi.worldbank.org/en/snapshots/country/kazakhstan (accessed 18 October 2022).

Figure 18 shows the number of PPP projects that have received payment in the form of user charges and government pay (offtake) in the road sector of Kazakhstan.

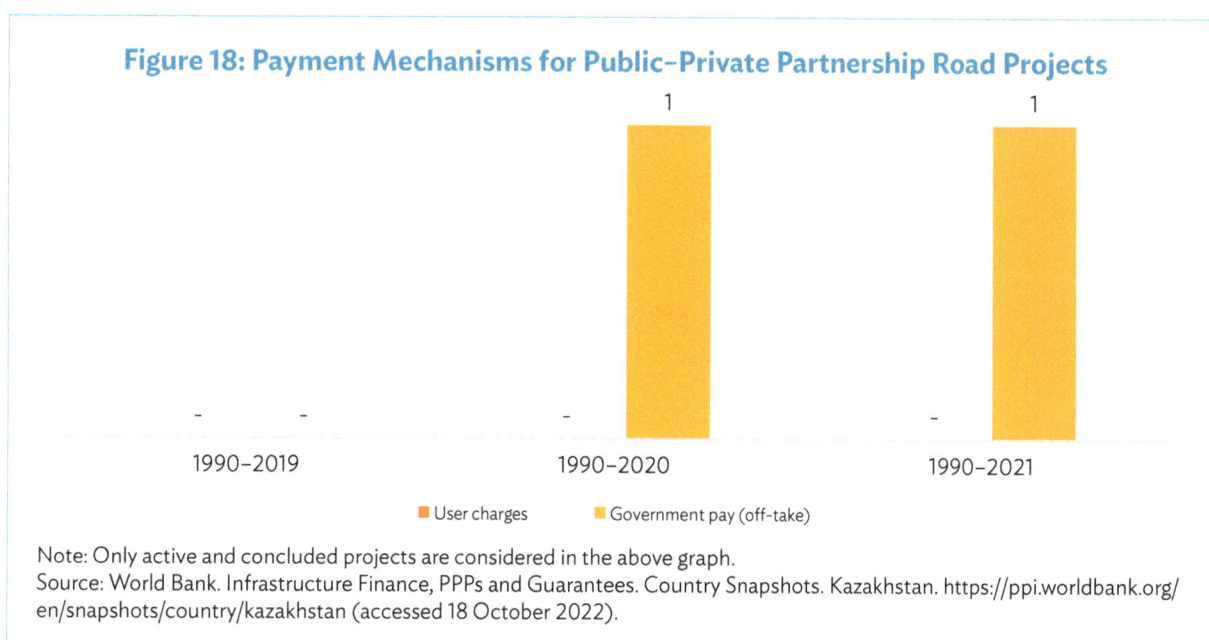

Figure 18: Payment Mechanisms for Public–Private Partnership Road Projects

Legend: User charges · Government pay (off-take)

Note: Only active and concluded projects are considered in the above graph.
Source: World Bank. Infrastructure Finance, PPPs and Guarantees. Country Snapshots. Kazakhstan. https://ppi.worldbank.org/en/snapshots/country/kazakhstan (accessed 18 October 2022).

The past PPP projects in the road sector according to the PPP Center's database, broken down by jurisdiction, is shown in Table 14.

Table 14: Summary of Projects Across Public–Private Partnership in Road Sector

Sector	Number of Projects	Total Cost (T million)	Total Cost ($ million)
Local level	9	1,571	3.3
Republican level	2	286,499	610
Grand total	11	288,070	613.3

Note: Currency equivalent is as of 1 September 2022.
Source: Kazakhstan Public–Private Partnership Center. PPP Project Database. http://www.kzppp.kz/projects (accessed 18 October 2022); Unicase Law LLP.

BAKAD (which reached financial close in 2020) is the only road project on a PPP modality that can be identified as bankable according to international standards and that is listed in the World Bank databank. The projects in the PPP Center's database include automotive bridge construction in North Kazakhstan oblast (signed in 2020), access road construction in Aktobe oblast (signed in 2018), construction of additional infrastructure on Almaty–Khorgos road (signed in 2017), and several service contracts in various regions (Almaty, West Kazakhstan oblast, Aktobe oblast, etc.).

4.1 Tariffs in the Road Sector

Currently, there are 12 toll roads in Kazakhstan, operated and maintained by KazAvtoZhol.[44] The tariffs have remained unchanged since their first introduction in 2013. They are effectively charged on a T per kilometer basis:

- For cars – T1 per km with the possibility of obtaining discounts on monthly passes.
- For buses, depending on the number of passenger seats – from T5 to T15 per km.[45] The buses on international regular routes are exempt from tolls.
- For freight vehicles – depending on load capacity, from T5 to T25 per km.[46]

The tariffs for end users are charged for the whole toll road section (tariff x length of the toll road section).

---

[44] Kazakhstan Strategy 2050 official website. https://strategy2050.kz/ru/news/platnye-dorogi-kak-oformit-godovoy-abonment/ (in Russian, accessed February 2022).
[45] Approximately $0.01 – $0.03.
[46] Approximately $0.01 – $0.05. See Sputnik.kz information website. https://ru.sputnik.kz/economy/20211123/18730980/Novyy-platnye-dorogi-zarabotali-v-Kazakhstane.html (in Russian).

4.2 Typical Risk Allocation for Public–Private Partnership Projects in the Road Sector

A typical risk allocation for road projects is shown in Table 15.[47]

Table 15: Risk Allocations to the Public and Private Sectors for Road Projects, by Risk Type

Risk	Private	Public	Shared
Land expropriation		✓	
Financing risk	✓		
Inflation and cost overruns	✓		
Commissioning of road; meeting hand-back standards	✓		
Availability of road; meeting operating standards	✓		
Traffic risk		✓	
Currency fluctuations			✓
Termination payment; discriminatory change in law	✓		

Source: Unicase Law LLP.

4.3 Financing Details for Public–Private Partnership Projects in the Road Sector

Parameter	1990–2019	1990–2020	1990–2021
PPP projects with foreign lending participation	–	1	1
PPP projects that received export credit agency/international financing institution support	–	1	1
Typical debt: equity ratio			78:22
Time for financial close			3 years
Typical concession period			20
Typical financial internal rate of return	UA	UA	UA

PPP = public–private partnership, UA = unavailable.
Source: Unicase Law LLP.

5. Challenges in the Road Sector

Some of the key challenges to the road sector PPP in Kazakhstan are as follows:

- The geographic conditions of Kazakhstan, which is a large sparsely populated country with an extremely continental climate, lead to high capital expenditures for road construction and reconstruction, and low traffic numbers, thus making road construction and operation commercially unattractive.

- Falling household incomes affect the tariff affordability and willingness to pay, making any traffic-related risk transfer commercially unattractive.

- Absence of a robust pipeline of PPP road projects reduces the interest of reputable private investors.

---

47   There is only one internationally recognized PPP project and that is BAKAD.

B. Railways

Parameter	Value	Unit
Length of total railway network	16,061	total route–km
Total number of passengers carried	19,110	Million passenger–km
Total volume of freight carried	2,19,927	Million ton–km
Quality of railways infrastructure	4.20	1(low) – 7(high)

Sources: The Economist Intelligence Unit 2019. Infrascope: Kazakhstan Country Report. https://infrascope.eiu.com/; The Global Economy. Railway Passengers—Country Rankings. https://www.theglobaleconomy.com/rankings/Railway_passengers/; The Global Economy. Railway Transport of Goods—Country Rankings. https://www.theglobaleconomy.com/rankings/Railway_transport_of_goods/; The Global Economy. Railroad Infrastructure Quality—Country Rankings. https://www.theglobaleconomy.com/rankings/railroad_quality/.

Railroads are the backbone of Kazakhstan's transport infrastructure. OECD estimates investment needs in developing the railway sector at $4.5 billion. Lack of access to sea, flat terrain, and sparsely located settlements are the main reasons behind putting priority emphasis to this transportation mode in the Soviet times, which now carries up to a half of the country's freight. Kazakhstan's railways run on the Russian standard gauge of 1,520 mm, which hinders the use of international investors and contractors in railroad construction and maintenance. For the country to increase its attractiveness in rail transportation, it will need to invest primarily in speed improvements, reduction of maintenance costs, electrification, and construction of new lines.[48]

1. Contracting Agencies in the Railway Sector

The Transport Committee under MIID is the key competent body responsible for regulatory, implementation, and control functions in implementing the state strategy in the railway transport. It is authorized to decide which railway passages can be procured as concession/PPP projects. The Transport Committee can hire consultants for preparing and structuring such projects and sign project agreements on behalf of the government.

Kazakhstan Temir Zholy JSC (KTZ), a quasi-state enterprise and a subsidiary of the national Wealth Management Fund Samruk-Kazyna, is the national railway network operator that carry out railway track operations and maintenance, locomotive traction and rolling stock operations, and railway track freight logistics. KTZ can be legally a part of PPP agreements as a joint venture party, offtaker, or guarantor of traffic risks.

2. Railway Sector Laws and Regulations

The main legislation governing the railway sector is the Law of the Republic of Kazakhstan "On Railway Transport," or the Law on Railways.

The November 2020 amendments to the Law on Railways included changes to the definition of "freight" and rules for freight transportation, which filled the legal gap that prevented KTZ from charging a transit tariff for the transportation of its own empty wagons. The amendment also extended the validity period of the temporary balancing charge. KTZ is currently undertaking a privatization program of its non-core assets.[49]

---

[48]   OECD. 2019. *Sustainable Infrastructure for Low-Carbon Development in Central Asia and the Caucasus: Hotspot Analysis and Needs Assessment.* Paris. https://doi.org/10.1787/d1aa6ae9-en.

[49]   Law of the Republic of Kazakhstan "On Amendments and Supplements to Certain Legal Acts of the Republic of Kazakhstan on Energy, Transport and State Awards" dated 9 November 2020.

2.1 Foreign Investment Restrictions in the Railway Sector

The ownership allowance in the railway sector is indicated below.

Parameter	2019	2020	2021
Maximum allowed foreign ownership of equity in greenfield projects	100%[a]	100%[a]	100%[a]

PPP = public–private partnership.
[a] Except for trunk railway network, which is not subject to concessions/PPPs and not subject to privatization/private participation.
Sources: ADB. 2019. *Public–Private Partnership Monitor*. Second Edition. Manila. https://www.adb.org/sites/default/files/publication/509426/ppp-monitor-second-edition.pdf; Unicase Law LLP.

2.2 Standard Contracts in the Railway Sector

Type of Contract	Availability
PPP/concession agreement	✗
Performance-based operation and maintenance contract	✗
Engineering procurement and construction contract	✗

✗ = no, PPP = public–private partnership.
Source: Unicase Law LLP.

There are no standard contracts specific to the railway sector yet.

3. Railway Sector Master Plan

Railway sector development in Kazakhstan is guided by two strategic documents:

(i) Nurly Zhol program, which proposes that KTZ shall, with the support from the republican budget, implement three investment projects, namely,

- modernization of the railway transit corridor section Dostyk–Moiynty,
- electrification of the railway sections Moiynty–Aktogay and Tobol–Nikeltau, and
- construction of a bypass railway line Kokpekty–Karagayly bypassing Lake Karasor.

Nurly Zhol also calls for the electrification of the existing railway lines using a PPP mechanism, as well as railway station development, operation, and maintenance.

(ii) The KTZ Strategy, effective until 2029, outlines three strategic directions:

- Improving the technological conditions for transit traffic along the trans-Eurasian corridors (e.g., increasing the speed of transit trains, optimizing the customs processing time).
- Eliminating the bottlenecks along the PRC–European Union–PRC transit route (Dostyk–Mointy section).
- Improving the regulatory environment for a competitive carrier market and deregulation of locomotive traction tariffs.
- Privatizing 28 out of 64 non-core subsidiaries.

3.1 Projects under Preparation and Procurement in the Railway Sector

Figure 19 shows the number of PPP projects that are under preparation and procurement in the railway sector of Kazakhstan.

Figure 19: Public–Private Partnership Railway Projects under Preparation and Procurement

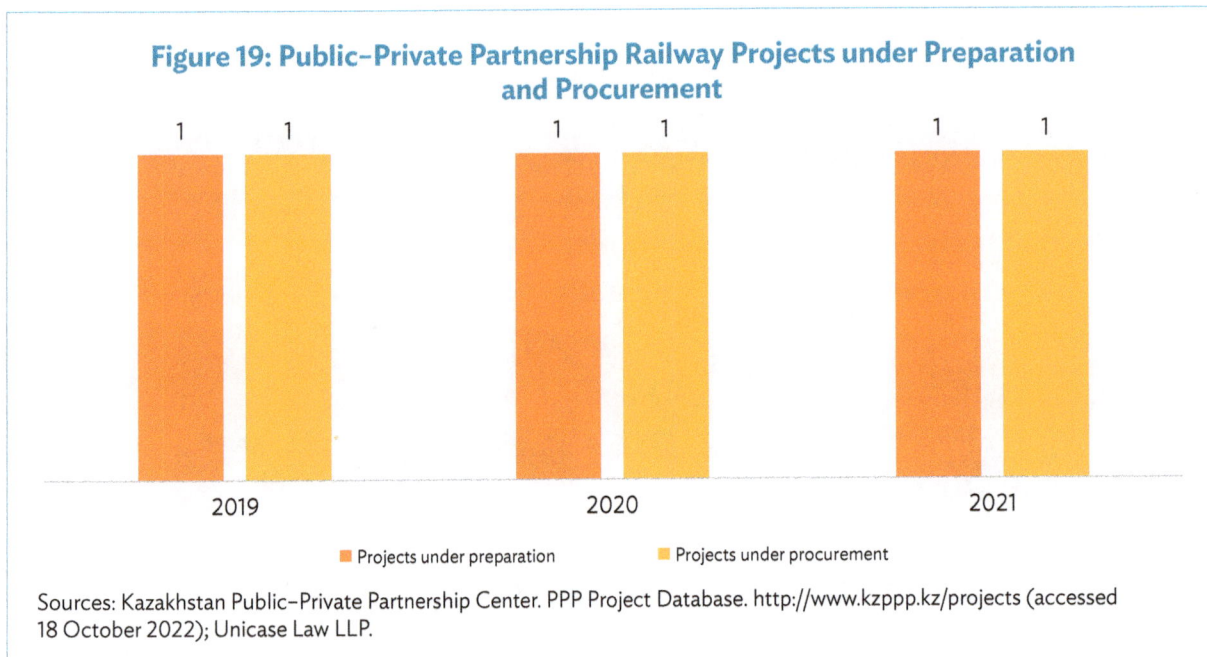

■ Projects under preparation   ■ Projects under procurement

Sources: Kazakhstan Public–Private Partnership Center. PPP Project Database. http://www.kzppp.kz/projects (accessed 18 October 2022); Unicase Law LLP.

4. Features of Past Public–Private Partnership Projects in the Railway Sector

Figure 20 shows the number of PPP projects procured through various modes, including direct appointment, unsolicited bids, and competitive bids in the railway sector of Kazakhstan.

Figure 20: Modes of Procurement for Public–Private Partnership Railway Projects

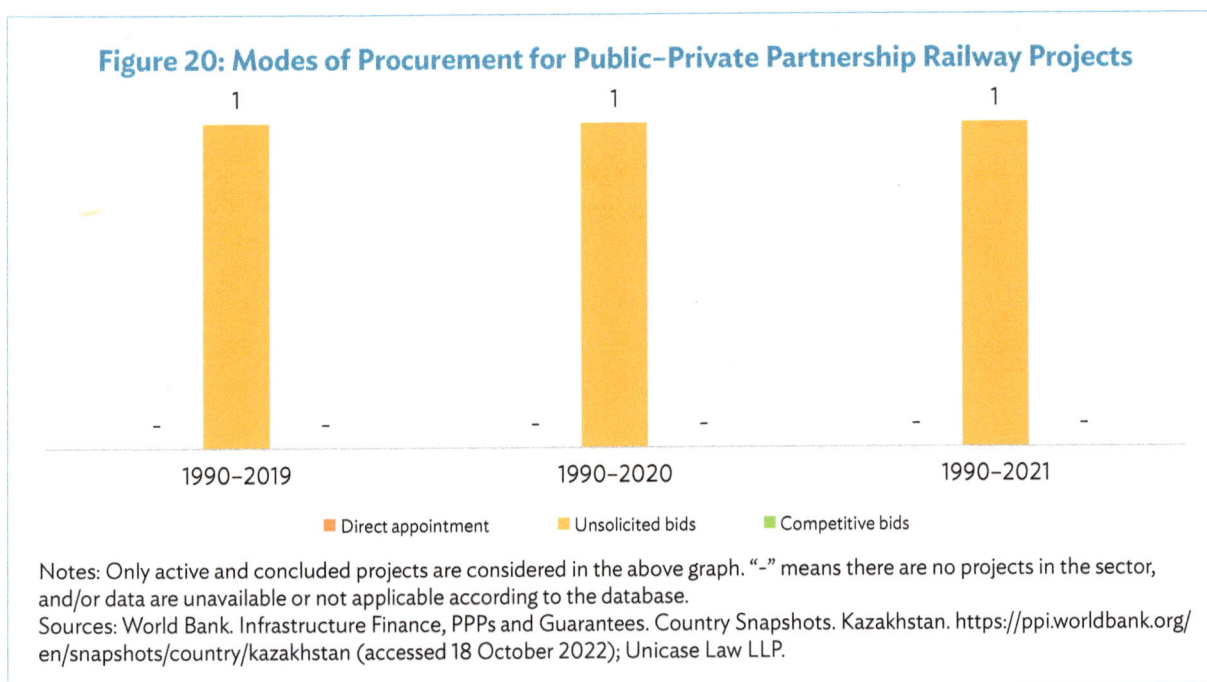

■ Direct appointment   ■ Unsolicited bids   ■ Competitive bids

Notes: Only active and concluded projects are considered in the above graph. "-" means there are no projects in the sector, and/or data are unavailable or not applicable according to the database.
Sources: World Bank. Infrastructure Finance, PPPs and Guarantees. Country Snapshots. Kazakhstan. https://ppi.worldbank.org/en/snapshots/country/kazakhstan (accessed 18 October 2022); Unicase Law LLP.

Figure 21 shows the number of PPP projects that have reached financial close and the total value of those projects in the railway sector of Kazakhstan.

Figure 21: Public–Private Partnership Railway Projects Reaching Financial Close

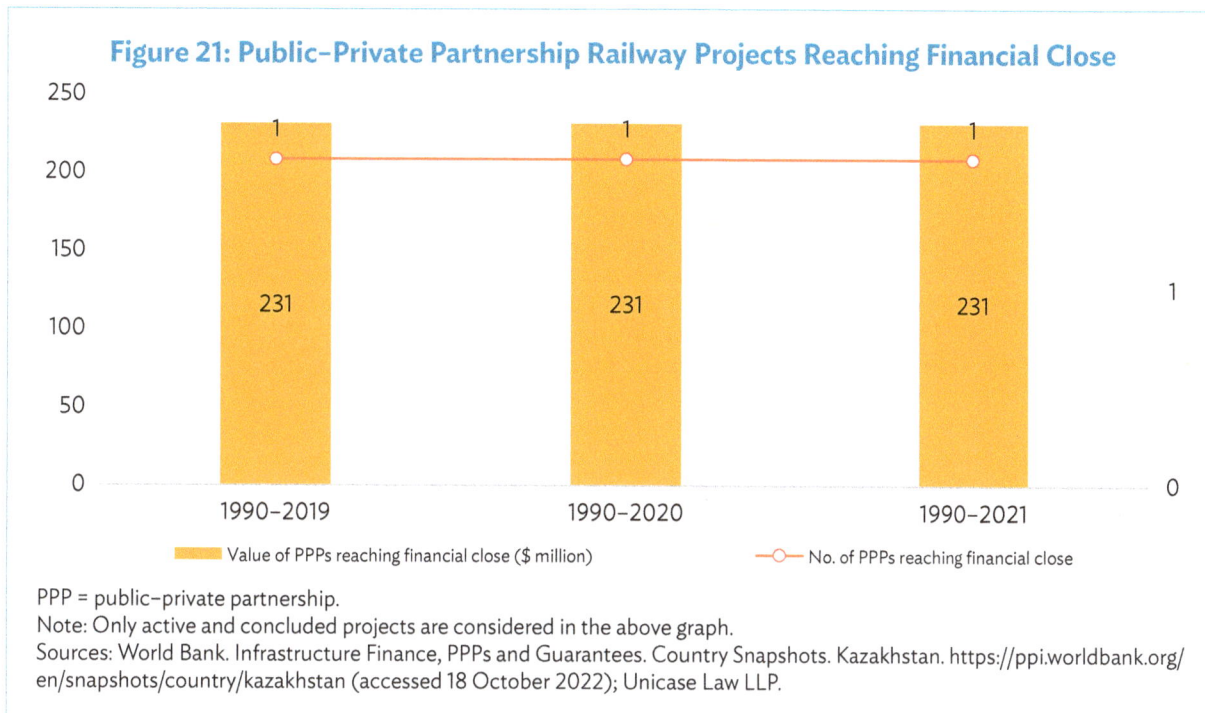

PPP = public–private partnership.
Note: Only active and concluded projects are considered in the above graph.
Sources: World Bank. Infrastructure Finance, PPPs and Guarantees. Country Snapshots. Kazakhstan. https://ppi.worldbank.org/en/snapshots/country/kazakhstan (accessed 18 October 2022); Unicase Law LLP.

Figure 22 shows the number of PPP projects that have received foreign sponsor participation in the railway sector of Kazakhstan.

Figure 22: Public–Private Partnership Railway Projects with Foreign Sponsor Participation

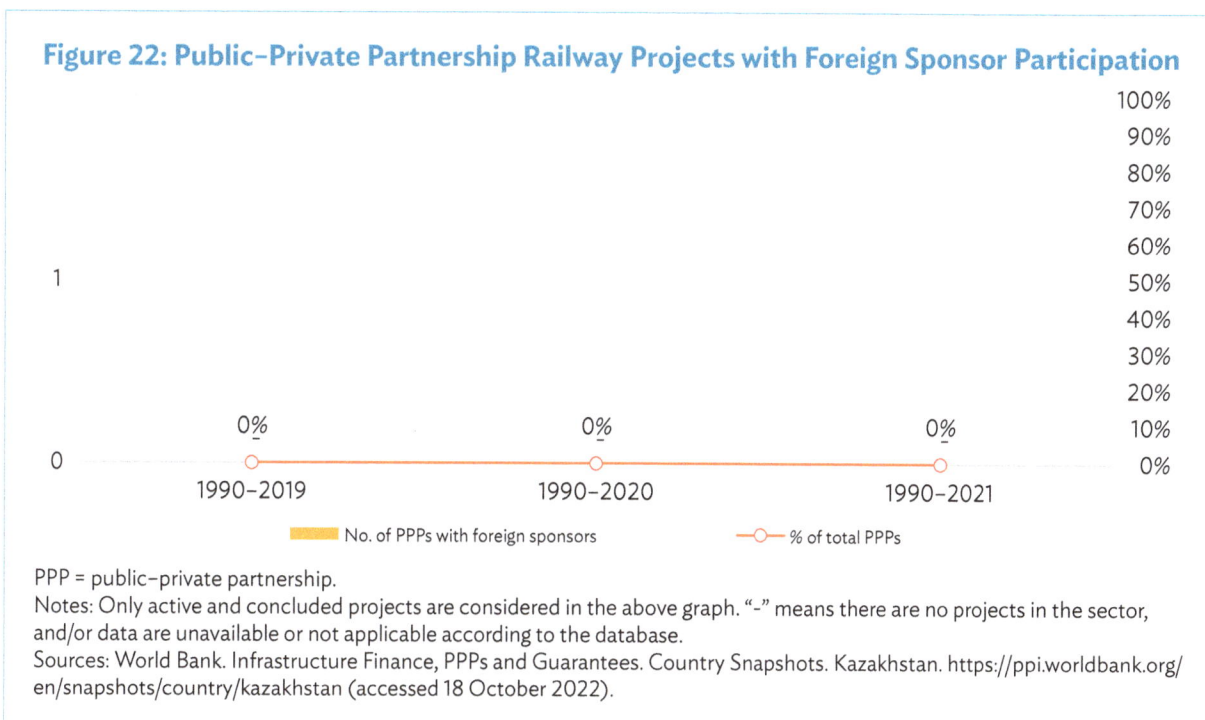

PPP = public–private partnership.
Notes: Only active and concluded projects are considered in the above graph. "-" means there are no projects in the sector, and/or data are unavailable or not applicable according to the database.
Sources: World Bank. Infrastructure Finance, PPPs and Guarantees. Country Snapshots. Kazakhstan. https://ppi.worldbank.org/en/snapshots/country/kazakhstan (accessed 18 October 2022).

The number of PPP projects that have received government support including VGF mechanism, government guarantees, and availability or performance payment in the railway sector of Kazakhstan are shown in Figure 23.

Figure 23: Government Support to Public–Private Partnership Railway Projects

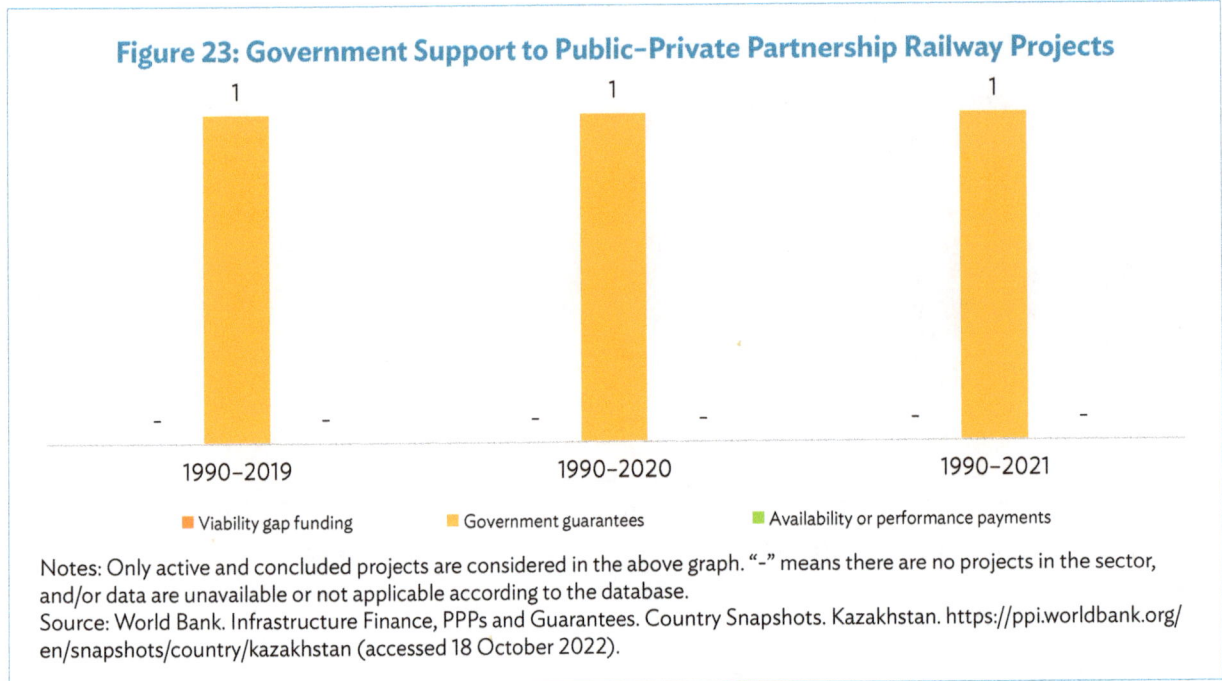

Notes: Only active and concluded projects are considered in the above graph. "-" means there are no projects in the sector, and/or data are unavailable or not applicable according to the database.
Source: World Bank. Infrastructure Finance, PPPs and Guarantees. Country Snapshots. Kazakhstan. https://ppi.worldbank.org/en/snapshots/country/kazakhstan (accessed 18 October 2022).

Figure 24 shows the number of PPP projects that have received payment in the form of user charges and government pay (offtake) in the railway sector of Kazakhstan.

Figure 24: Payment Mechanism for Public–Private Partnership Railway Projects

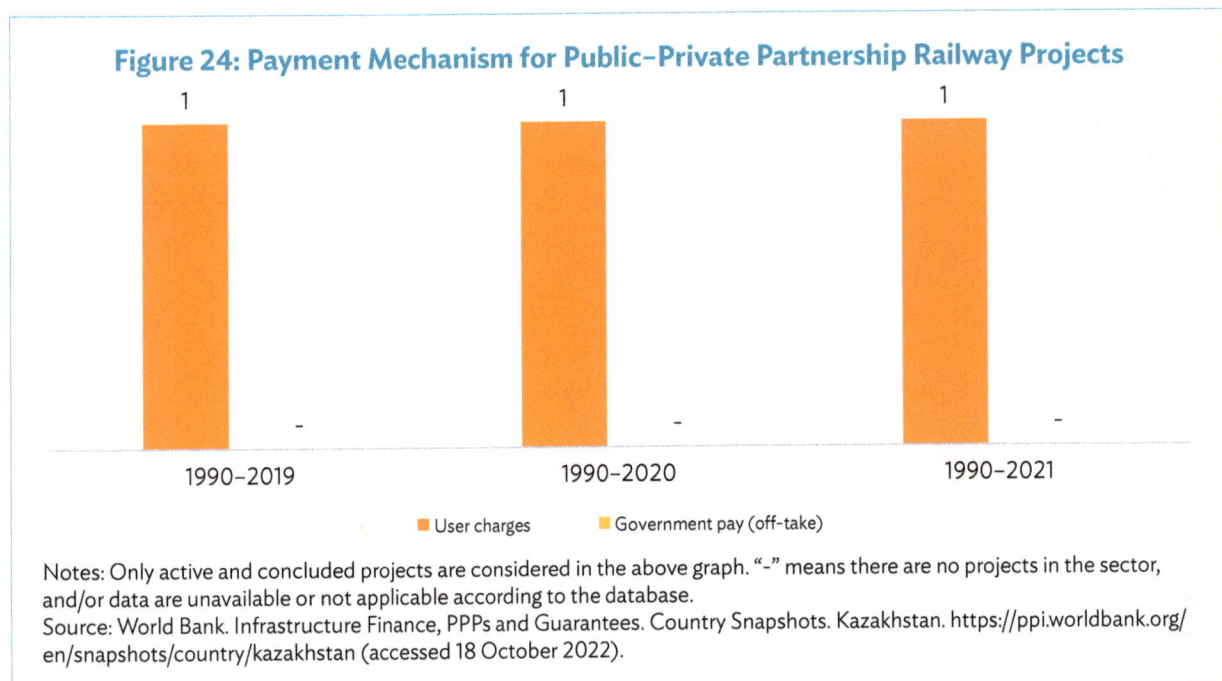

Notes: Only active and concluded projects are considered in the above graph. "-" means there are no projects in the sector, and/or data are unavailable or not applicable according to the database.
Source: World Bank. Infrastructure Finance, PPPs and Guarantees. Country Snapshots. Kazakhstan. https://ppi.worldbank.org/en/snapshots/country/kazakhstan (accessed 18 October 2022).

The past PPP projects in the railway sector according to the PPP Center's database, classified based on the jurisdiction, is provided in Table 16.

Table 16: Summary of Projects Across Public–Private Partnerships in the Railway Sector

Sector	Number of Projects	Total Cost (T million)	Total Cost ($ million)
Local level	1	468	1
Republican level	1	55,231	117.6
Grand total	**2**	**55,699**	**118.6**

Note: Currency equivalent is as of 1 September 2022.
Sources: Kazakhstan Public–Private Partnership Center. PPP Project Database. http://www.kzppp.kz/projects (accessed 18 October 2022); Unicase Law LLP.

The railway sector in Kazakhstan has one major PPP project, the construction of 153-kilometer rail line Shar–Oskemen, signed in 2005.

4.1 Tariffs in the Railway Sector

Railway tariffs are partly market-based and partly regulated as a natural monopoly:

- Infrastructure is regarded as a natural monopoly; the regulator CREM sets infrastructure tariffs, subject to change every 5 years or more.

- Tariffs for traction, commercial, and freight services are regulated to protect competition. The regulator CREM updates the associated tariffs, generally at intervals of a year or more.

- Tariffs for domestic, export, and import freight railway operations are subject to regulation to protect competition, while tariffs for transit and container operations are unregulated.[50]

There are many elements to railway tariffs in Kazakhstan, and the calculation is complex, based on distance, type of locomotive traction, and type of cargo and freight, among others.[51]

4.2 Typical Risk Allocation for Public–Private Partnership Projects in the Railway Sector

A typical risk allocation for railway sector projects is unavailable.

---

[50]   CAREC. 2021. *Railway Sector Assessment for Republic of Kazakhstan.*
[51]   A detailed calculation methodology along with the current tariff levels is available at KTZ's website: https://www.ktzh-gp.kz/new-ru/shippers/cargo-transportation/.

4.3 Financing Details for Public–Private Partnership Projects in the Railway Sector

Parameter	1990–2019	1990–2020	1990–2021
PPP projects with foreign lending participation	–	–	–
PPP projects that received export credit agency/international financing institution support	–	–	–
Typical debt to equity ratio	UA	UA	UA
Time for financial close	UA	UA	UA
Typical concession period	23	23	23
Typical financial internal rate of return	UA	UA	UA

PPP = public–private partnership, UA = unavailable.
Source: World Bank. Infrastructure Finance, PPPs and Guarantees. Country Snapshots. Kazakhstan. https://ppi.worldbank.org/en/snapshots/country/kazakhstan (accessed 18 October 2022).

5. Challenges in the Railway Sector

The railway sector faces the following challenges:

- The railway tariffs are not set to reflect the costs, and tariff setting practices are inflexible. Certain types of freight are cross-subsidized (e.g., coal vs. oil products), resulting in inefficient capacity utilization and reduced profitability of the sector.

- The dominance of KTZ in all areas of railway transportation deters private companies and investors from investing in the sector.

- Legal restrictions to private sector participation in track ownership, operation, and maintenance limit the use of PPP procurement mode and restrict private financing.

- The 1,520-millimeter track gauge limits the investor base and choice of equipment and technologies.

C. Airports

Parameter	Value	Unit
No. of airports	23	No.
Total passenger capacity	6.80	million passengers
Quality of air transport infrastructure	4.30	1(low) – 7 (high)
Total number of projects with cumulative lending, grant, and technical assistance commitments in the transport sector	28	Number
Total amount of cumulative lending, grant, and technical assistance commitments in the transport sector	2,038	$ million

Sources: City Population. 2021 https://www.citypopulation.de/en/world/bymap/Airports.html; World Bank. 2020 https://data.worldbank.org/indicator/IS.AIR.PSGR?locations=BD-KH-GE-KZ-MM-PK-PG-LK-UZ-VN-CN-IN-ID-PH-TH; The Global Economy. Compare Countries. Compare countries | TheGlobalEconomy.com; Asian Development Bank. Cumulative Lending, Grant, and Technical Assistance Commitments. https://data.adb.org/dataset/cumulative-lending-grant-and-technical-assistance-commitments.

Out of 23 airports in Kazakhstan, 15 are admitted to servicing international flights, and two airports (those of Almaty and Astana) comply with the International Civil Aviation Organization (ICAO) IIIA and IIIB standards.

1. Contracting Agencies in the Airport Sector

The Civil Aviation Committee under MIID is responsible for the overall sector policies, strategy, and general oversight. The main objectives of the Committee are coordination and regulation of civil aviation, ensuring the safe use of Kazakhstan's airspace, certification, and control and monitoring of the performance of industry participants.

The contracting authority for airports depends on the airport ownership allocation:

- MIID, via its Civil Aviation Committee, for republican projects and if the ownership is directly by the state.
- Local *akimats*, for regional projects, or if the airport is owned by regional authorities.
- Republican State Enterprise Kazaeronavigatsia has the exclusive rights to provide air navigation services in Kazakhstan. It has 15 subsidiaries registered in different regions of the country with its head office in Astana.

2. Airport Sector Laws and Regulations

The main legal act governing airport sector in Kazakhstan is the Law of the Republic of Kazakhstan "On use of airspace of the Republic of Kazakhstan and aviation activity" No. 339-IV dated 15 July 2010 (Aviation Law). It covers the following:

- State regulation and state control of airspace management and aviation operations
- Organization of airspace management, international flights, aircraft, aviation personnel, operators, airports, air services, and aviation work
- Legal requirements in air services, including activities that affect flight operating services, air accidents and their investigation, and rescue works in relation to aircrafts, their passengers, and crew members.

Generally, the airports' assets or ownership are regarded as either of "strategic" or of "socioeconomic significance for the development of Kazakh society," which restricts private sector participation. However, not all of them are formally included in the list of strategic objects banned from privatization, as currently established by the Government of Kazakhstan. Transfer of ownership of the airports in that list is subject to additional approvals by the government.[52]

2.1 Foreign Investment Restrictions in the Airport Sector

Parameter	2019	2020	2021
Maximum allowed foreign ownership of equity in greenfield projects	100%	100%	100%

Sources: ADB. 2019. *Public–Private Partnership Monitor*. Second Edition. Manila. https://www.adb.org/sites/default/files/publication/509426/ppp-monitor-second-edition.pdf; Unicase Law LLP.

Airports can be owned by the state and/or private legal entities, including foreign legal entities, according to Article 5 and Article 64 of the Aviation Law.

---

[52]   Asian Development Bank. 2019. *Public–Private Partnership Monitor*. Second Edition. Manila.

2.2 Standard Contracts in the Airport Sector

Type of Contract	Availability
PPP/concession agreement	✗
Performance-based operation and maintenance contract	✗
Engineering, procurement, and construction contract	✗

✗ = no, PPP = public–private partnership.
Source: Unicase Law LLP.

There are no standard contract forms for PPPs in the airport sector yet.

3. Airport Sector Master Plan

There is no specific airport sector master plan. The sector development plans are outlined in the second stage of the Nurly Zhol program, which highlights the need for reconstruction and modernization of the existing airfield infrastructure and construction of new ones, to ensure development of regional air transportation.

Under the first stage of the program (2015–2019), a number of significant infrastructure projects have been implemented in the civil aviation industry, including the construction of a new terminal at Astana airport, and reconstruction and modernization of the runways of airports in the cities of Almaty, Semey, Taraz, Uralsk, and Petropavlovsk. There are plans to develop transit service infrastructure through the air hubs of Astana, Aktobe, Atyrau, Aktau, and Almaty with the opening of additional international and transit routes, and modernization and renewal of the fleet of Kazakhstan's air carriers operating international flights.

3.1 Projects under Preparation and Procurement in the Airport Sector

Figure 25 shows the number of PPP projects that are under preparation and procurement in the airport sector of Kazakhstan.

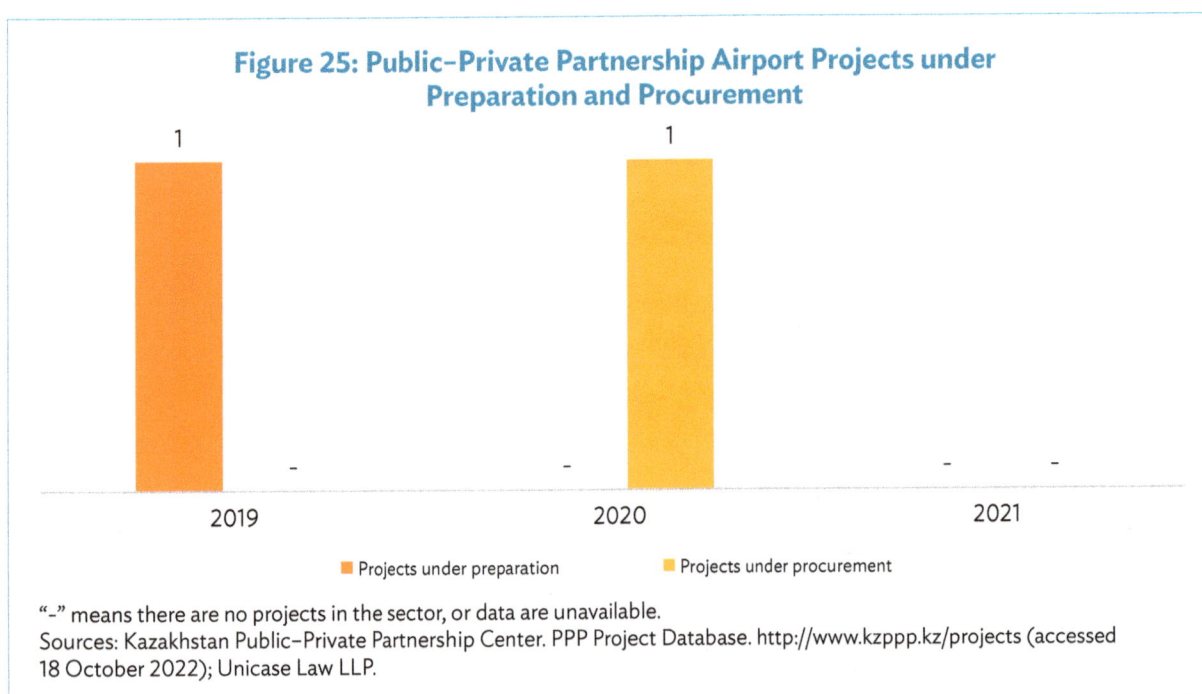

Figure 25: Public–Private Partnership Airport Projects under Preparation and Procurement

■ Projects under preparation   ■ Projects under procurement

"-" means there are no projects in the sector, or data are unavailable.
Sources: Kazakhstan Public–Private Partnership Center. PPP Project Database. http://www.kzppp.kz/projects (accessed 18 October 2022); Unicase Law LLP.

4. Features of Past Public–Private Partnership Projects in the Airport Sector

Figure 26 shows the features of PPP in the airport sector of Kazakhstan.

Figure 26: Modes of Procurement for Public–Private Partnership Airport Projects

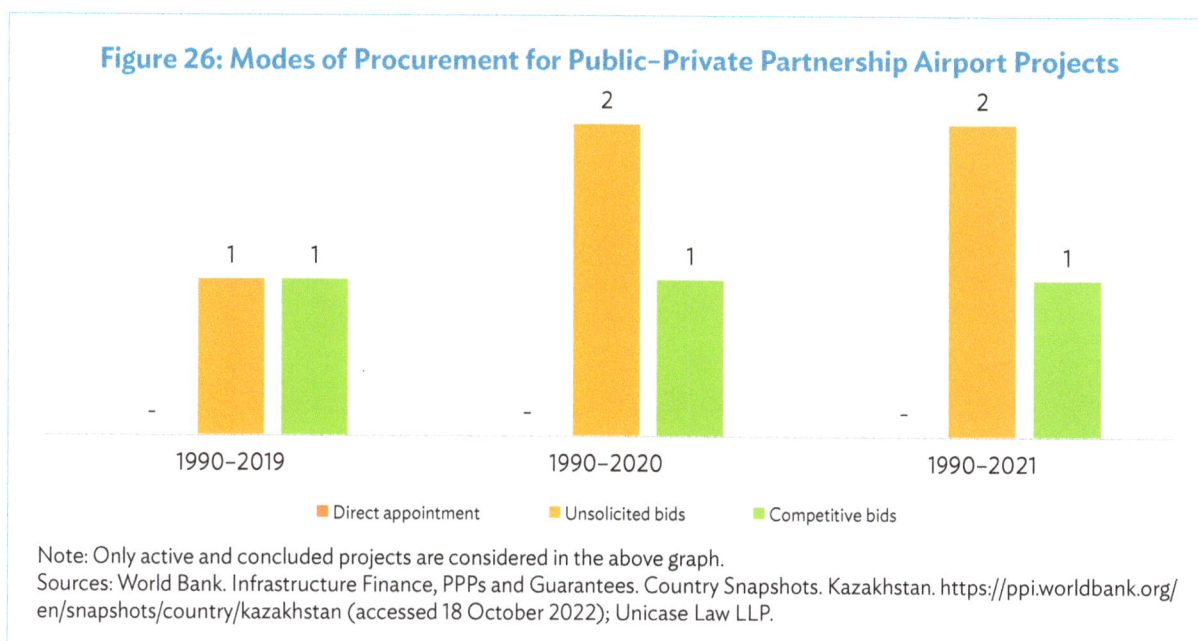

Note: Only active and concluded projects are considered in the above graph.
Sources: World Bank. Infrastructure Finance, PPPs and Guarantees. Country Snapshots. Kazakhstan. https://ppi.worldbank.org/en/snapshots/country/kazakhstan (accessed 18 October 2022); Unicase Law LLP.

Figure 27 shows the number of PPP projects that have reached financial close and the total value of those projects in the airport sector of Kazakhstan.

Figure 27: Public–Private Partnership Airport Projects Reaching Financial Close

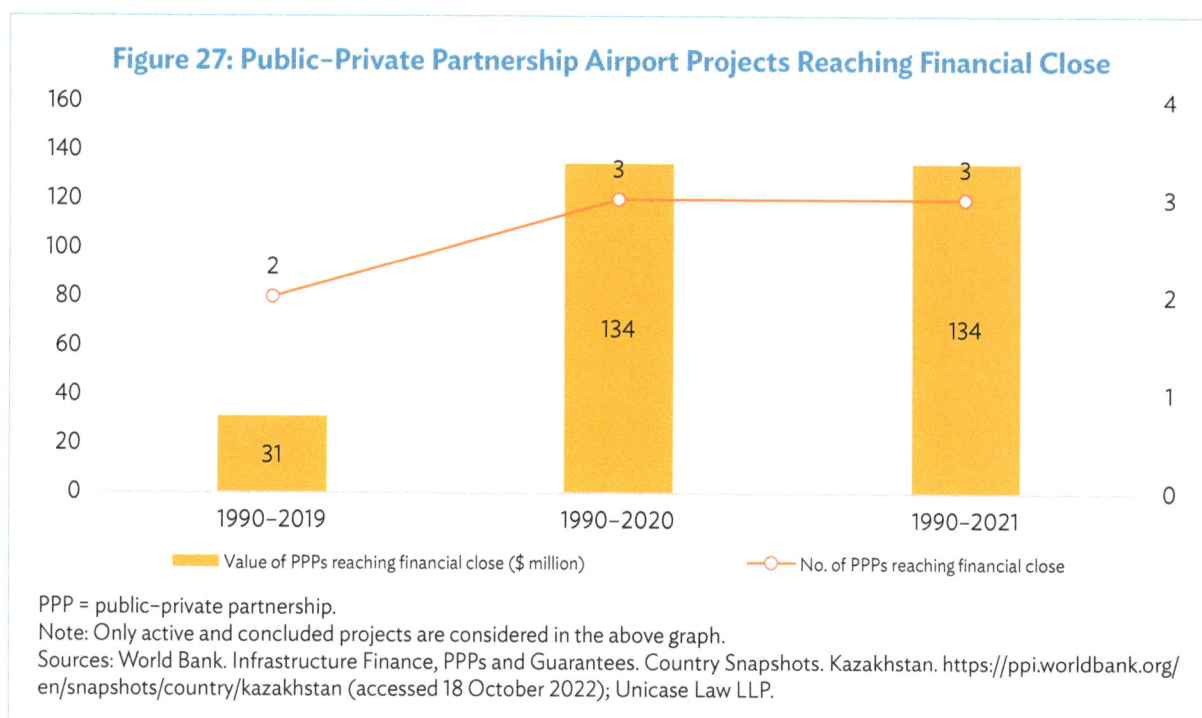

PPP = public–private partnership.
Note: Only active and concluded projects are considered in the above graph.
Sources: World Bank. Infrastructure Finance, PPPs and Guarantees. Country Snapshots. Kazakhstan. https://ppi.worldbank.org/en/snapshots/country/kazakhstan (accessed 18 October 2022); Unicase Law LLP.

Figure 28 shows the number of PPP projects that have received foreign sponsor participation in the airport sector of Kazakhstan.

Figure 28: Public–Private Partnership Airport Projects with Foreign Sponsor Participation

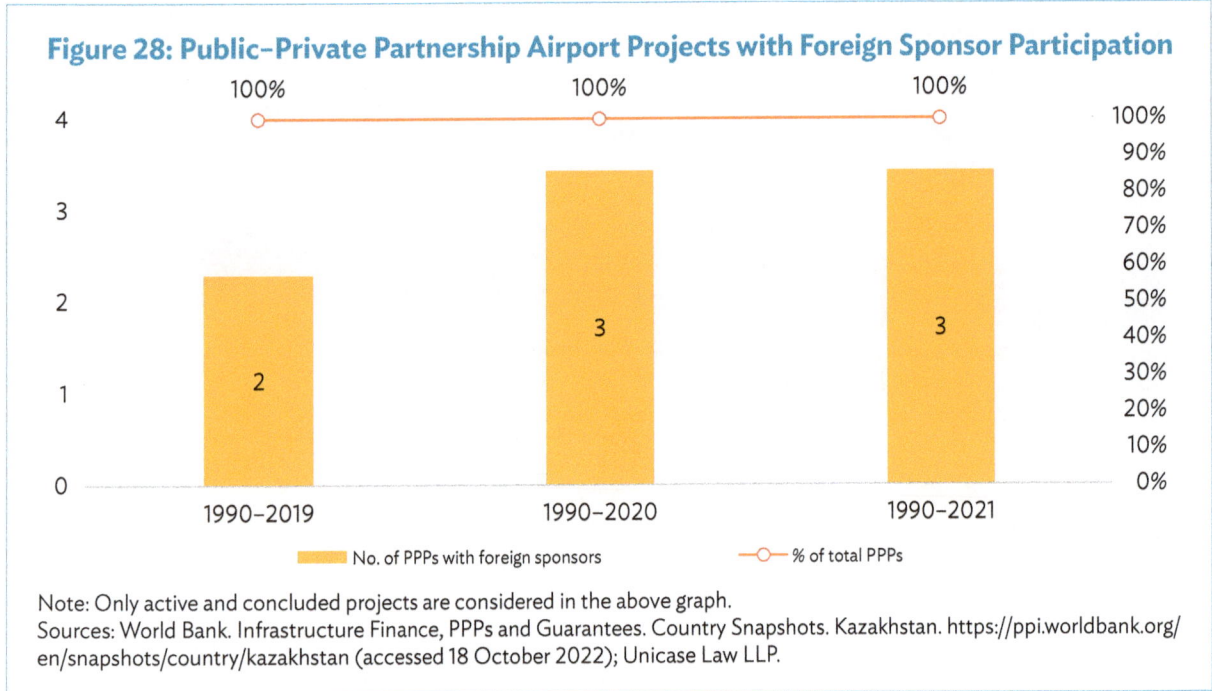

Note: Only active and concluded projects are considered in the above graph.
Sources: World Bank. Infrastructure Finance, PPPs and Guarantees. Country Snapshots. Kazakhstan. https://ppi.worldbank.org/en/snapshots/country/kazakhstan (accessed 18 October 2022); Unicase Law LLP.

The number of PPP projects that have received government support, including VGF mechanism, government guarantees, and availability or performance payment in the airport sector, are shown in Figure 29.

Figure 29: Government Support to Public–Private Partnership Airport Projects

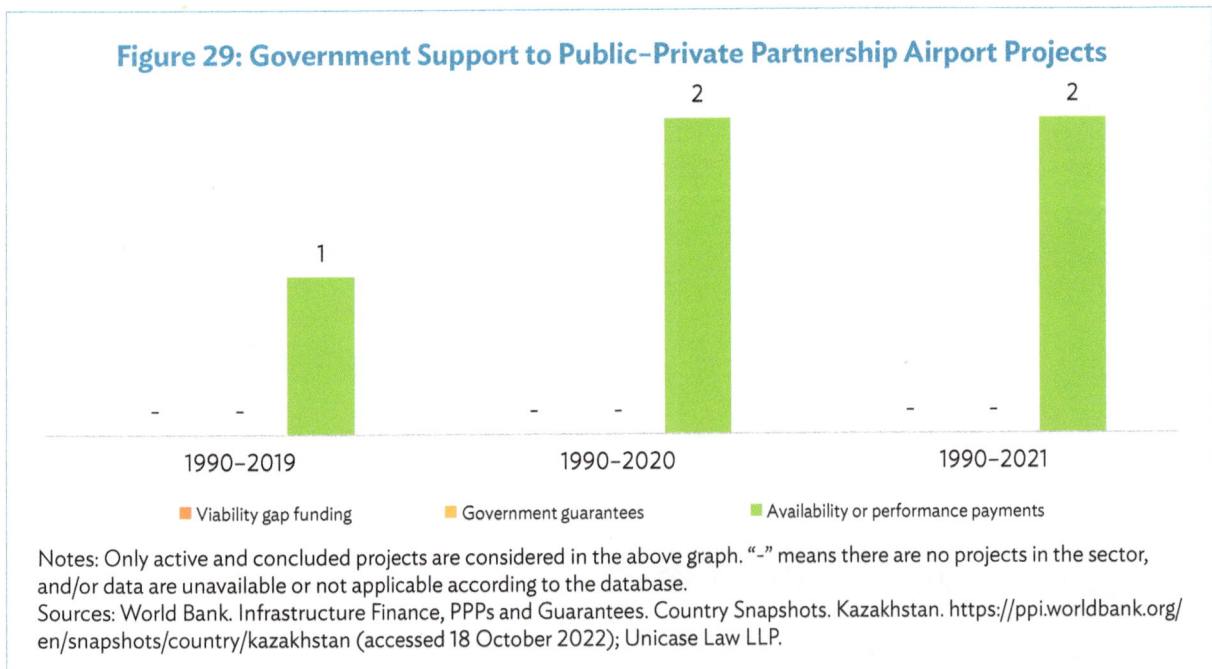

Notes: Only active and concluded projects are considered in the above graph. "-" means there are no projects in the sector, and/or data are unavailable or not applicable according to the database.
Sources: World Bank. Infrastructure Finance, PPPs and Guarantees. Country Snapshots. Kazakhstan. https://ppi.worldbank.org/en/snapshots/country/kazakhstan (accessed 18 October 2022); Unicase Law LLP.

Figure 30 shows the number of PPP projects that have received payments in the form of user charges and government pay (offtake) in the airport sector of Kazakhstan.

Figure 30: Payment Mechanisms for Public–Private Partnership Airport Projects

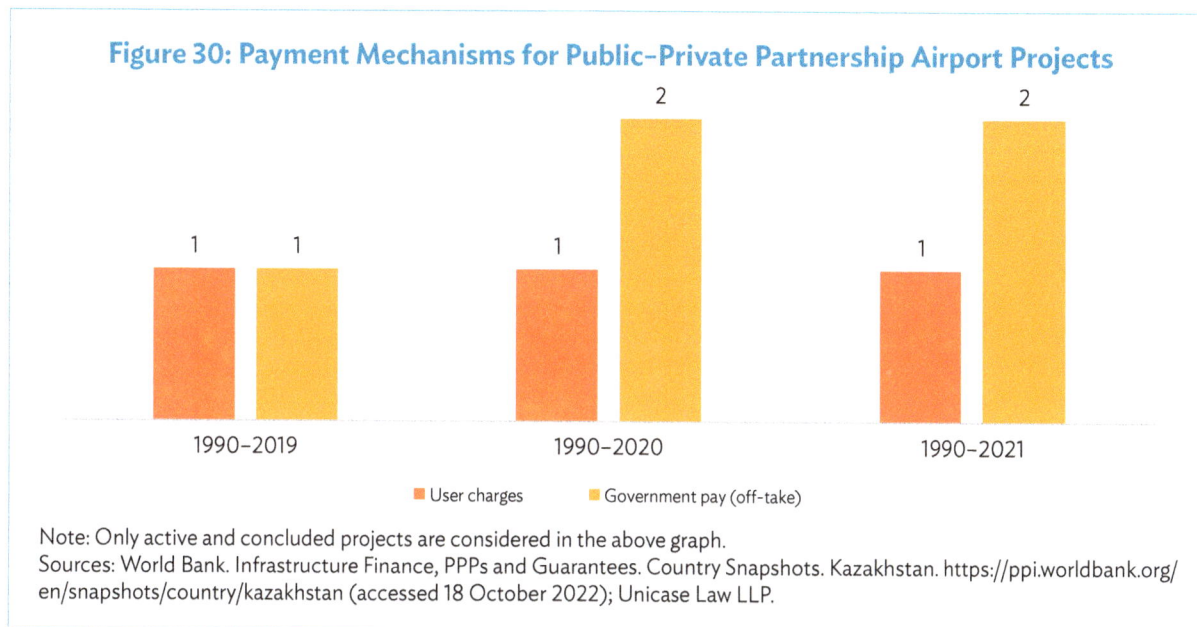

Note: Only active and concluded projects are considered in the above graph.
Sources: World Bank. Infrastructure Finance, PPPs and Guarantees. Country Snapshots. Kazakhstan. https://ppi.worldbank.org/en/snapshots/country/kazakhstan (accessed 18 October 2022); Unicase Law LLP.

The past PPP projects in the airport sector according to the PPP Center's database, broken down by jurisdiction, is provided in Table 17.

Table 17: Summary of Projects Across Public–Private Partnership in the Airport Sector

Sector	Number of Projects	Total Cost (T million)	Total Cost ($ million)
Local level	2	134,217	286
Republican level	2	8,344	18
Grand Total	**4**	**142,561**	**304**

Note: Currency equivalent is as of 1 September 2022.
Sources: Kazakhstan Public–Private Partnership Center. PPP Project Database. http://www.kzppp.kz/projects (accessed 18 October 2022); Unicase Law LLP.

According to the PPP Center's database, the list of projects in the airport sector includes Aktau airport (signed in 2007) and Turkestan airport (signed in 2020). There are also smaller PPP projects at airports providing information systems. Although there are intentions to start the preparation process for an airport in Northern Kazakhstan, this project is not yet listed in the PPP database.

4.1 Tariffs in the Airport Sector

Airport services are subject to natural monopoly regulation. In 2017, the commercial regulation of airport tariffs has been transferred from CREM to the Committee of Civil Aviation under MIID, which sets tariffs for the following activities:

- provision of take-off and landing services for aircraft
- provision of aviation security
- provision of parking area for aircraft over a certain time limit (for more than 3 hours after landing for passenger aircraft and for more than 6 hours for cargo certified aircraft with cargo [post] to be handled [loading and/or uploading] at the airport)
- provision of parking area for the aircraft at the base airport.

All other tariffs are either subject to anti-monopoly regulation (ground-handling services) or are non-regulated (non-aviation revenue).

4.2 Typical Risk Allocation for Public–Private Partnership Projects in the Airport Sector

A typical risk allocation for airport sector projects is unavailable.

4.3 Financing Details for Public–Private Partnership Projects in the Airport Sector

Parameter	1990–2019	1990–2020	1990–2021
PPP projects with foreign lending participation	–	–	–
PPP projects that received export credit agency/ international financing institution support	–	–	–
Typical debt to equity ratio	UA	UA	UA
Time for financial close	UA	UA	UA
Typical concession period	30 years for Aktau; 3 years for Turkestan; 10 years for Astana		
Typical financial internal rate of return	UA	UA	UA

PPP = public–private partnership, UA = unavailable.
Sources: World Bank. Infrastructure Finance, PPPs and Guarantees. Country Snapshots. Kazakhstan. https://ppi.worldbank.org/en/snapshots/country/kazakhstan (accessed 18 October 2022); Unicase Law LLP.

5. Challenges in the Airport Sector

The airport sector faces these key challenges:

- Low population density and urbanization hamper internal passenger growth. Around 70% of current passenger traffic is concentrated in two airports—Almaty and Astana.
- Aviation services are cross-subsidized by fuel sales. Low tariffs for aircraft and passenger handling services make it unprofitable to operate majority of airports in the country.
- Local airports are unattractive to transit freight and passenger flows due to high fuel costs.

D. Energy

Parameter	Value	Unit
Electric power consumption	5,599.90	kilowatt-hour per capita
Share of clean energy	1.56	% of total energy use
Access to electricity	100.00	% of population
Getting electricity (score out of 100)		Number
Energy imports	–116.89	% of total energy use
Investment in energy with private participation	28	current $ million
Total number of projects with cumulative lending, grant, and technical assistance commitments in the energy sector	9	Number
Total amount of cumulative lending, grant, and technical assistance commitments in the energy sector	164	$ million

Sources: Economist Intelligence Unit. 2019. Infrascope: Kazakhstan Country Report. https://infrascope.eiu.com/; The Global Economy. Share of Clean Energy. Country Rankings. https://www.theglobaleconomy.com/rankings/Share_of_clean_energy/; World Bank. Access to Electricity. https://data.worldbank.org/indicator/EG.ELC.ACCS.ZS?end=2018&locations=MM-KH-UZ-CN-BD-GE-IN-ID-KZ-PK-PH-LK-TH-VN&start=2018&view=bar; The Global Economy. Energy Imports. https://www.theglobaleconomy.com/rankings/Energy_imports/; Asian Development Bank. Cumulative Lending, Grant, and Technical Assistance Commitments. https://data.adb.org/dataset/cumulative-lending-grant-and-technical-assistance-commitments.

The entire population has access to electricity. Kazakhstan has been a net exporter of power generation until 2021 (it is projected to face a deficit for the coming 5 years). It has transmission connections to all its neighbors except the People's Republic of China. Electric power distribution systems are also sufficient to provide adequate access to power for all regions. However, the long-term sustainability of the system is at risk due to underinvestment in modernization and capacity replacement. Another important threat to sustainability is its heavy reliance on coal. More than 70% of generation capacities are coal-fired, which will require investment in decarbonization. For the country to be able to absorb all planned renewable capacity, given its unstable generation profiles, Kazakhstan will need to invest in the modernization of its grid, supply of balancing sources, and interregional power trade.

1. Contracting Agencies in the Energy Sector

In terms of private sector participation, Kazakhstan's power market is mature—generation is delivered mainly by private companies, with more than half of distribution also being in private hands. The only exclusion is the high-voltage transmission and dispatch where private ownership above 49% is not allowed by law. Past attempts to structure PPP in renewable energy have been unsuccessful due to the need of asset transfer to the state at the end of the contract, which is not customary in the power sector of Kazakhstan.

The key policymaking and supervision authority in the power sector in Kazakhstan is the Ministry of Energy (MOE). There are several committees and departments with different roles and functions within the Ministry as listed below:

- The Department of Electric Power Development sets the state power sector policy and strategy (including heat supply), proposes long-term sector development plans, supervises the implementation of sector-specific state budget programs, and decides on the procurement mode of investment projects initiated by the state (including decisions on PPP).

- The Department for Renewable Energy is responsible for the state policy in supporting renewable energy, coordination of such support with other government entities and market stakeholders, drafting of renewable energy-related regulatory and legal acts, and implementing international cooperation in the renewable energy sector.

- The Committee for Atomic and Energy Supervision and Control is responsible for technical supervision and control over the power industry. It sets the technical rules of operations, issues licenses, approves commissioning of new facilities, and grants operation permissions for power generation, transmission, and dispatch.

There are several legal entities in the power sector with the special status of a national operator:

- Kazakhstan Electricity Grid Operating Company JSC (KEGOC) is the system operator of the country's unified power system. It owns and manages the assets of the national power grid. The company operates as a natural monopoly and employs more than 4,000 people. KEGOC is a subsidiary of Samruk–Kazyna and is listed on the Kazakhstan Stock Exchange.

- Kazakhstan Electricity and Power Market Operator JSC (KOREM) is the national operator of centralized trades with energy and capacity. Apart from running the platform for spot trades in energy and capacity, KOREM is also responsible for organizing and conducting renewable energy auctions for new generation.

- Financial Settlement Center of Renewable Energy LLP (FSC) is the single buyer of renewable energy and guaranteed power capacity.[53] FSC on-sells the renewable energy at levelized prices to "conditional purchasers," the carbon fuel-based power plants.

2. Energy Sector Laws and Regulations

The main legal acts governing the energy sector in Kazakhstan are

- Law of the Republic of Kazakhstan No. 588 "On Electric Power Industry" dated 9 June 2004 (Electricity Law); and

- Law of the Republic of Kazakhstan No. 165-VI "On Support of the Use of Renewable Energy Sources" dated 4 July 2009 (Renewable Energy Law).

The Electricity Law sets the wholesale power market in four segments: (i) decentralized market for energy, (ii) centralized market for energy and for (iii) capacity, and (iv) the balancing market. The decentralized energy market is dominated by bilateral agreements between generators and large consumers at prices not exceeding the ceiling tariffs set by the MOE. The balancing market is for hourly financial and physical control over power imbalances on a single grid, currently operating in pilot mode. Both centralized markets for energy and for capacity are operated by KOREM with equal access to large-scale generators and consumers. The trades there can be of three types: short-term sales (T+day), medium-term (T+week, T+month), and long-term sales (quarter, year).

Majority of renewable energy projects are supported by guaranteed offtake of all generated energy by FSC, thus making them de facto PPPs. However, since these projects have not relied on the provisions of either the Concessions Law or the PPP Law, they are not regarded as PPP under Kazakhtan's law or considered as such by the government and local authorities. The Renewable Energy Law also allows for conclusion of direct bilateral PPAs, but this option is yet to be tested. The amendments to Renewable Energy Law introduced in 2018 launched the auctions mechanism for all future renewable energy projects willing to have access to guaranteed offtake from FSC. The bidding process on the electronic platform consists of acceptance and consideration of bids from local and

---

[53]   Guaranteed power capacity is the capacity that can be always made available, as verified by the Committee for Atomic and Energy Supervision and Control.

foreign organizations that should be below the maximum auction price established by the state. The PPAs of such projects include a tariff indexation mechanism in accordance with changes in the exchange rate and inflation.[54]

The Renewable Energy Law also guarantees renewable energy facilities with free and nondiscriminatory access to the nearest point of connection to electrical or thermal grids of transmission companies. The law, however, does not give a clear guidance on the curtailment risks of the network operators.

2.1 Foreign Investment Restrictions in the Energy Sector

Maximum allowed foreign ownership of equity in greenfield projects	2019	2020	2021
Power generation	100%	100%	100%
Power transmission	0%	0%	0%
Power distribution	100%	100%	100%
Oil and gas	100%	100%	100%

Sources: ADB. 2019. *Public–Private Partnership Monitor*. Second Edition. Manila. https://www.adb.org/sites/default/files/publication/509426/ppp-monitor-second-edition.pdf; Unicase Law LLP.

The 2003 Law on Investments established a single investment regime for domestic and foreign investors. The Electricity Law forbids private ownership of power lines above 220 kilovolts (kV). The law also restricts privatization of KEGOC above 49% of ownership.

2.2 Standard Contracts in the Energy Sector

Type of Contract	Availability
PPP concession agreement	✗
Power purchase agreement	✓[a]
Capacity take-or-pay contract	✗
Fuel supply agreement	✓
Transmission and use of system agreement	✓
Performance-based operation and maintenance (O&M) contract	✗
Engineering, procurement, and construction contract	✗

✓ = yes, ✗ = no, NA = not applicable, UA = unavailable.
[a] Template for a long-term power purchase agreement (PPA) is available only for renewable energy projects with Financial Settlement Center of Renewable Energy LLP. Template for PPAs available at KOREM's website are up to 1 year.
Sources: ADB. 2019. *Public–Private Partnership Monitor*. Second Edition. Manila. https://www.adb.org/sites/default/files/publication/509426/ppp-monitor-second-edition.pdf; Unicase Law LLP.

3. Energy Sector Master Plan

The use of coal as the main fuel for generating electricity and heat has significant environmental and climate consequences, thus Kazakhstan is pursuing a policy to gradually replace coal with natural gas and renewable energy sources. The concept for the transition to a "green" economy, adopted in 2013, has set ambitious goals to significantly reduce Kazakhstan's share of coal generation and has been the basis for the country's new energy policy. In October 2021, Kazakhstan unveiled its Doctrine for Carbon Neutrality by 2060 and updated

---

[54] Grata. 2016. *Report—Renewable Energy Projects in Kazakhstan*. http://www.gratanet.com/en/publications/details/renewable_kazakhstan_2016.

its Nationally Determined Contributions (NDCs) which call for a series of ambitious interim targets (e.g., a 15% reduction in greenhouse gas emissions by 2030).[55]

However, the development of sources with a variable nature of generation, depending on weather conditions and time of day, such as wind and solar stations, exacerbates the existing problem of regulation and stability of the energy system in the face of a shortage of maneuvering capacities.

The new edition of the Environmental Code sets a large-scale task to modernize power plants through transition to the principles of "best available technologies" (BAT) and through a significant reduction in pollutant emissions. Commitments under the Paris Climate Agreement impose significant challenges for Kazakhstan to decarbonize the economy and the power industry, the fulfillment of which depends on the pace of reforming pricing policy and reviewing the mechanisms for ensuring the stability of investments in the sector.

3.1 Projects under Preparation and Procurement in the Energy Sector

No energy projects under preparation and procurement are listed in the PPP Center's database (Figure 31). However, each year, the MOE publishes schedules of planned renewable energy auctions. These renewable energy projects are not considered as PPP in Kazakhstan.

Figure 31: Public–Private Partnership Energy Projects under Preparation and Procurement

2019   2020   2021

■ Projects under preparation   ■ Projects under procurement

"-" means there are no projects in the sector, or data are unavailable.
Sources: Kazakhstan Public–Private Partnership Center. PPP Project Database. http://www.kzppp.kz/projects (accessed 18 October 2022); Unicase Law LLP.

The only energy sector project regarded as a PPP in Kazakhstan is the high-voltage transmission line, Northern Kazakhstan – Aktobe Oblast (Batys Transit), signed in 2005. No power projects are currently listed as PPP under preparation and procurement.

4. Features of Past Public–Private Partnership Projects in the Energy Sector

The World Bank database contains all energy projects with private sector participation. The projects involving divestitures and fully-private merchant greenfield projects have been removed. The private renewable energy

---

55   UN Partnership for Action on Green Economy. Kazakhstan Unveils Doctrine for Carbon Neutrality by 2060. https://www.un-page.org/kazakhstan-unveils-doctrine-carbon-neutrality-2060.

projects supported by state-guaranteed PPAs are not listed as PPP in the PPP Center's database but are included in the World Bank database. They have been kept in the analysis Figure 32–36. On this premise, Figure 32 shows the number of PPP projects procured through various modes, including direct appointment, unsolicited bids, and competitive bids, in the power sector of Kazakhstan.

Figure 32: Modes of Procurement for Public–Private Partnership Energy Projects

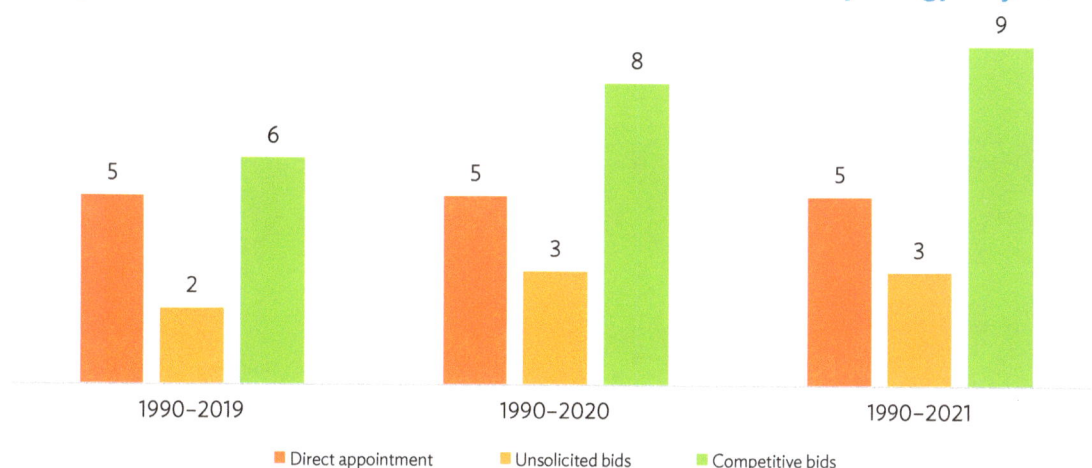

Note: Only active and concluded projects are considered in this graph.
Sources: World Bank. Infrastructure Finance, PPPs and Guarantees. Country Snapshots. Kazakhstan. https://ppi.worldbank.org/en/snapshots/country/kazakhstan (accessed 18 October 2022); Unicase Law LLP.

Figure 33 shows the number of PPP projects that have reached financial close and the total value of those projects in the power sector of Kazakhstan.

Figure 33: Public–Private Partnership Energy Projects Reaching Financial Close

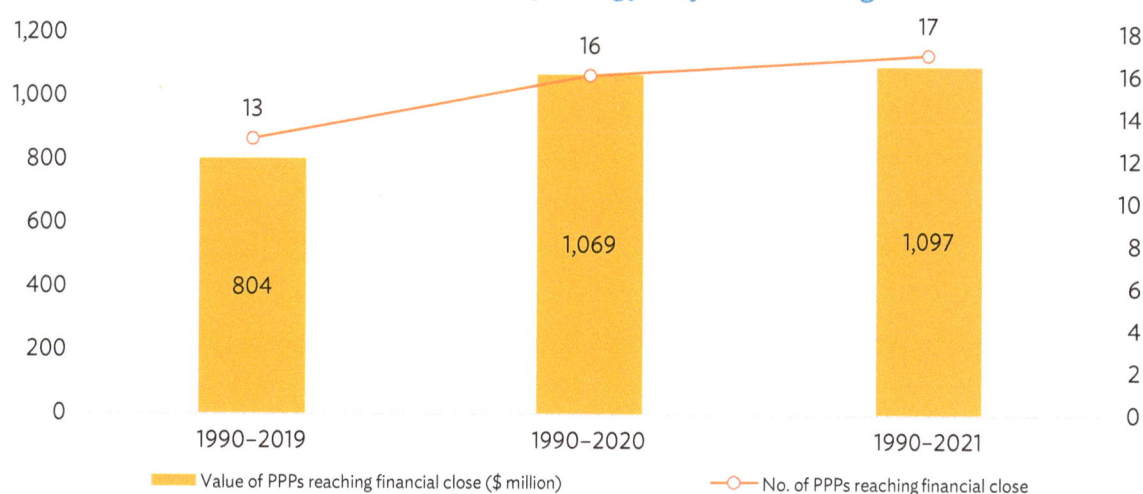

Note: Only active and concluded projects are considered in the above graph.
Sources: World Bank. Infrastructure Finance, PPPs and Guarantees. Country Snapshots. Kazakhstan. https://ppi.worldbank.org/en/snapshots/country/kazakhstan (accessed 18 October 2022); Unicase Law LLP.

Figure 34 provides the number of PPP projects that have received foreign sponsor participation in the energy sector of Kazakhstan.

Figure 34: Public–Private Partnership Energy Projects with Foreign Sponsor Participation

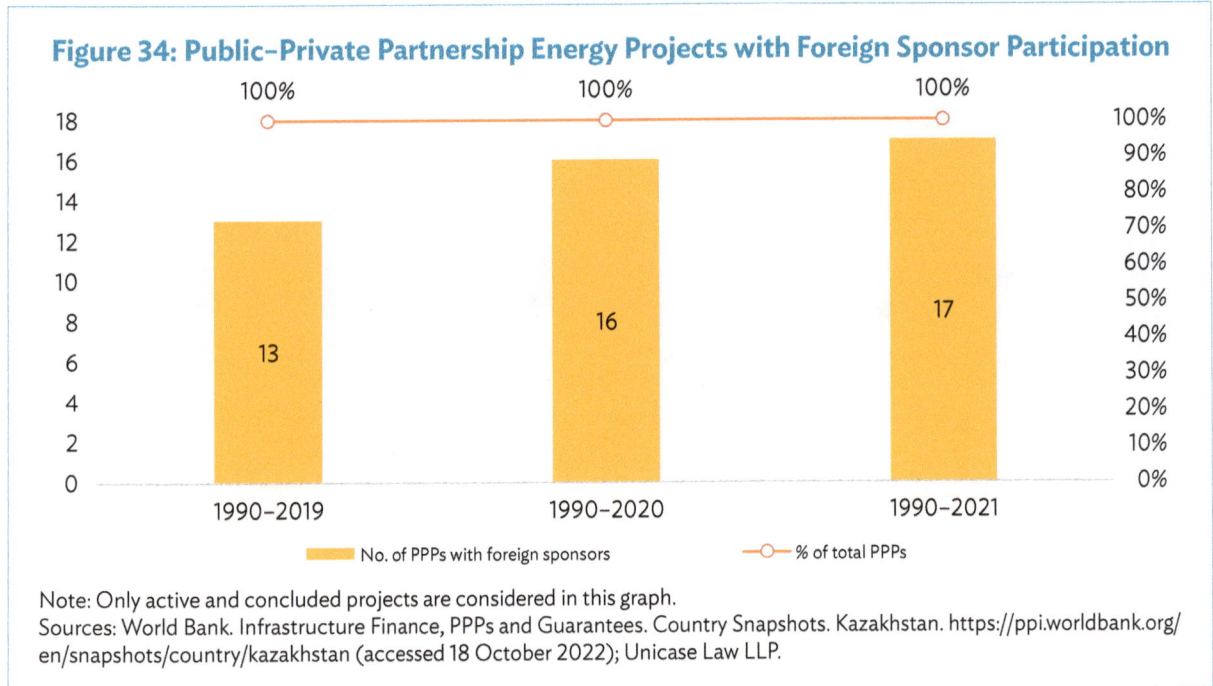

Note: Only active and concluded projects are considered in this graph.
Sources: World Bank. Infrastructure Finance, PPPs and Guarantees. Country Snapshots. Kazakhstan. https://ppi.worldbank.org/en/snapshots/country/kazakhstan (accessed 18 October 2022); Unicase Law LLP.

The number of PPP projects that have received government support, including VGF mechanism, government guarantees, and availability or performance payment, in the energy sector are shown in Figure 35.

Figure 35: Government Support to Public–Private Partnership Energy Projects

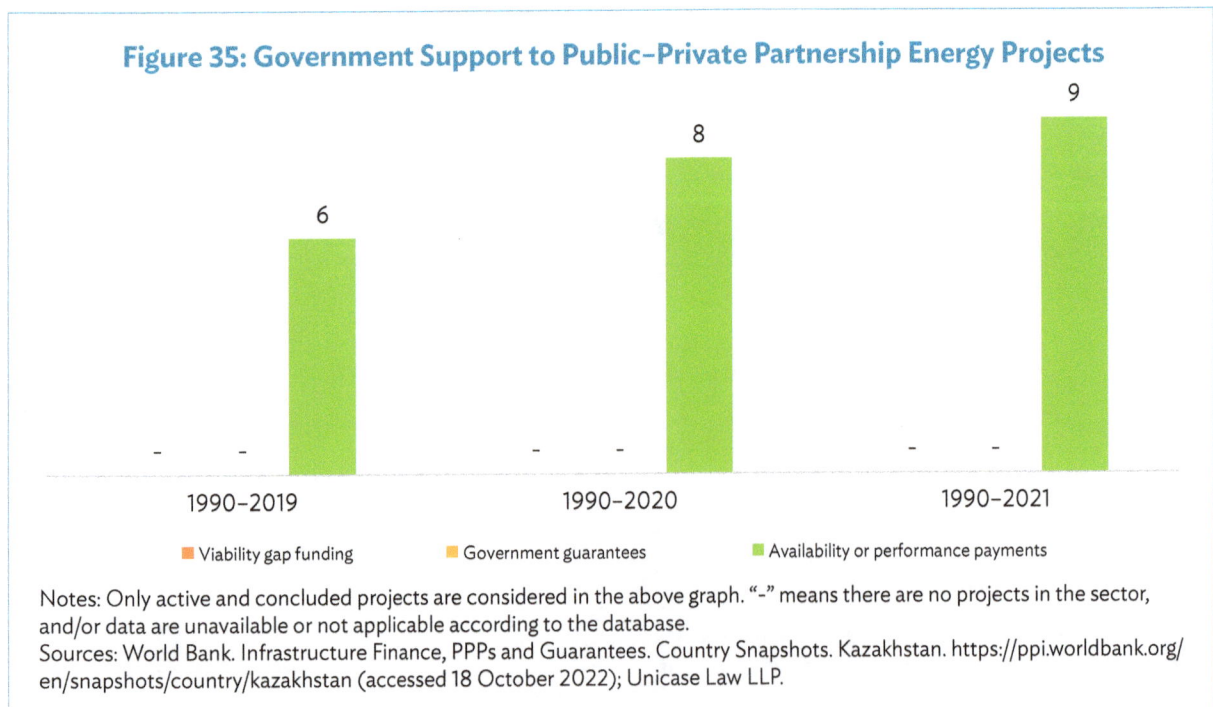

Notes: Only active and concluded projects are considered in the above graph. "-" means there are no projects in the sector, and/or data are unavailable or not applicable according to the database.
Sources: World Bank. Infrastructure Finance, PPPs and Guarantees. Country Snapshots. Kazakhstan. https://ppi.worldbank.org/en/snapshots/country/kazakhstan (accessed 18 October 2022); Unicase Law LLP.

Figure 36 shows the number of PPP projects that have received payment in the form of user charges and government pay (offtake) in the energy sector of Kazakhstan.

Figure 36: Payment Mechanisms for Public–Private Partnership Energy Projects

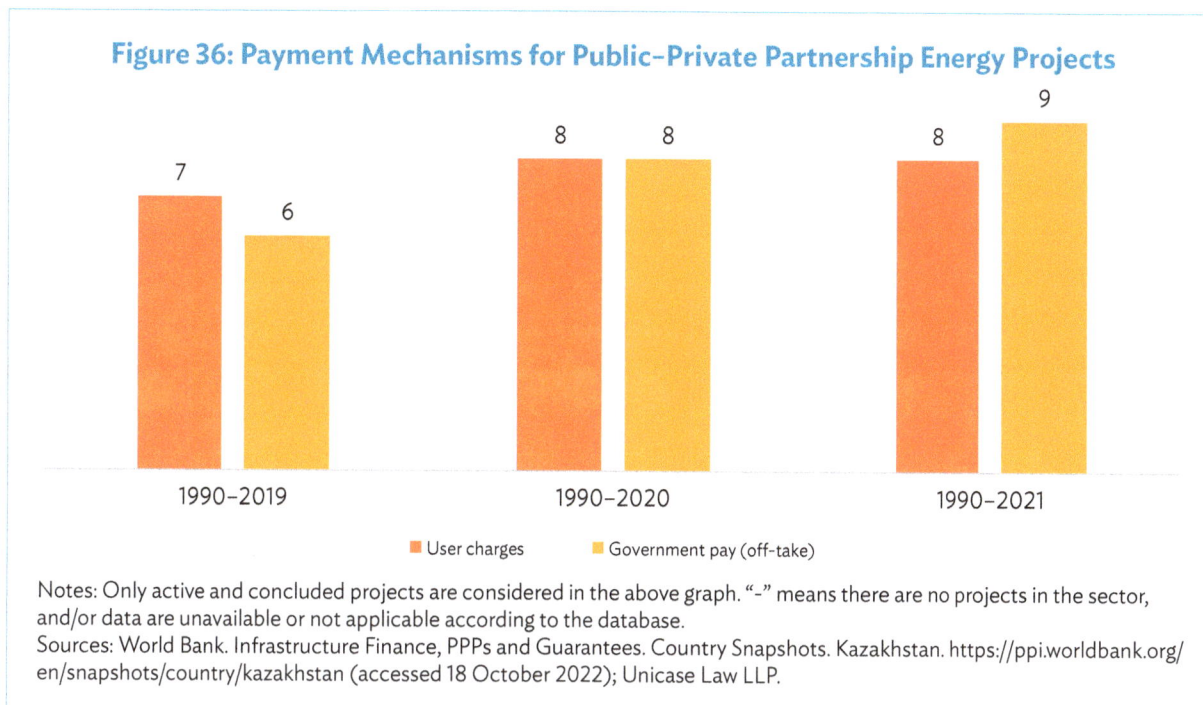

Notes: Only active and concluded projects are considered in the above graph. "–" means there are no projects in the sector, and/or data are unavailable or not applicable according to the database.
Sources: World Bank. Infrastructure Finance, PPPs and Guarantees. Country Snapshots. Kazakhstan. https://ppi.worldbank.org/en/snapshots/country/kazakhstan (accessed 18 October 2022); Unicase Law LLP.

The past PPP projects in the energy sector according to the PPP Center's database, broken down between republican and regional, is provided in Table 18.

Table 18: Summary of Projects Across Public–Private Partnerships in the Energy Sector

Sector	Number of Projects	Total Cost (T million)	Total Cost ($ million)
Local level	1	22,684	48
Republican level	1	2,320	5
Grand total	2	25,004	53

Note: Currency equivalent is as of 1 September 2022.
Source: Kazakhstan Public–Private Partnership Center. PPP Project Database. http://www.kzppp.kz/projects (accessed 18 October 2022).

4.1 Tariffs in the Energy Sector

The tariffs for power generation are capped by the Order of the MOE which splits all generators into 49 groups. The caps are revised annually as a measure to curb the growth of electricity tariffs due to considerations of social policy. The tariffs for distribution, transmission, and dispatch are regulated according to NML. The renewable energy tariffs from auctions held in 2020 are presented in the table below.

Renewable Source	Tariff (T/kWh)	Tariff ($/kWh)
Wind	21.53	0.046
Solar PV	16.96	0.036
Hydropower plant	15.2	0.032

kWh = kilowatt-hour, PV = photovoltaic.
Source: Financial Settlement Center database (accessed September 2022).

4.2 Typical Risk Allocation for Public–Private Partnership Projects in the Energy Sector

A typical risk allocation for energy projects is unavailable.

4.3 Financing Details for Public–Private Partnership Projects in the Energy Sector

Parameter	1990–2019	1990–2020	1990–2021
PPP projects with foreign lending participation	1	6	11
PPP projects that received export credit agency/international financing institution support	UA	UA	UA
Typical debt to equity ratio	70/30	70/30	80/20
Time for financial close	< 1 year	< 6 months	< 6 months
Typical concession period	UA	15	20
Typical financial internal rate of return	UA	UA	UA

PPP = public–private partnership, UA = unavailable.
Sources: World Bank. Infrastructure Finance, PPPs and Guarantees. Country Snapshots. Kazakhstan. https://ppi.worldbank.org/en/snapshots/country/kazakhstan (accessed 18 October 2022); Unicase Law LLP.

5. Challenges in the Energy Sector

Some of the key challenges impacting the energy sector are as follows:

- The absence of a coherent sector development strategy with a clear energy transition plan that is consistent with the country's Nationally Determined Contributions hinders investment planning.

- The prevalent policy of curbing the growth of electricity tariffs for the benefit of the broader social considerations makes investments in the power sector risky and unattractive.

- The absence of ancillary service markets (e.g., balancing, capacity, peak power) creates additional curtailment risks.

- The absence of carbon pricing creates distortions in the true cost of power for renewable energy and limits financing possibilities.

- The legal requirement to transfer the project assets to the state at the end of the PPP contract makes this procurement mode unattractive to the private sector, limiting the potential upside.

E. Water And Wastewater

Parameter	Value	Unit
Improved water source access	97.30	% of population with access
Improved sanitation facilities access	98.00	% of population with access
Investment in water and sanitation with private participation	UA	current $ million
Total number of projects with cumulative lending, grant, and technical assistance commitments in water and other urban infrastructure and services	7	Number
Total amount of cumulative lending, grant, and technical assistance commitments in water and other urban infrastructure and services	38	$ million

UA = unavailable.
Sources: Asian Development Bank. Cumulative Lending, Grant, and Technical Assistance Commitments. https://data.adb.org/dataset/cumulative-lending-grant-and-technical-assistance-commitments; Asian Development Bank. 2017. *Country Partnership Strategy, 2017–2021*. https://www.adb.org/sites/default/files/institutional-document/357421/cps-kaz-2017-2021.pdf; Unicase Law LLP.

Water infrastructure is relatively well-developed in Kazakhstan, including dams, levees, pump stations, reservoirs, irrigation distribution, and drainage system. According to the 2019 OECD report, Kazakhstan's population is less vulnerable to unsafe drinking water than the neighboring Central Asian countries. However, climate change is already affecting the reliability of water supply in some regions of Kazakhstan.[56]

1. Contracting Agencies in the Water and Wastewater Sector

The Republican state institution "Committee for construction and housing and communal services" under MIID (the Construction Committee) is the main competent body responsible for the policy and supervision of water utilities in Kazakhstan, along with its other functions relating to control of architectural, urban planning, and construction activities; housing relations; utilities; and solid waste management.[57]

The contracting authority will depend on the asset/utility ownership allocation:

- The Construction Committee on behalf of MIID, in the case of republic-level projects.
- Local *akimats*, in the case of regional-level projects (i.e., water and wastewater utilities are on the balance of regional authorities).[58]
- Joint Stock Company, KazCenter ZhKH, is the national operator for implementing various reforms in housing and utilities. It is 100% owned by the Construction Committee and provides project preparation and approval services to MIID for projects financed out of the Nurly Zhol and Nurly Zher programs.

[56] OECD. 2019. *Sustainable Infrastructure for Low-Carbon Development in Central Asia and the Caucasus: Hotspot Analysis and Needs Assessment*. Green Finance and Investment. Paris: OECD Publishing. https://doi.org/10.1787/d1aa6ae9-en.
[57] Government of Kazakhstan, Ministry of Industry and Infrastructural Development, Construction and Housing-Communal Services Affairs Committee. https://www.gov.kz/memleket/entities/kds/about?lang=en.
[58] Municipal water utilities can become parties to various contracts, but those contracts will be structured in accordance with the Civil Code, not the Concessions Law or the PPP Law.

2. Water and Wastewater Sector Laws and Regulations

Parameter	
Can the private sector be given water abstraction rights?	✗
Are there regulations in place on raw water extraction?	✓
Are there regulations in place on the release of treated effluents?	✓

✓ = yes, ✗ = no.
Sources: Asian Development Bank. Cumulative Lending, Grant, and Technical Assistance Commitments. https://data.adb.org/dataset/cumulative-lending-grant-and-technical-assistance-commitments; Asian Development Bank. 2017. *Country Partnership Strategy, 2017–2021*. https://www.adb.org/sites/default/files/institutional-document/357421/cps-kaz-2017-2021.pdf; Unicase Law LLP.

The water and wastewater sector is regulated by two key legislative acts:

- Water Code of the Republic of Kazakhstan No. 481 dated 9 July 2003
- Environmental Code of the Republic of Kazakhstan No. 400-VI 3PK dated 2 January 2021.

2.1 Foreign Investment Restrictions in the Water and Wastewater Sector

Parameter	2019	2020	2021
Maximum allowed foreign ownership of equity in greenfield projects			
– Bulk water supply and treatment	100%	100%	100%
– Water distribution	100%	100%	100%
– Wastewater treatment	100%	100%	100%
– Wastewater collection	100%	100%	100%

Sources: Water Code of Kazakhstan; Environmental Code of Kazakhstan; Unicase Law LLP.

2.2 Standard Contracts in the Water and Wastewater Sector

Type of Contract	Availability
PPP/concession agreement	✗
Performance-based operation and maintenance contract	✗
Engineering, procurement, and construction contract	✗

✗ = no, PPP = public–private partnership.
Source: Unicase Law LLP.

There are no standard contract forms for PPPs in the water and wastewater sector yet.

3. Water and Wastewater Sector Master Plan

The Nurly Zher state program is the main document that describes the further development of water and wastewater sector. It aims to improve the quality of living standards in Kazakhstan.

The program covers district heating, water and wastewater, and housing and construction sectors.

For the water and wastewater sector, along with the modernization and expansion of water supply infrastructure, the program envisages the construction and reconstruction of 53 wastewater treatment plants in 49 settlements.[59] Overall, it pursues the following key performance indicators (KPIs):

- Provide 100% access to centralized water supply in urban areas by 2025.
- Provide 97.7% access to centralized water supply in rural areas by 2025.
- Provide 2.3% access to decentralized water supply in rural areas by 2025.
- Provide 100% access to the centralized wastewater services in urban areas by 2023.
- Decrease the share of obsolete water and wastewater networks to 47%.

Some of the challenges in the water and wastewater sector mentioned in the program include lack of skilled workforce, high accident rates, low automation, unclear division of responsibilities for water pollution, and weak enforcement of environmental standards for discharge leading to inability to manage environmental risks.

3.1 Projects under Preparation and Procurement in the Water and Wastewater Sector

Figure 37 provides the number of PPP projects that are under preparation and procurement in the water and wastewater sector of Kazakhstan according to the PPP Center's database (there is no information on such projects in the World Bank project database).

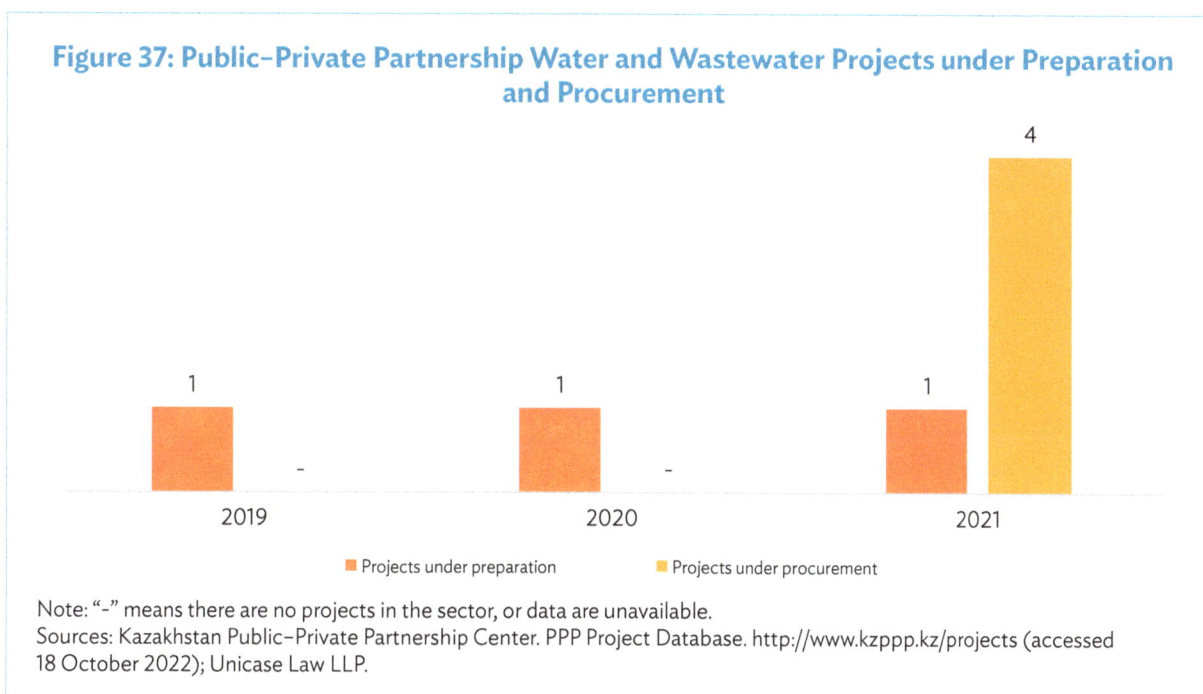

Figure 37: Public–Private Partnership Water and Wastewater Projects under Preparation and Procurement

Note: "–" means there are no projects in the sector, or data are unavailable.
Sources: Kazakhstan Public–Private Partnership Center. PPP Project Database. http://www.kzppp.kz/projects (accessed 18 October 2022); Unicase Law LLP.

Four out of five PPP projects in water and wastewater are located in Almaty region (three projects are for the reconstruction of water network, and one project is for the reconstruction of wastewater treatment facilities in Kapchagay City, Almaty region). The remaining one is the reconstruction of wastewater treatment facilities in

---

[59]   While the government has designated JSC KazCenter ZhKH as the program operator, the decisions are yet to be made on financing sources, procurement mode, or possible role of water utilities as borrowers or as public parties to the PPP arrangements.

Kokshetau City (Akmola region). All projects are promoted by local *akimats* and are on a short-term basis (for construction). There is no project at the republican-level.

4. Features of Past Public–Private Partnership Projects in the Water and Wastewater Sector

Figure 38 shows the number of PPP projects procured through various modes, including direct appointment, unsolicited bids, and competitive bids, in the water and wastewater sector of Kazakhstan (based on the World Bank PPI database).

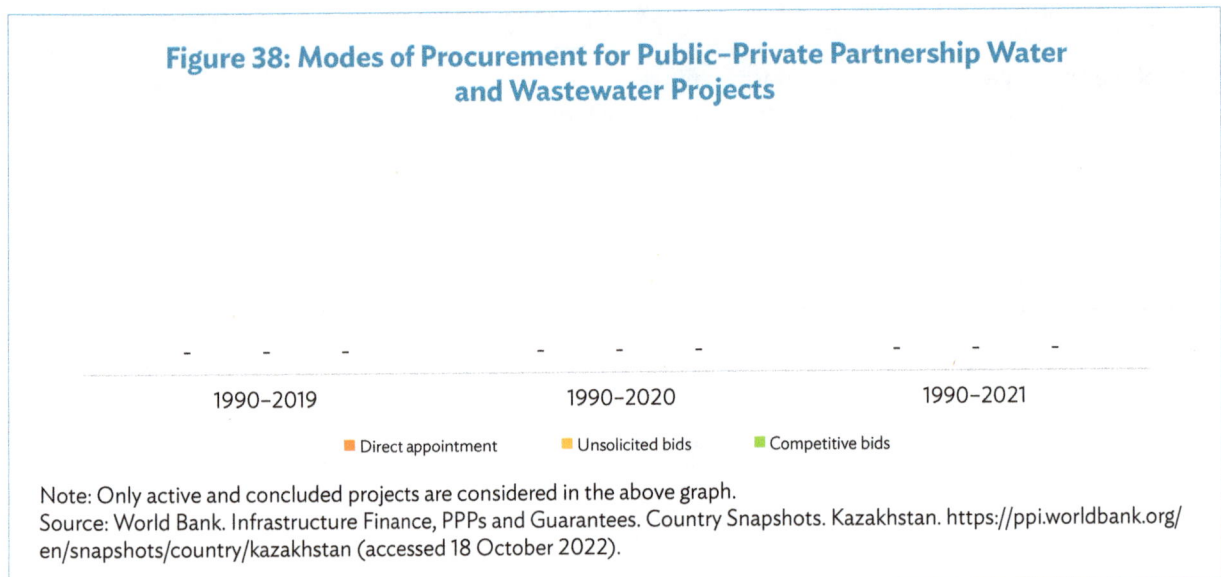

Figure 38: Modes of Procurement for Public–Private Partnership Water and Wastewater Projects

1990–2019   1990–2020   1990–2021

■ Direct appointment   ■ Unsolicited bids   ■ Competitive bids

Note: Only active and concluded projects are considered in the above graph.
Source: World Bank. Infrastructure Finance, PPPs and Guarantees. Country Snapshots. Kazakhstan. https://ppi.worldbank.org/en/snapshots/country/kazakhstan (accessed 18 October 2022).

Figure 39 shows the number of PPP projects that have reached financial close and the total value of those projects in the water and wastewater sector of Kazakhstan.

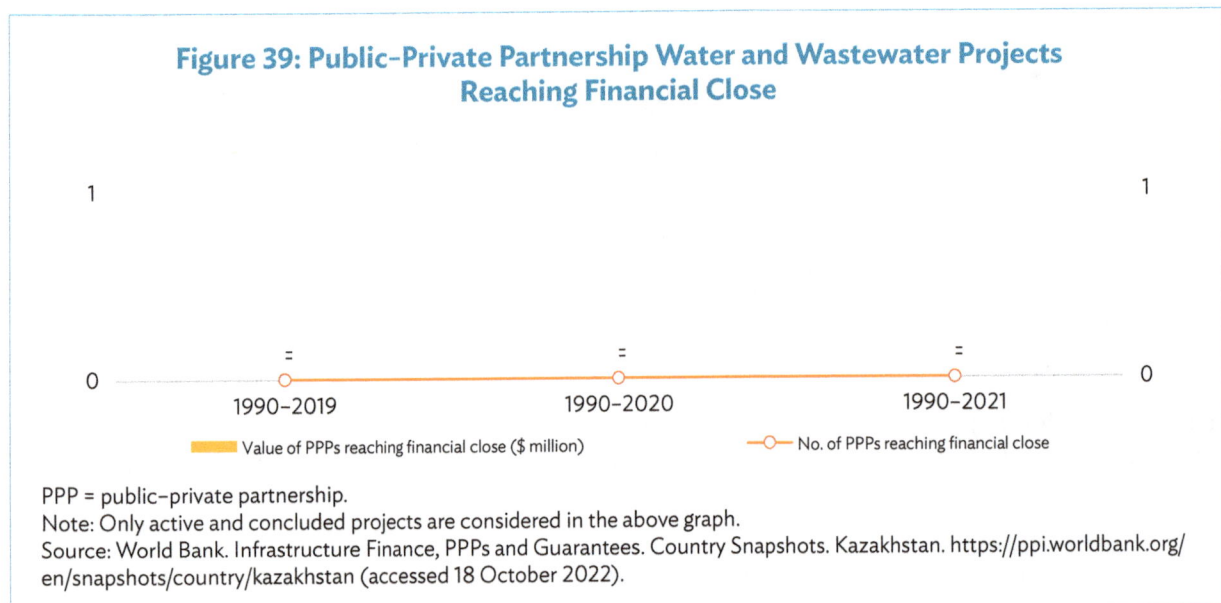

Figure 39: Public–Private Partnership Water and Wastewater Projects Reaching Financial Close

1   1

0   0
    1990–2019   1990–2020   1990–2021

▬ Value of PPPs reaching financial close ($ million)   ─O─ No. of PPPs reaching financial close

PPP = public–private partnership.
Note: Only active and concluded projects are considered in the above graph.
Source: World Bank. Infrastructure Finance, PPPs and Guarantees. Country Snapshots. Kazakhstan. https://ppi.worldbank.org/en/snapshots/country/kazakhstan (accessed 18 October 2022).

Figure 40 shows the number of PPP projects that have received foreign sponsor participation in the water and wastewater sector of Kazakhstan.

Figure 40: Public–Private Partnership Water and Wastewater Projects with Foreign Sponsor Participation

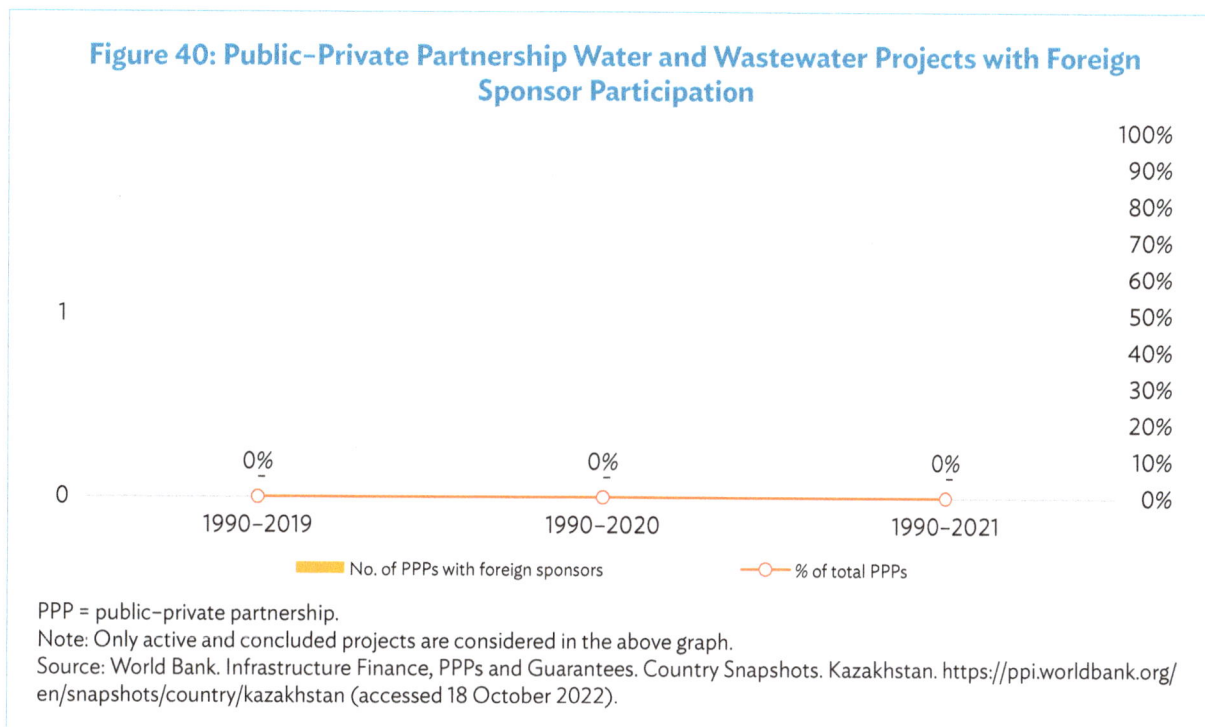

PPP = public–private partnership.
Note: Only active and concluded projects are considered in the above graph.
Source: World Bank. Infrastructure Finance, PPPs and Guarantees. Country Snapshots. Kazakhstan. https://ppi.worldbank.org/en/snapshots/country/kazakhstan (accessed 18 October 2022).

The number of PPP projects that have received government support, including VGF mechanism, government guarantees, and availability or performance payment, in the water and wastewater sector are shown in Figure 41.

Figure 41: Government Support to Public-Private Partnership Water and Wastewater Projects

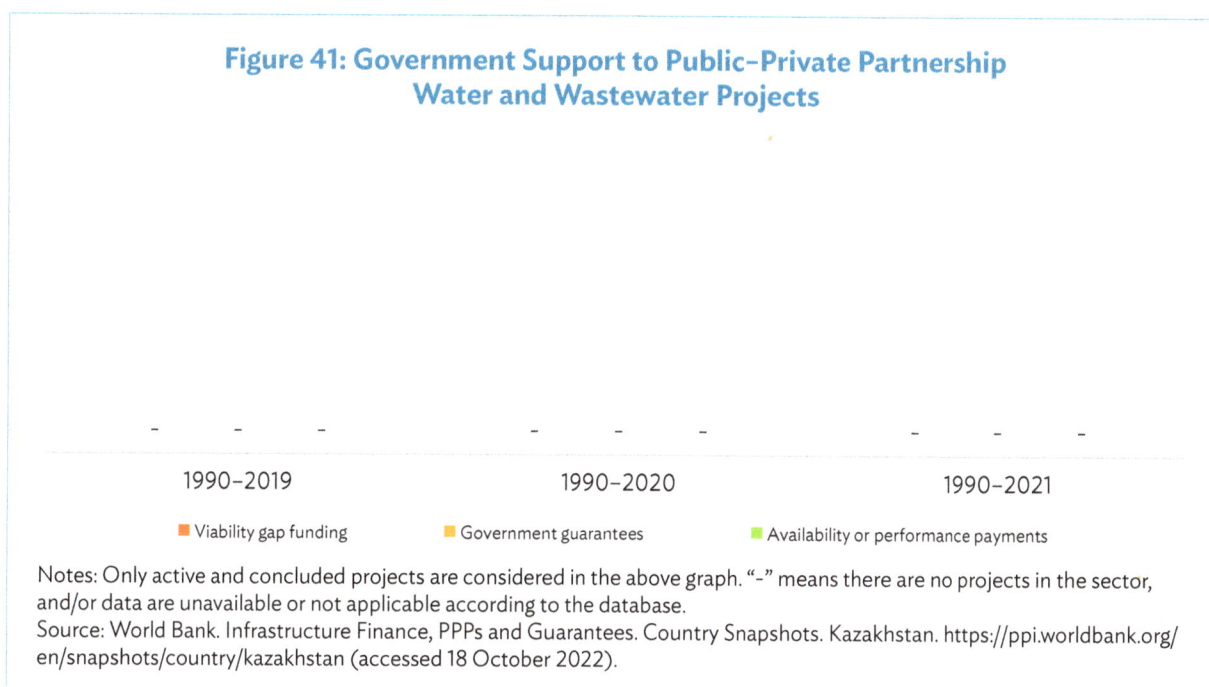

Notes: Only active and concluded projects are considered in the above graph. "-" means there are no projects in the sector, and/or data are unavailable or not applicable according to the database.
Source: World Bank. Infrastructure Finance, PPPs and Guarantees. Country Snapshots. Kazakhstan. https://ppi.worldbank.org/en/snapshots/country/kazakhstan (accessed 18 October 2022).

Figure 42 shows the number of PPP projects that have received payment in the form of user charges and government pay (offtake) in the water and wastewater sector of Kazakhstan.

Figure 42: Payment Mechanisms for Public–Private Partnership Water and Wastewater Projects

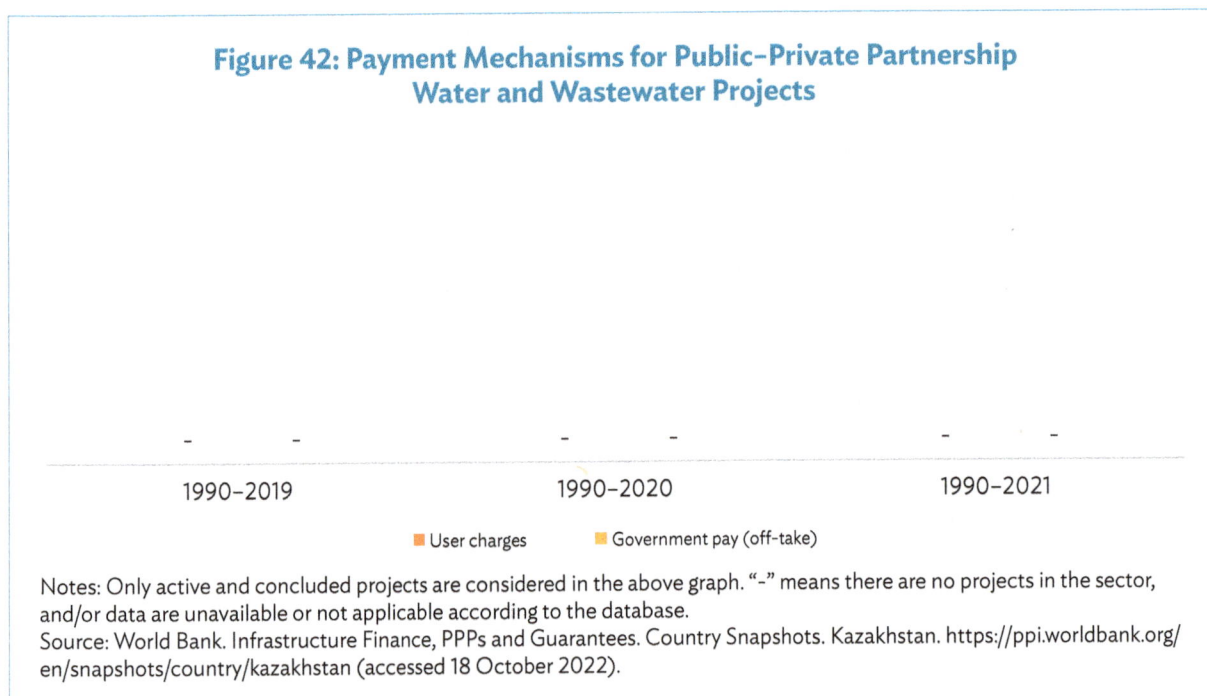

| 1990–2019 | 1990–2020 | 1990–2021 |

■ User charges   ■ Government pay (off-take)

Notes: Only active and concluded projects are considered in the above graph. "–" means there are no projects in the sector, and/or data are unavailable or not applicable according to the database.
Source: World Bank. Infrastructure Finance, PPPs and Guarantees. Country Snapshots. Kazakhstan. https://ppi.worldbank.org/en/snapshots/country/kazakhstan (accessed 18 October 2022).

There are no past PPP projects in the water and wastewater sector found in the database of the PPP Center (Table 19).

Table 19: Summary of Projects Across Public–Private Partnership in Water and Wastewater Sector

Sector	Number of Projects	Total Cost (T million)	Total Cost ($ million)
Local level	–	–	–
Republican level	–	–	–
Grand total	–	–	–

– = no project.
Sources: Kazakhstan Public–Private Partnership Center. PPP Project Database. http://www.kzppp.kz/projects (accessed 18 October 2022); Unicase Law LLP.

4.1 Tariffs in the Water and Wastewater Sector

All water and wastewater services are subject to natural monopoly regulation, therefore CREM sets their tariffs. There are more than 60 water utilities in Kazakhstan, each with their own tariff structures approved at least annually, published on their websites. The water and wastewater tariffs are generally set separately. There are some utilities where the wastewater tariffs are further split into collection and treatment.

The current tariff setting practices do not allow the water utilities to recover their investment costs and do not encourage water saving.

4.2 Typical Risk Allocation for Public–Private Partnership Projects in the Water and Wastewater Sector

A typical risk allocation for water and wastewater sector projects is unavailable.

4.3 Financing Details for Public–Private Partnership Projects in the Water and Wastewater Sector

Parameter	1990–2019	1990–2020	1990–2021
PPP projects with foreign lending participation	–	–	–
PPP projects that received export credit agency/international financing institution support	–	–	–
Typical debt to equity ratio	UA	UA	UA
Time for financial close	UA	UA	UA
Typical concession period	UA	UA	UA
Typical financial internal rate of return	UA	UA	UA

– = no project, PPP = public–private partnership, UA = unavailable.
Source: World Bank. Infrastructure Finance, PPPs and Guarantees. Country Snapshots. Kazakhstan. https://ppi.worldbank.org/en/snapshots/country/kazakhstan (accessed 18 October 2022).

5. Challenges in the Water and Wastewater Sector

The key challenges in the water and wastewater sector are the following:

- Due to climate change, Kazakhstan is expected to experience more severe droughts and greater deficits of fresh water in the future.
- The current tariff setting practices do not allow the water utilities to recover their investment costs and do not encourage water saving.
- The weak financial standing of water utilities undermines their ability to become parties to design–build–operate (DBO) agreements with private parties or to borrow directly from banks.
- Lack of skilled workforce results in inefficient water management, high accident rates, and low automation.
- Unclear division of responsibilities for water pollution and weak enforcement of environmental standards for discharge lead to inability to manage environmental risks.

F. Information And Communication Technology

Parameter	Value	Unit
Telephone subscribers	16.00	per 100 inhabitants
Cellular phone subscribers	129.00	per 100 inhabitants
Cellular network coverage	86.60	% of population covered
Internet subscribers (fixed broadband)	13.96	per 100 inhabitants
Internet bandwidth per internet user	51.49	Kbps

continued on next page

continued from previous page

Parameter	Value	Unit
Total number of projects with cumulative lending, grant, and technical assistance commitments in ICT sector	UA	Number
Total amount of cumulative lending, grant, and technical assistance commitments in ICT sector	UA	$ million

ICT = information and communication technology, Kbps = kilobits per second, UA = unavailable.
Sources: World Bank. Telephone Subscribers 2020. https://data.worldbank.org/indicator/IT.MLT.MAIN?locations=KZ; The Global Economy. Mobile Phone Subscribers. https://www.theglobaleconomy.com/rankings/Mobile_phone_subscribers_per_100_people/; The Global Economy. Mobile Network Coverage. https://www.theglobaleconomy.com/rankings/Mobile_network_coverage/; The Global Economy. Internet Subscribers. https://www.theglobaleconomy.com/rankings/Internet_subscribers_per_100_people/; The Global Economy. Internet Bandwidth. https://www.theglobaleconomy.com/rankings/Internet_bandwidth/.

ICT is Kazakhstan's most developed infrastructure segment. The World Economic Forum ranks Kazakhstan 44th among 141 countries in ICT adoption.[60] All of the country's administrative regions have access to 3G and 4G networks.

1. Contracting Agencies in the Information and Communication Technology Sector

The Telecommunications Committee of the Ministry of Digital Development, Innovations, and Aerospace Industry is one of the key entities in the ICT sector and a contracting agency. It is responsible for the implementation of public policy in the ICT sector, including communication and informatization, and e-government services. The Committee also oversees compliance with the legislation of the Republic of Kazakhstan within the sector and exerts public control.[61]

There are additional joint stock companies under the ministry which work toward achieving various mandates of the Ministry:

- Zerde National Infocommunication Holding JSC (Zerde) is the largest ICT company in Kazakhstan, a national operator and e-government service integrator, and the main driver of digitalization. Zerde is responsible for implementing government digitalization programs and development initiatives in the sector.

- State Corporation "Government for Citizens" JSC, is a digital integrator and single provider of digital public services to the citizens of Kazakhstan.

- JSC Kazakhtelecom is the largest telecommunications company in Kazakhstan and has the status of a national telecommunications operator, with 51% of ownership belonging to Samruk-Kazyna.[62] JSC Kazakhtelecom controls 93% of fixed-line telephony and broadband internet,[63] including the National Information Superhighway, which is a transport fiber-optic ring that connects large cities of Kazakhstan with digital streams with high data transmission speed.[64]

---

[60] Klaus Schwab. 2019. *The Global Competitiveness Report. World Economic Forum.* Geneva. http://www3.weforum.org/docs/WEF_TheGlobalCompetitivenessReport2019.pdf.
[61] Government of Kazakhstan, Ministry of Digital Development, Innovations and Aerospace Industry, Telecommunications Committee. https://www.gov.kz/memleket/entities/telecom/about?lang=en.
[62] Kazakhtelecom. The Main Shareholders Structure. https://telecom.kz/en/pages/11893/172452 (accessed February 2022).
[63] OECD. 2017. *Reforming Kazakhstan: Progress, Challenges and Opportunities.* Paris.
[64] Kazakhtelecom. Facts About the Company. https://telecom.kz/en/about/list.

2. Information and Communication Technology Sector Laws and Regulations

The Law of the Republic of Kazakhstan No. 418 dated 24 November 2015 "On Informatization" defines and regulates public relations in the ICT sector between state bodies, individuals, and legal entities during the creation, development, and operation of informatization objects. The law also defines the measures for state support in the development of the ICT industry.

2.1 Foreign Investment Restrictions in the Information and Communication Technology Sector

Parameter	2019	2020	2021
Maximum allowed foreign ownership of equity in greenfield projects			
– Fixed line infrastructure	49%	49%	49%
– Fixed line services	49%	49%	49%
– Wireless/mobile infrastructure	100%	100%	100%
– Wireless/mobile services	100%	100%	100%

Sources: ADB. 2019. *Public–Private Partnership Monitor*. Second Edition. Manila. https://www.adb.org/sites/default/files/publication/509426/ppp-monitor-second-edition.pdf; Unicase Law LLP.

There are no legal restrictions to foreign involvement in the ICT sector.

2.2 Standard Contracts in the Information and Communication Technology Sector

Parameter	
What standardized contracts are available and used in the market?	
– PPP/concession agreement	✕
– Performance-based operation and maintenance contract	✕
– Engineering, procurement, and construction contract	✕
– License agreement	✕

✕ = no, PPP = public–private partnership.
Source: Unicase Law LLP.

There are no sector-specific templates available for the ICT sector.

3. Information and Communication Technology Sector Master Plan

The state program, Digital Kazakhstan, sets the objectives to accelerate the pace of economic development and improve the quality of life through promoting digital technologies in the medium term. It also aims to shift the country's economy to a fundamentally new development trajectory, ensuring the creation of a digital economy from a long-term perspective.

Digital Kazakhstan is being implemented through a mix of republican and local government budgets, private sector initiatives, and public–private partnership programs. Below are some of the projects proposed to be developed and implemented using a PPP mechanism:

- Electronic labor exchange (consolidation of IP systems "Labor market," Enbek.kz portal, private employment agencies, and online Internet sites)
- Automated system for collecting data on air passengers
- Industrial Automation and Digitalization Institute (to be created based on existing infrastructure)
- e-Residence project.[65]

3.1 Projects under Preparation and Procurement in the Information and Communication Technology Sector

Figure 43 shows the number of PPP projects that are under preparation and procurement in the ICT sector of Kazakhstan.

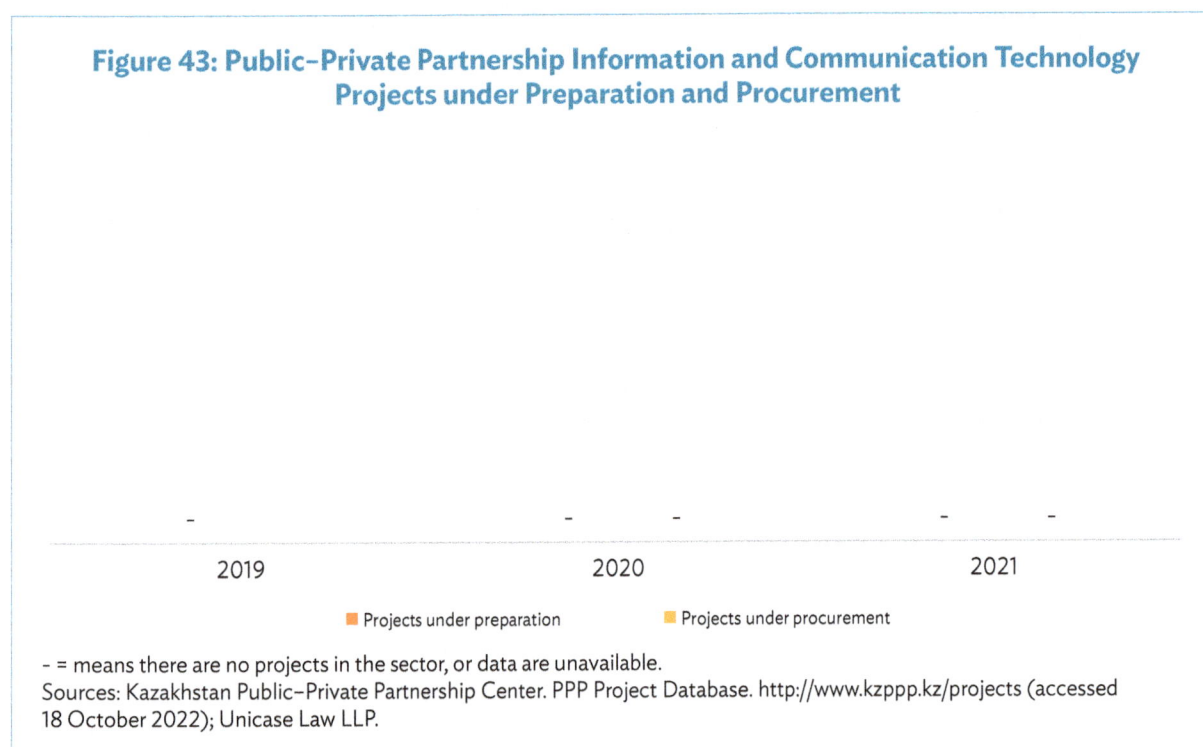

Figure 43: Public–Private Partnership Information and Communication Technology Projects under Preparation and Procurement

2019   2020   2021

■ Projects under preparation   ■ Projects under procurement

- = means there are no projects in the sector, or data are unavailable.
Sources: Kazakhstan Public–Private Partnership Center. PPP Project Database. http://www.kzppp.kz/projects (accessed 18 October 2022); Unicase Law LLP.

The list of PPP projects in the ICT sector includes the project on the Provision of Broadband Access to Rural Settlements with fiber-optic communication lines technology (signed in 2018).

4. Features of Past Public–Private Partnership Projects in the Information and Communication Technology Sector

The World Bank data contains all ICT projects with private sector participation. For the purposes of this section, projects involving divestitures and fully-private mobile operators have been removed. The project on the Provision of Broadband Access to Rural Settlements with fiber-optic communication lines technology (signed in 2018) has been added.

---

[65] Digital Kazakhstan. 2020. *Plan of Activities for Implementation of the Program.* Astana. https://digitalkz.kz/wp-content/uploads/2020/03/%D0%9F%D0%9C%20%D0%A6%D0%9A%20eng%20(2).pdf.

Figure 44 shows the features of PPP in the ICT sector of Kazakhstan.

Figure 44: Modes of Procurement for Public–Private Partnership Information and Communication Technology Projects

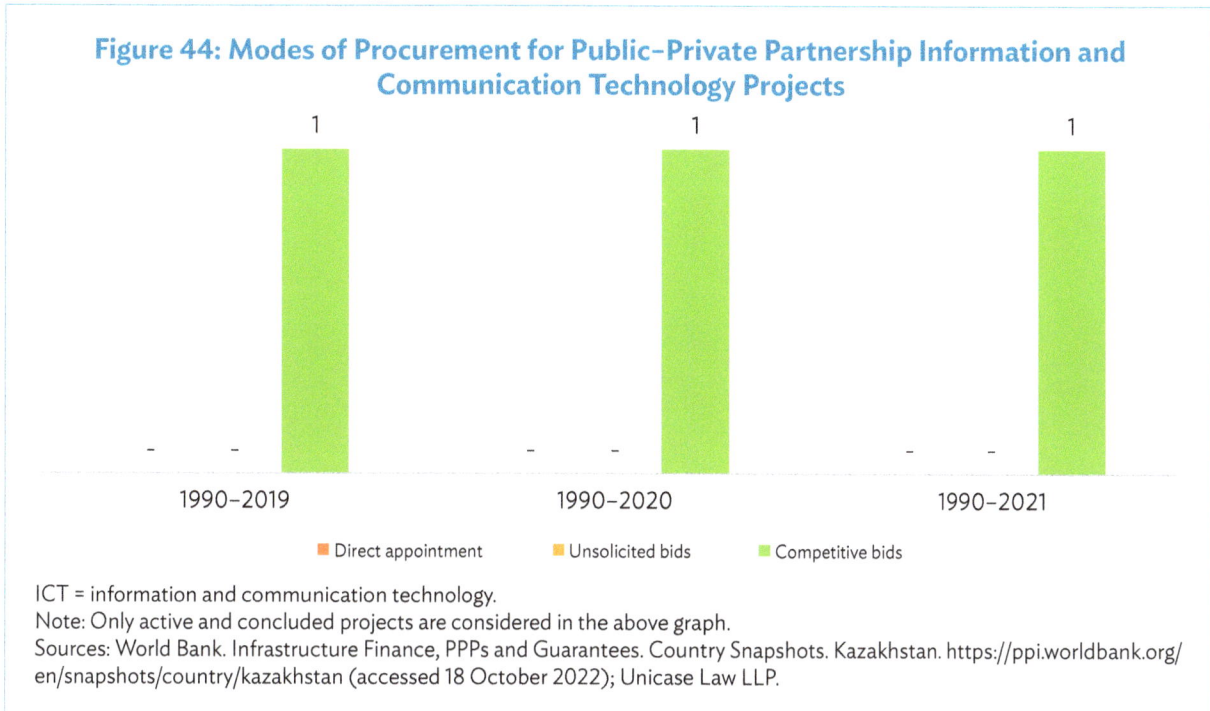

ICT = information and communication technology.
Note: Only active and concluded projects are considered in the above graph.
Sources: World Bank. Infrastructure Finance, PPPs and Guarantees. Country Snapshots. Kazakhstan. https://ppi.worldbank.org/en/snapshots/country/kazakhstan (accessed 18 October 2022); Unicase Law LLP.

Figure 45 shows the number of PPP projects that have reached financial close and the total value of those projects in the ICT sector of Kazakhstan.

Figure 45: Public–Private Partnership Information and Communication Technology Projects Reaching Financial Close

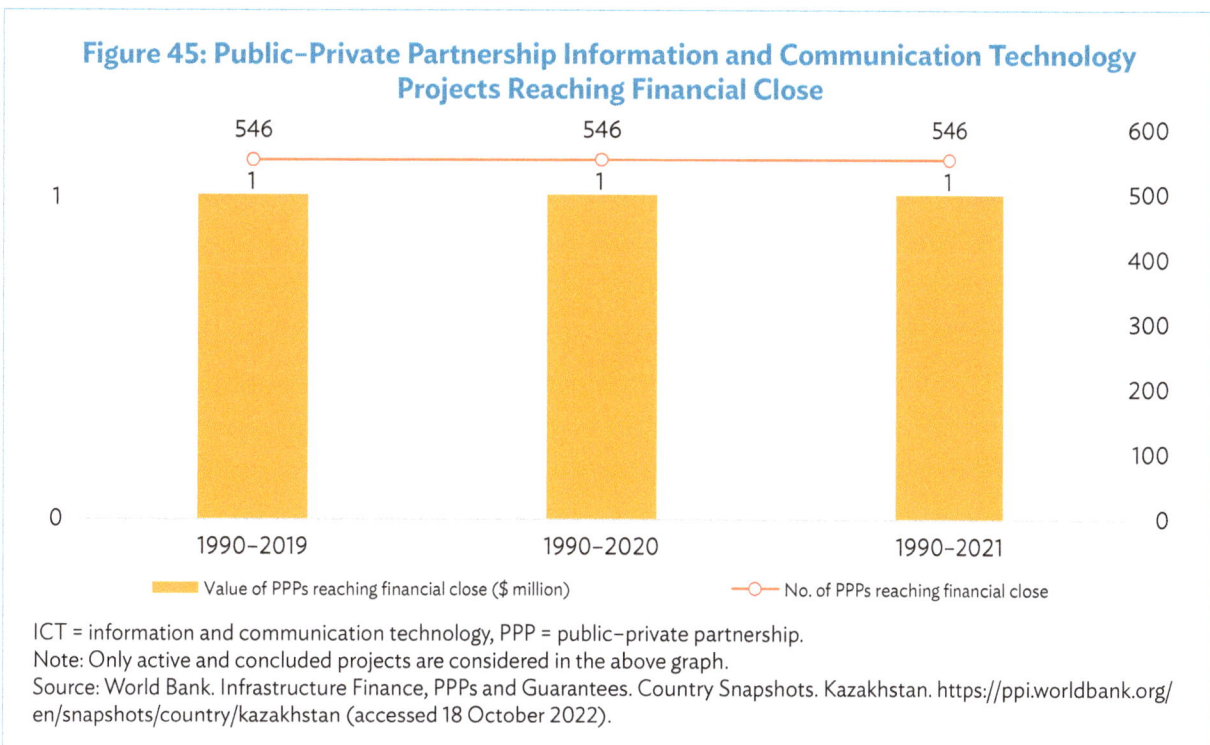

ICT = information and communication technology, PPP = public–private partnership.
Note: Only active and concluded projects are considered in the above graph.
Source: World Bank. Infrastructure Finance, PPPs and Guarantees. Country Snapshots. Kazakhstan. https://ppi.worldbank.org/en/snapshots/country/kazakhstan (accessed 18 October 2022).

Figure 46 shows the number of PPP projects that have received foreign sponsor participation in the ICT sector of Kazakhstan.

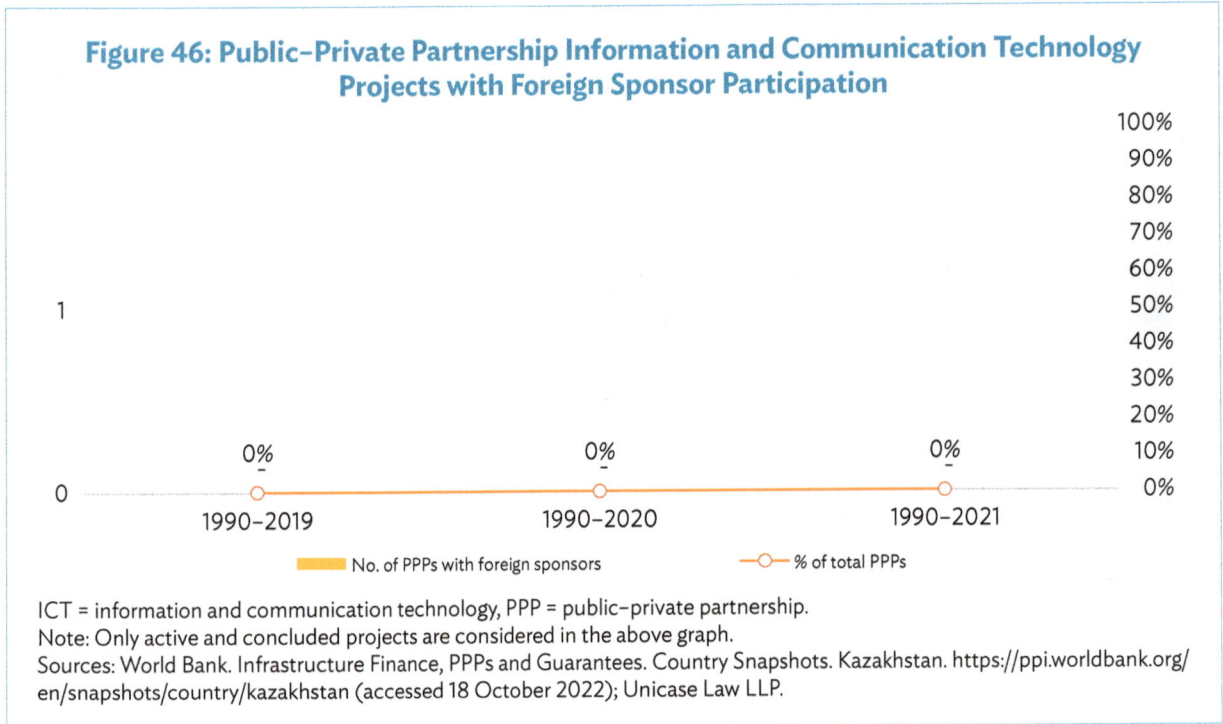

Figure 46: Public–Private Partnership Information and Communication Technology Projects with Foreign Sponsor Participation

ICT = information and communication technology, PPP = public–private partnership.
Note: Only active and concluded projects are considered in the above graph.
Sources: World Bank. Infrastructure Finance, PPPs and Guarantees. Country Snapshots. Kazakhstan. https://ppi.worldbank.org/en/snapshots/country/kazakhstan (accessed 18 October 2022); Unicase Law LLP.

The number of PPP projects that have received government support, including VGF mechanism, government guarantees, and availability or performance payment, in the ICT sector are shown in Figure 47.

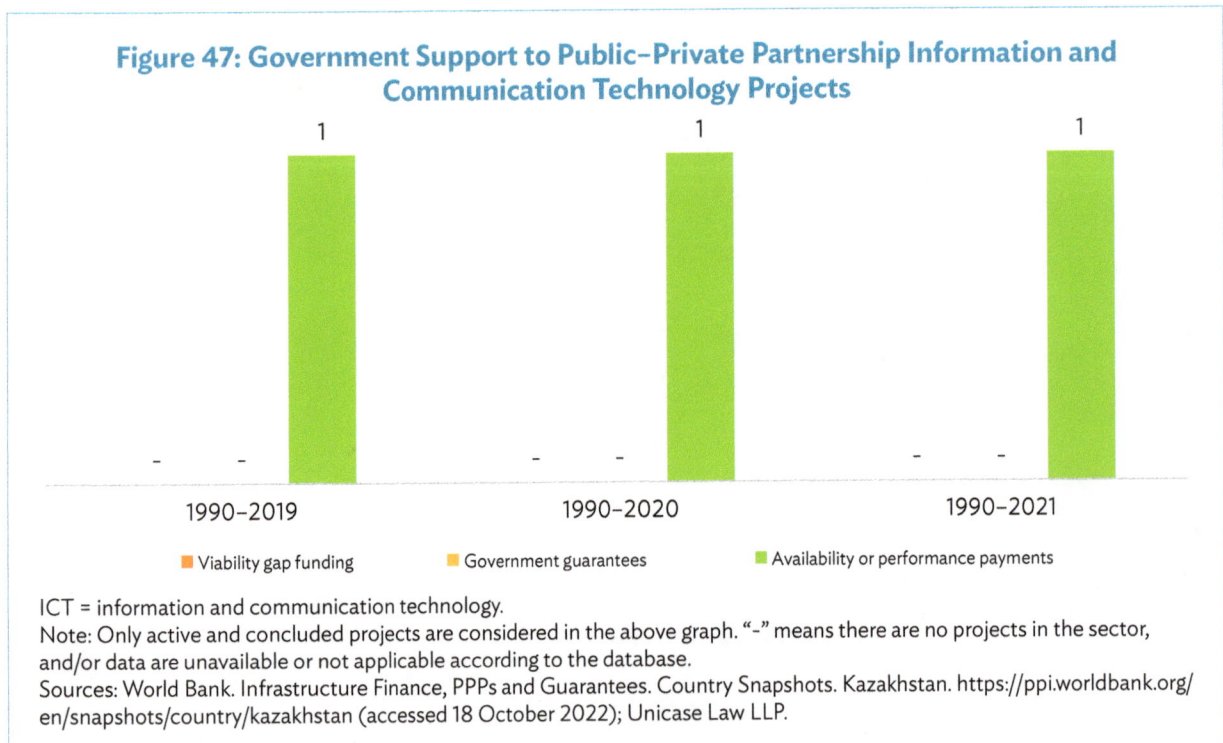

Figure 47: Government Support to Public–Private Partnership Information and Communication Technology Projects

ICT = information and communication technology.
Note: Only active and concluded projects are considered in the above graph. "-" means there are no projects in the sector, and/or data are unavailable or not applicable according to the database.
Sources: World Bank. Infrastructure Finance, PPPs and Guarantees. Country Snapshots. Kazakhstan. https://ppi.worldbank.org/en/snapshots/country/kazakhstan (accessed 18 October 2022); Unicase Law LLP.

Figure 48 shows the number of PPP projects that have received payment in the form of user charges and government pay (offtake) in the ICT sector of Kazakhstan.

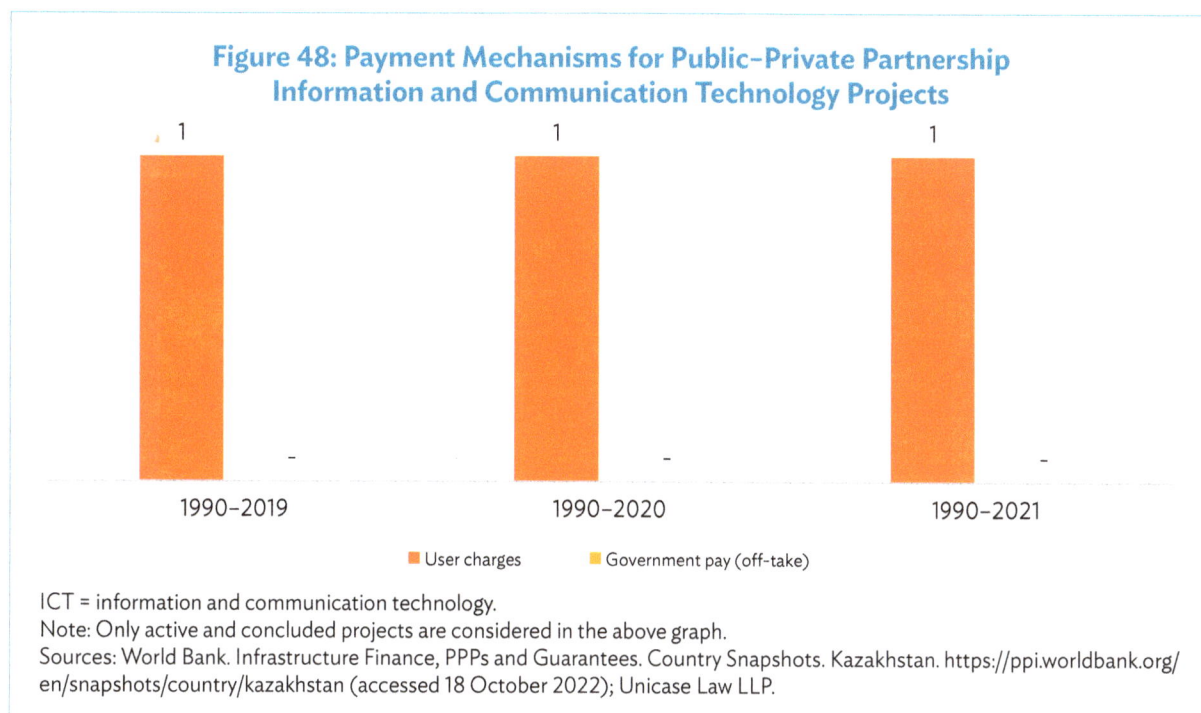

Figure 48: Payment Mechanisms for Public–Private Partnership Information and Communication Technology Projects

ICT = information and communication technology.
Note: Only active and concluded projects are considered in the above graph.
Sources: World Bank. Infrastructure Finance, PPPs and Guarantees. Country Snapshots. Kazakhstan. https://ppi.worldbank.org/en/snapshots/country/kazakhstan (accessed 18 October 2022); Unicase Law LLP.

The past PPP projects in the ICT sector according to the PPP Center's database, classified based on the jurisdiction, is provided in the Table 20.

Table 20: Summary of Projects Across Public–Private Partnership in Information and Communication Technology Sector

Sector	Number of Projects	Total Cost (T million)	Total Cost ($ million)
Local level	0	0	0
Republican level	1	209,118	445[a]
Grand total	**1**	**209,118**	**445**[a]

Note: Currency equivalent is as of 1 September 2022.
[a] The discrepancy in the project cost in US dollars between the graph and this table is because of the difference in the exchange rate used in this report and in the data sources.
Source: Kazakhstan Public–Private Partnership Center. PPP Project Database. http://www.kzppp.kz/projects (accessed 18 October 2022).

4.1 Tariffs in the Information and Communication Technology Sector

According to Worldwide Mobile Data Pricing 2020, the average cost of 1 gigabyte of mobile data in Kazakhstan was estimated at $0.46, which puts the country sixth out of 228 countries in the ranking.[66]

---

[66] Cable.co.uk. 2021. *Worldwide Mobile Data Pricing*. London.

4.2 Typical Risk Allocation for Public–Private Partnership Projects in the Information and Communication Technology Sector

A typical risk allocation for ICT sector projects is unavailable.

4.3 Financing Details for Public–Private Partnership Projects in the ICT Sector

Parameter	1990–2019	1990–2020	1990–2021
PPP projects with foreign lending participation	–	–	–
PPP projects that received export credit agency/international financing institution support	–	–	–
Typical debt to equity ratio	UA	UA	UA
Time for financial close	UA	UA	UA
Typical concession period	UA	UA	UA
Typical financial internal rate of return	UA	UA	UA

– = no project, ICT = information and communication technology, PPP = public–private partnership, UA = unavailable.
Source: World Bank. Infrastructure Finance, PPPs and Guarantees. Country Snapshots. Kazakhstan. https://ppi.worldbank.org/en/snapshots/country/kazakhstan (accessed 18 October 2022).

5. Challenges in the Information and Communication Technology Sector

The increasing state ownership in the ICT sector and the market power of the state-owned operator, combined with the absence of an independent regulatory authority, may have adverse consequences for the overall competitiveness of the economy, thus deterring private investors.

G. Social Infrastructure

Parameter	Value	Unit
Government expenditure on education	2.80	% of GDP
Education spending as % of government spending	11.42	%
Primary school gross enrollment	99.20	%
Adult literacy rate	99.80	%
Total number of projects with cumulative lending, grant, and technical assistance commitments in the education sector	7.00	Number
Total amount of cumulative lending, grant, and technical assistance commitments in the education sector	67.34[a]	$ million
Total health expenditure	2.79[b]	% of GDP
Health spending per capita	272.97[b]	$
Out-of-pockets expenditure	33.86[c]	% of total health expenditure
Maternal mortality ratio (modeled estimates per 100,000 live births)	10.00[c]	(per 100,000 live births)
Infant mortality rate	9[c]	(below 1 year/per 1,000 live births)
Life expectancy at birth	72.00[c]	(years)
Child malnutrition	2.60[c]	(% below 5 years old)

continued on next page

continued from previous page

Parameter	Value	Unit
Total number of projects with cumulative lending, grant, and technical assistance commitments in the health sector	2[a]	Number
Total amount of cumulative lending, grant, and technical assistance commitments in the health sector	6.04[a]	$ million
Existing no. of affordable housing units	UA	Number
Affordable housing gap	UA	

GDP = gross domestic product, UA = unavailable.
Sources:
[a] Asian Development Bank. Cumulative Lending, Grants, and Technical Assistance Commitments. https://data.adb.org/dataset/cumulative-lending-grant-and-technical-assistance-commitments (accessed 18 October 2022).
[b] World Health Organization. Global Health Expenditure Database. https://apps.who.int/nha/database/country_profile/Index/en (accessed 18 October 2022).
[c] World Bank Databank. Kazakhstan. https://data.worldbank.org/country/kazakhstan (accessed 18 October 2022).

Social infrastructure includes healthcare, education, public housing, and government building infrastructure. Where possible, the following analysis will be split into these subsectors. Since there is no data on social infrastructure projects available in the World Bank database, the analysis on the number of projects will be based on the PPP Center's database (accessed in October 2022).

1. Contracting Agencies in Social Infrastructure Sector

Healthcare

Healthcare facilities in Kazakhstan are largely owned and operated by the public sector, represented by the Ministry of Healthcare (MOH). PPP projects in healthcare may be contracted through the following:

- MOH for republican projects
- Local *akimats* for regional projects
- Turar Healthcare is the national medical operator under MOH responsible for providing medical services in facility management PPPs. It may also be a part of the contractual structure. According to legislation, Turar may also provide advisory support for healthcare projects.

Education

Education facilities in Kazakhstan are largely owned and operated by the public sector, represented by the Ministry of Education (MinEdu) and local *akimats*. PPP projects in education may be contracted through the following:

- MinEdu for republican projects
- Local *akimats* for regional projects
- JSC Financial Center under MinEdu is responsible for setting subsidy financing in education PPPs (per capita expenditures). It is also the designated national operator of the programmatic PPP process, which entails developing a series of PPPs based on standard requirements, contracts, and procedures, for student dormitories and schools.
- Talap, a nonprofit state-owned company, also has the national operator status and promotes the development of technical and vocational education and training.

Public Housing

The Republican state institution "Committee for Construction and Housing and Communal Services of the MIID" is the key agency that performs control and implementation functions in the field of architectural, urban planning, and construction activities; housing relations; utilities; and municipal waste management within its competence, in accordance with the legislation of the Republic of Kazakhstan.

PPP projects in public housing may be contracted through the following:

- MIID for republican projects
- Local *akimats* for regional projects.

2. Social Infrastructure Sector Laws and Regulations

Healthcare

The key legal act that provides overall regulation of the healthcare sector is the Healthcare Code (No. 360-VI ZRK dated 7 July 2020). Detailed regulation is provided via decrees and orders issued by MOH.

Education

The key legal act that provides overall regulation of the education sector is the Law "On education" No. 318-III ZRK dated 27 July 2007. Detailed regulation is provided via decrees and orders of the Minister of Education and Science.

Public Housing

The key legal act that provides overall regulation of the public housing sector is the Law "On housing relations" No. 94 ZRK dated 16 April 1997.

2.1 Standard Contracts in the Social Infrastructure Sector

Healthcare

Parameter	Availability
What standardized contracts are available and used in the market?	
– PPP/concession agreement	✓
– Performance-based operation and maintenance contract	✕
– Engineering procurement and construction contract	✕

✓ = yes, ✕ = no, PPP = public–private partnership.
Source: Unicase Law LLP.

Order No. 724 dated 25 November 2015 contains the PPP agreement templates for healthcare facilities (primary healthcare).

Education

Parameter	Availability
What standardized contracts are available and used in the market?	
– PPP/concession agreement	✓
– Performance-based operation and maintenance contract	✗
– Engineering, procurement, and construction contract	✗

✓ = yes, ✗ = no, PPP = public–private partnership.
Source: Unicase Law LLP.

Order No. 724 dated 25 November 2015 contains the PPP agreement templates for education facilities (dormitories, kindergartens, sports facilities). The Programmatic PPP promoted by JSC Financial Center under MinEdu also features templates for tender documents, procedures, and designs.

Public Housing

Parameter	Availability
What standardized contracts are available and used in the market?	
– PPP/concession agreement	✓
– Performance-based operation and maintenance contract	✗
– Engineering, procurement, and construction contract	✗

✓ = yes, ✗ = no, PPP = public–private partnership.
Source: Unicase Law LLP.

Order No. 724 dated 25 November 2015 contains the PPP agreement templates for the public housing sector.

2.2 Foreign Investment Restrictions in the Social Infrastructure Sector

Parameter	2019	2020	2021
Maximum allowed foreign ownership of equity in greenfield projects			
– Construction of healthcare facilities[a]	100%	100%	100%
– Services, including hospital management, specialist hospital/clinic, mental hospital, dental clinic, and laboratory and medical check-up services	100%	100%	100%
– Private maternity hospital, clinic general medical services/ public hospital/public medical clinic, residential health services, and basic healthcare services facility	100% (public hospitals and medical clinics – via facility management model)	100% (public hospitals and medical clinics – via facility management model)	100% (public hospitals and medical clinics – via facility management model)
– Construction of education facilities	100%	100%	100%
– Non-formal education services (vocational training, computer education, and language education)	100%	100%	100%
– Formal education services	100%	100%	100%

continued on next page

continued from previous page

Parameter	2019	2020	2021
– Government buildings (including prisons and correction centers)	100%	100%	100%
– Public housing	100%	100%	100%

[a] Except radiotherapy departments which cannot be privately owned.
Source: Unicase Law LLP.

3. Social Infrastructure Sector Master Plan

Healthcare

Healthcare infrastructure faces a growing gap and requires increased private investments in the sector. The national project "Good-quality and affordable healthcare for each citizen—Healthy nation" provides insights on key KPIs for the healthcare system in the Republic of Kazakhstan:[67]

- Increase in private investment in healthcare from T121.5 billion (about $259 million) in 2020 to T783.3 billion (about $1,668 million) in 2025

- Creation of 13,000 new permanent jobs

- Increase in the share of domestic pharmaceutical products from 17% in 2020 to 50% in 2025

- Increase in life expectancy of citizens from 71.37 years in 2020 to 75 years in 2025.

- Increase in the level of satisfaction of the population with the quality of medical services from 53.3% in 2020 to 80% in 2025

Hospital PPP is a part of the Ministry of Healthcare national project indicated above. It envisages a pipeline of 20 greenfield hospital PPPs (most of them are via unsolicited proposals) across the country, including four teaching hospitals.[68]

Education

The national project "Good Quality Education—Educated Nation" provides insights on the key performance indicators for the education system in the Republic of Kazakhstan:[69]

- Investments in fixed assets in the education sector in 2025—174.8% (% of real growth compared to 2019)

- Private funding in the education sector—T4,830 billion (about $10.2 billion)

- Number of jobs created through the construction (extension)/opening of educational facilities by 2025—103,905

---

[67]   https://adilet.zan.kz/rus/docs/P2100000725#z10 (in Russian).
[68]   The program was reduced to five teaching hospitals in December 2021.
[69]   https://adilet.zan.kz/rus/docs/P2100000726#z5 (in Russian).

- Coverage of children ages 3–6 years with preschool education and training—100%
- Ratio of the salary of a teacher to the average monthly salary in the economy—102.9%.

Public Housing

Under the Nurly Zher program, the key program objectives for public housing revolve around providing housing facilities and renovation of housing stock. Key performance indicators for the public housing are the following:

- Increase in the annual volume of housing commissioning from all sources of financing by 2025—20.7 million square meters.
- Availability of housing by 2025—26 square meters per resident.
- Reduction in the share of objects, condominiums requiring major repairs by 2025—18.1%.

3.1 Projects under Preparation and Procurement in the Social Infrastructure Sector

Figure 49 shows the number of PPP projects that are under preparation and procurement in the social infrastructure sector of Kazakhstan (all three subsectors). Data is derived from the PPP Center's project database. Figures 50–52 provide details for each of the three subsectors.

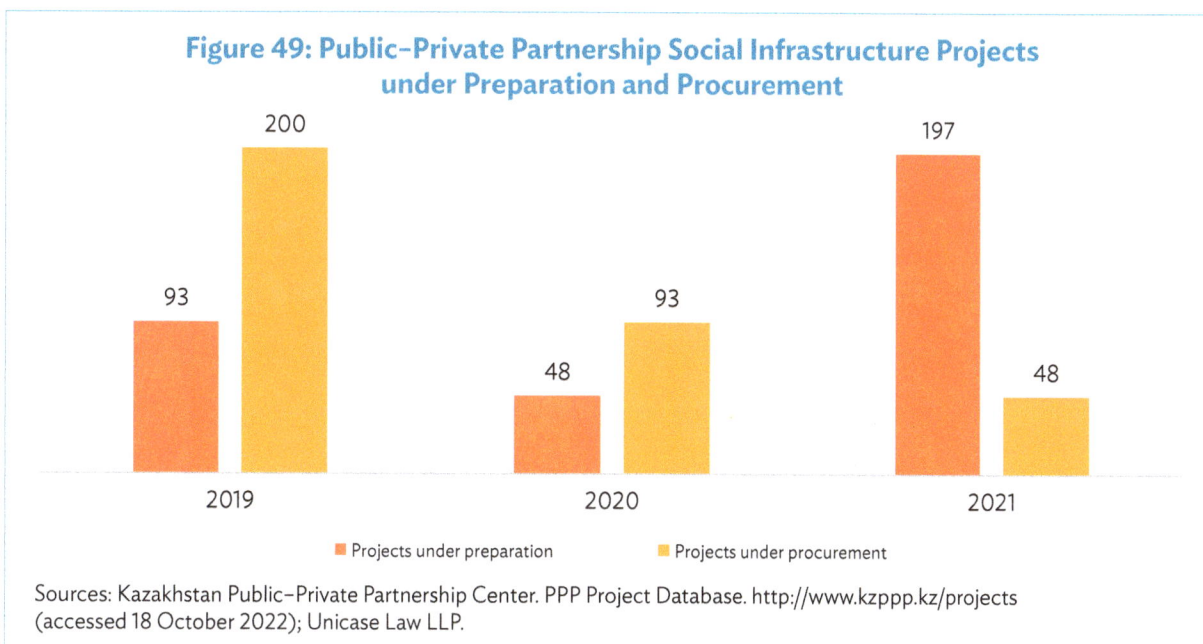

Figure 49: Public–Private Partnership Social Infrastructure Projects under Preparation and Procurement

Sources: Kazakhstan Public–Private Partnership Center. PPP Project Database. http://www.kzppp.kz/projects (accessed 18 October 2022); Unicase Law LLP.

Figure 50: Public–Private Partnership Healthcare Infrastructure Projects under Preparation and Procurement

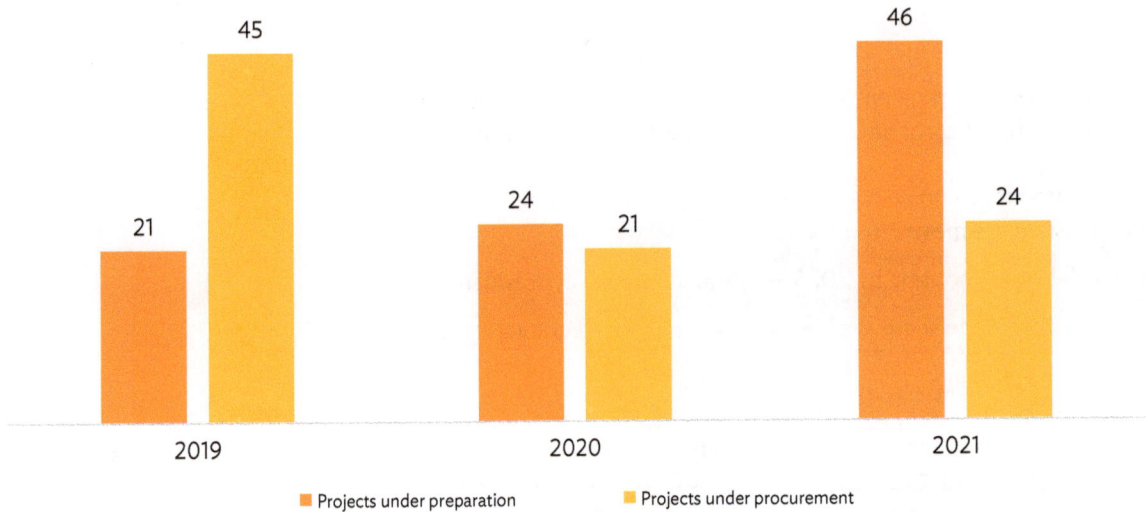

Sources: Kazakhstan Public–Private Partnership Center. PPP Project Database. http://www.kzppp.kz/projects (accessed 18 October 2022); Unicase Law LLP.

Figure 51: Public–Private Partnership Education Infrastructure Projects under Preparation and Procurement

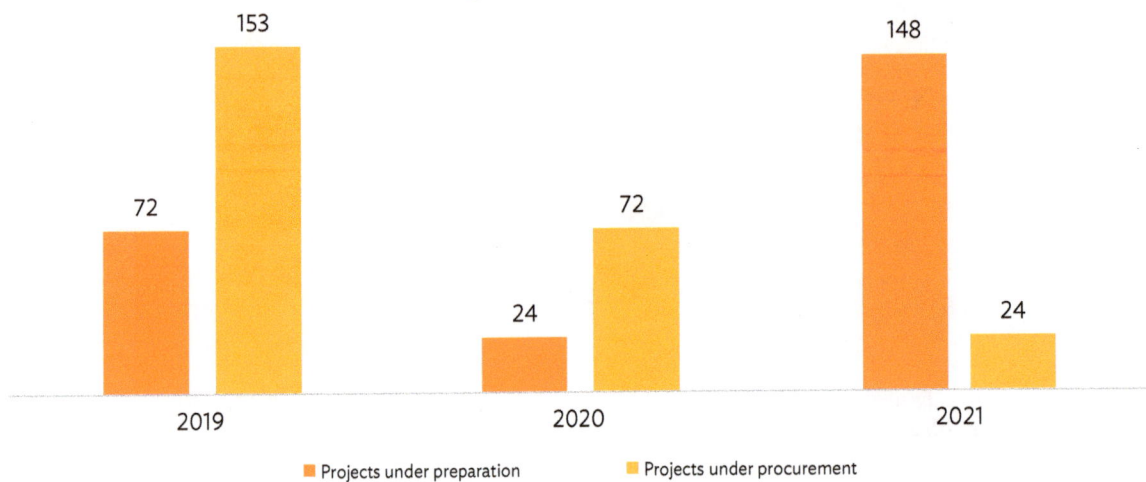

Sources: Kazakhstan Public–Private Partnership Center. PPP Project Database. http://www.kzppp.kz/projects (accessed 18 October 2022); Unicase Law LLP.

Figure 52: Public–Private Partnership Public Housing and Other Social Infrastructure Projects under Preparation and Procurement

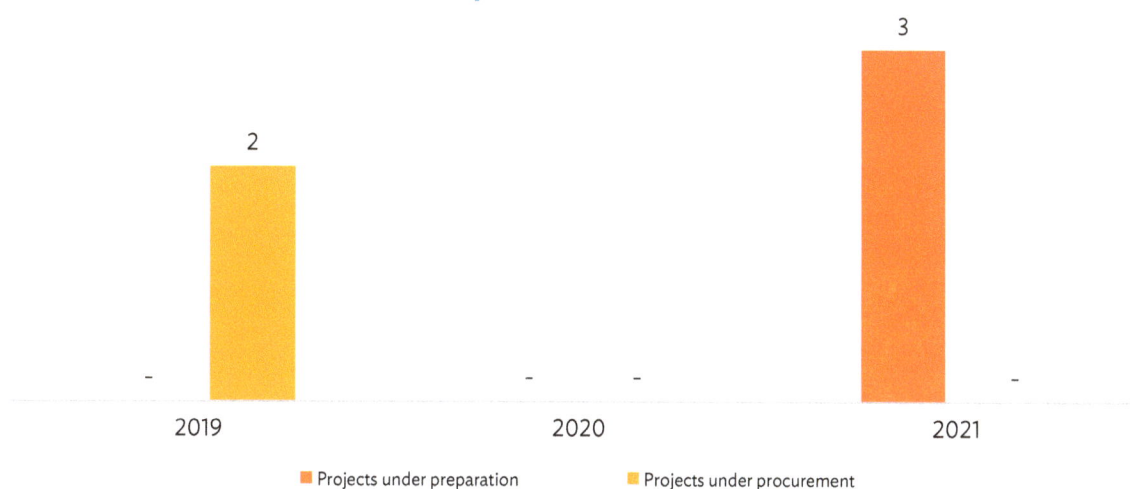

Note: "-" means there are no projects in the sector, or data are unavailable.
Sources: Kazakhstan Public–Private Partnership Center. PPP Project Database. http://www.kzppp.kz/projects (accessed 18 October 2022); Unicase Law LLP.

Most of the social PPP projects in the pipeline are small regional projects (e.g., kindergartens, school canteens, sports facilities) and are structured based on unsolicited proposals.

4. Features of Past Public–Private Partnership Projects in the Social Infrastructure Sector

For purposes of consistency and cross-country comparability, the Figures 53–57 are based on the World Bank PPI databank. PPP projects from social infrastructure sector in Kazakhstan are however not reported in this database.

Figure 53: Modes of Procurement for Public–Private Partnership Social Infrastructure Projects

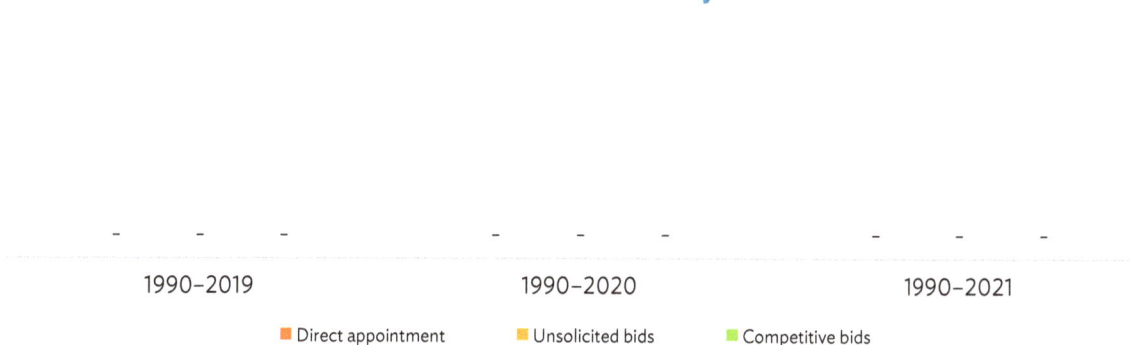

Notes: Only active and concluded projects are considered in the above graph. "-" means there are no projects in the sector, and/or data are unavailable or not applicable according to the database.
Source: World Bank. Infrastructure Finance, PPPs and Guarantees. Country Snapshots. Kazakhstan. https://ppi.worldbank.org/en/snapshots/country/kazakhstan (accessed 18 October 2022).

Figure 54: Public–Private Partnership Social Infrastructure Projects Reaching Financial Close

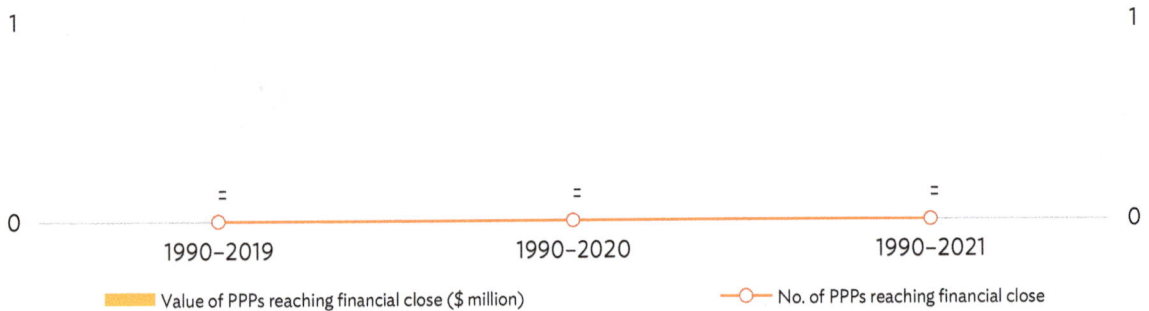

Value of PPPs reaching financial close ($ million)   —○— No. of PPPs reaching financial close

PPP = public–private partnership.
Notes: Only active and concluded projects are considered in the above graph. "-" means there are no projects in the sector, and/or data are unavailable or not applicable according to the database.
Source: World Bank. Infrastructure Finance, PPPs and Guarantees. Country Snapshots. Kazakhstan. https://ppi.worldbank.org/en/snapshots/country/kazakhstan (accessed 18 October 2022).

Figure 55: Public–Private Partnership Social Infrastructure Projects with Foreign Sponsor Participation

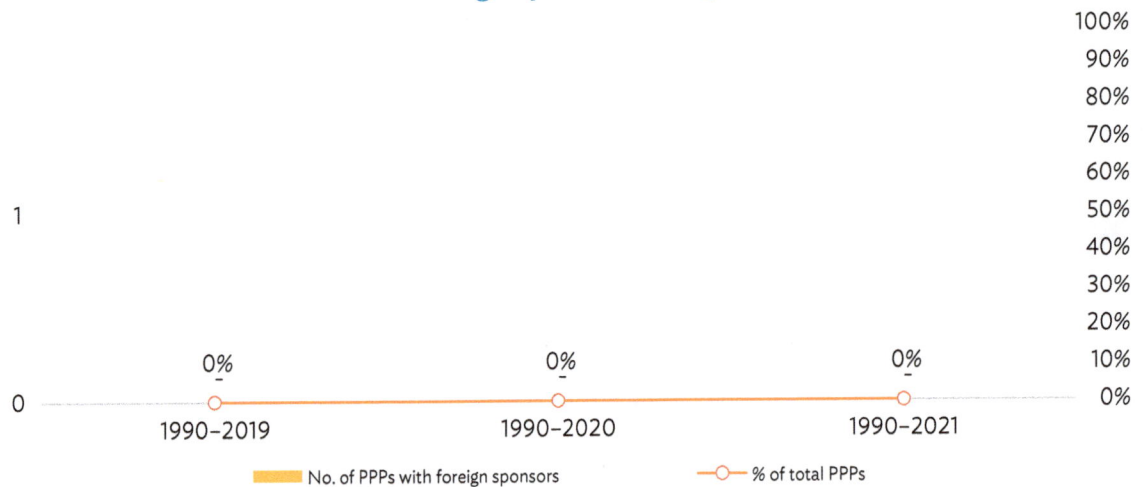

No. of PPPs with foreign sponsors   —○— % of total PPPs

PPP = public–private partnership.
Notes: Only active and concluded projects are considered in the above graph. "-" means there are no projects in the sector, and/or data are unavailable or not applicable according to the database.
Source: World Bank. Infrastructure Finance, PPPs and Guarantees. Country Snapshots. Kazakhstan. https://ppi.worldbank.org/en/snapshots/country/kazakhstan (accessed 18 October 2022).

**Figure 56: Government Support to Public–Private Partnership
Social Infrastructure Projects**

1990–2019   1990–2020   1990–2021

■ Viability gap funding   ■ Government guarantees   ■ Availability or performance payments

Notes: Only active and concluded projects are considered in the above graph. "-" means there are no projects in the sector, and/or data are unavailable or not applicable according to the database.
Source: World Bank. Infrastructure Finance, PPPs and Guarantees. Country Snapshots. Kazakhstan. https://ppi.worldbank.org/en/snapshots/country/kazakhstan (accessed 18 October 2022).

**Figure 57: Payment Mechanisms for Public–Private Partnership
Social Infrastructure Projects**

1990–2019   1990–2020   1990–2021

■ User charges   ■ Government pay (off-take)

Notes: Only active and concluded projects are considered in the above graph. "-" means there are no projects in the sector, and/or data are unavailable or not applicable according to the database.
Source: World Bank. Infrastructure Finance, PPPs and Guarantees. Country Snapshots. Kazakhstan. https://ppi.worldbank.org/en/snapshots/country/kazakhstan (accessed 18 October 2022).

The past PPP projects in the social infrastructure sector according to the PPP Center's database, classified based on the jurisdiction, is provided in Table 21.

Table 21: Summary of Projects Across Public–Private Partnerships in the Social Infrastructure Sector

Sector	Number of Projects	Total Cost (T million)	Total Cost ($ million)
Healthcare			
Local level	198	74,858	159
Republican level	0	0	0
Total – Healthcare	**198**	**74,858**	**159**
Education			
Local level	611	92,627	197
Republican level	2	1,400	3
Total – Education	**613**	**94,027**	**200**
Public Housing and Other Social			
Local level	84	51,708	110
Republican level	0	0	0
Total – Public Housing and Other Social	**84**	**51,708**	**110**
Total			
Local level	893	219,193	466
Republican level	2	1,400	3
Grand Total	**895**	**220,593**	**469**

Note: Currency equivalent is as of 1 September 2022.
Sources: Kazakhstan Public–Private Partnership Center. PPP Project Database. http://www.kzppp.kz/projects (accessed 18 October 2022); Unicase Law LLP.

4.1 Tariffs in the Social Infrastructure Sector

- In the healthcare sector, tariffs for guaranteed volume of free medical services financed out of the state budget are regulated by Order of the Acting Minister of Healthcare of the Republic of Kazakhstan No. KR DCM-170/2020 dated 30 October 2020.

- In the education sector, the education tariffs (regulatory per capita expenditures) are regulated by Order of the Minister of Education and Science of the Republic of Kazakhstan No. 596 dated 27 November 2017.

- The tariffs for public housing tend to be determined by the market and are not regulated.

4.2 Typical Risk Allocation for Public–Private Partnership Projects in the Social Infrastructure Sector

The table below shows the typical risk allocation for the social infrastructure sector (Almaty hospital PPP, planning stage).

Risk	Private	Public	Shared
Political		✓	
Project site/land		✓	
Design	✓		
Construction	✓		
Demand		✓	
Operation/maintenance	✓		
Financing/refinancing	✓		
Changes in interest rates after financial close	✓		
Inflation during operation		✓	
Currency (within 5% corridor, outside – public partner)			✓
Discriminatory changes in legislation and taxes		✓	
Natural force majeure			✓
Early termination (grantor's fault)		✓	
Early termination (concessionaire's fault)	✓		

✓ = Yes.
Source: *Concession Project: Construction and Operation of 300-Bed University Hospital in Almaty.* Presentation at Almaty Hospital PPP Roadshow. 2020

4.3 Financing Details for Public–Private Partnership Projects in the Social Infrastructure Sector

Parameter	1990–2019	1990–2020	1990–2021
PPP projects with foreign lending participation	NA	NA	NA
PPP projects that received export credit agency/international financing institution support	NA	NA	NA
Typical debt to equity ratio		NA	
Time for financial close		NA	
Typical concession period		NA	
Typical financial internal rate of return		NA	

NA = not applicable, PPP = public–private partnership.

5. Challenges in the Social Infrastructure Sector

Healthcare

- The tariff setting practices for medical services financed by the state do not provide assurances of cost recovery for the private sector, especially for capital expenditures.
- The procedures for involving private sector players in the provision of medical services guaranteed by the state are cumbersome and bureaucratic.
- There is no clarity about the sources of compensation against specific costs—between the state budget, the state insurance system, or out-of-pocket payments on the revenues side, and between the private facility operator and the state medical services provider, on the costs side.

- The increasing lack of medical personnel—and their low salaries—also pose challenges for the development of Kazakhstan's healthcare.

Education

- The current legislation does not allow for a PPP facility management model in education.
- Lack of teaching personnel is the sector's greatest risk. Without modernizing the teachers' professional development, and without raising the educators' status within the society in general and increasing their remuneration, the future of the education sector will remain in jeopardy.
- The COVID-19 pandemic had a negative impact on equal access to education. Meanwhile, the quality of education suffers from the lack of teachers' ability to adapt to distance learning and online lessons. This is partly caused by low adoption of ICT competencies in training programs.

Public Housing

- Relatively high housing construction costs make affordability a serious challenge for this sector. According to the Nurly Zher program, it takes about 11 years for an average household to save for a 54-square-meter apartment.
- Current legislation does not allow for a PPP facility management model in the housing sector.
- Black-market rentals are relatively high (60% to 70% according to the Nurly Zher program).
- Green housing—encompassing energy efficiency, universal accessibility, and inclusive design—will be needed, requiring regulations, building codes and certification, as well as new skills and capacity in the private sector.

H. Other Infrastructure: Municipal Solid Waste

1. Contracting Agencies

The Committee on Environmental Regulation and Control under the Ministry of Ecology, Geology and Natural Resources is the competitive body in the sector responsible for the following tasks:

- Monitoring of the quality of the environment, environmental safety, preservation of natural resources, and achievement of a favorable level of environmentally sustainable development of society
- Environmental legislation and regulation, state environmental control within its competence, and organization and conduct of state environmental expertise in accordance with the requirements of the current legislation
- Coordination, regulation of emissions, and implementation of the issuance of environmental permits; implementation of state environmental control.

PPP projects in the municipal solid waste sector may be contracted through the following:

- Ministry of Ecology, Geology and Natural Resources for republican projects
- Local *akimats* for regional projects
- Certain projects may be structured via Operator Zhasyl Damu (100% owned by the government), which is responsible for managing a unified system of integrated waste management of products/goods.

2. Laws and Regulations

The Environmental Code is the key legislative document of the municipal solid waste sector.[70] The Code guides and governs all stages of waste handling. The Environmental Code introduces the concepts of waste collection, transportation, recovery, disposal, and auxiliary operations in waste management. The Code also defines the licensing requirements for entities involved in waste management.

2.1 Standard Contracts and Licenses

Parameter	Availability
What standardized contracts are available and used in the market?	
– PPP/concession agreement	✗
– Power purchase agreement	✗
– Long-term waste supply contract	✗
– Capacity take-or-pay contract	✗
– Transmission and use of system agreement	✗
– Performance-based operations and maintenance contract	✗
– Engineering, procurement, and construction contract	✗

✗ = no, PPP = public–private partnership.
Source: Unicase Law LLP.

There are no standard contracts specific to municipal solid waste sector yet.

2.2 Foreign Investment Restrictions

The ownership allowance in the municipal solid waste sector is indicated below.

Parameter	2019	2020	2021
Maximum allowed foreign ownership of equity in greenfield projects	100%	100%	100%

Sources: ADB. 2019. *Public–Private Partnership Monitor*. Second Edition. Manila. https://www.adb.org/sites/default/files/publication/509426/ppp-monitor-second-edition.pdf; Unicase Law LLP.

---

[70] Environmental Code of the Republic of Kazakhstan No. 400-VI 3PK, dated 2 January 2021.

3. Master Plan

The key document that regulates the development of the solid waste management sector is the Concept for Transition of the Republic of Kazakhstan to "Green Economy," approved by Presidential Decree of the Republic of Kazakhstan No. 577 dated 30 May 2013. The Concept aims to increase resource efficiency, upgrade existing infrastructure, and address climate change and other environmental issues.

Implementation of the Green Economy Concept has three stages:

- 2013–2020: During the first stage, the main priority of the state was to optimize the resource use and increase the efficiency of environment protection activities, and to establish green infrastructure.
- 2020–2030: The second stage proposes transformation of the national economy, based on the green infrastructure built during the first stage with focus on rational water use, and broad implementation of renewable energy and energy efficient technologies.
- 2030–2050: Transition of the national economy, according to the principles of Third Industrial Revolution, requires the use of natural resources on the condition of renewability and sustainability. For the municipal solid waste sector in particular, the Concept proposes development of a brand new integrated waste management system.

3.1 Projects under Preparation and Procurement in Municipal Solid Waste Sector

Figure 58 shows the number of PPP projects that are under preparation and procurement in the municipal solid waste sector of Kazakhstan.

Figure 58: Public–Private Partnership Municipal Solid Waste Projects under Preparation and Procurement

2019   2020   2021

■ Projects under preparation   ■ Projects under procurement

Note: "-" means there are no projects in the sector, or data are unavailable.
Sources: Kazakhstan Public–Private Partnership Center. PPP Project Database. http://www.kzppp.kz/projects (accessed 18 October 2022); Unicase Law LLP.

4. Features of Past Public–Private Partnership Projects

Figure 59 shows the number of PPP projects procured through various modes, including direct appointment, unsolicited bids, and competitive bids, in the municipal solid waste sector of Kazakhstan.

Figure 59: Modes of Procurement for Public–Private Partnership Municipal Solid Waste Projects

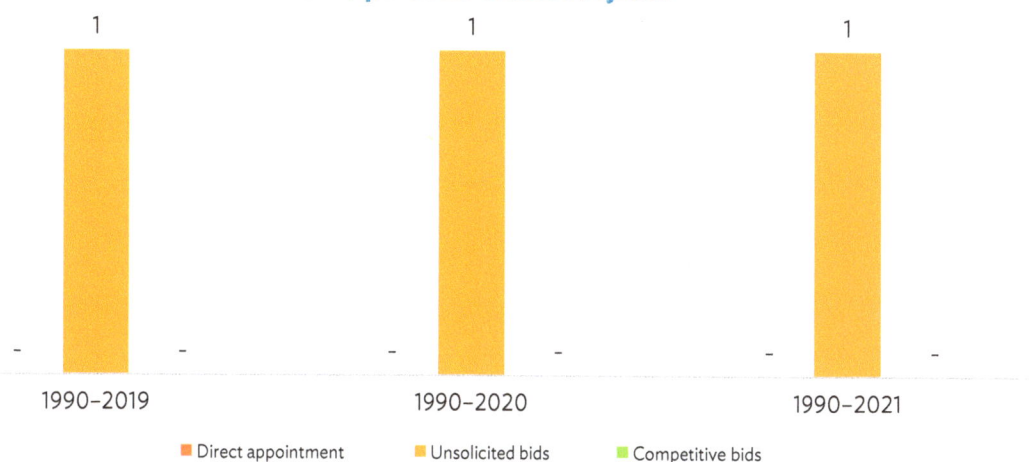

Notes: Only active and concluded projects are considered in the above graph. "–" means there are no projects in the sector, and/or data are unavailable or not applicable according to the database. Award method information on only project (up to 2020) is not available in the database and is therefore excluded from the above graph.
Source: World Bank. Infrastructure Finance, PPPs and Guarantees. Country Snapshots. Kazakhstan. https://ppi.worldbank.org/en/snapshots/country/kazakhstan (accessed 18 October 2022).

Figure 60 shows the number of PPP projects that have reached financial close and the total value of those projects in the municipal solid waste sector of Kazakhstan.

Figure 60: Public–Private Partnership Municipal Solid Waste Projects Reaching Financial Close

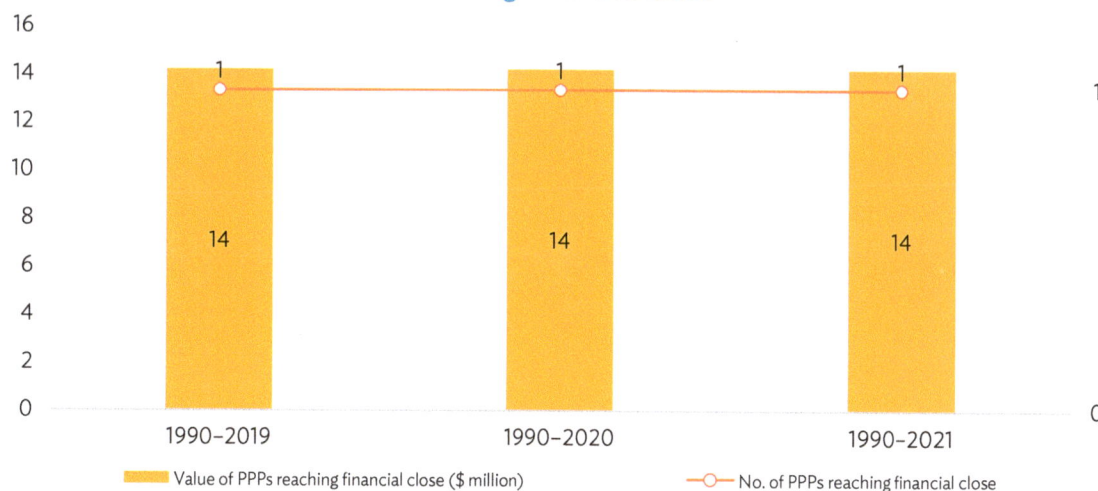

Note: Only active and concluded projects are considered in the above graph.
Source: World Bank. Infrastructure Finance, PPPs and Guarantees. Country Snapshots. Kazakhstan. https://ppi.worldbank.org/en/snapshots/country/kazakhstan (accessed 18 October 2022).

Figure 61 shows the number of PPP projects that have received foreign sponsor participation in the municipal solid waste sector of Kazakhstan.

Figure 61: Public–Private Partnership Municipal Solid Waste Projects with Foreign Sponsor Participation

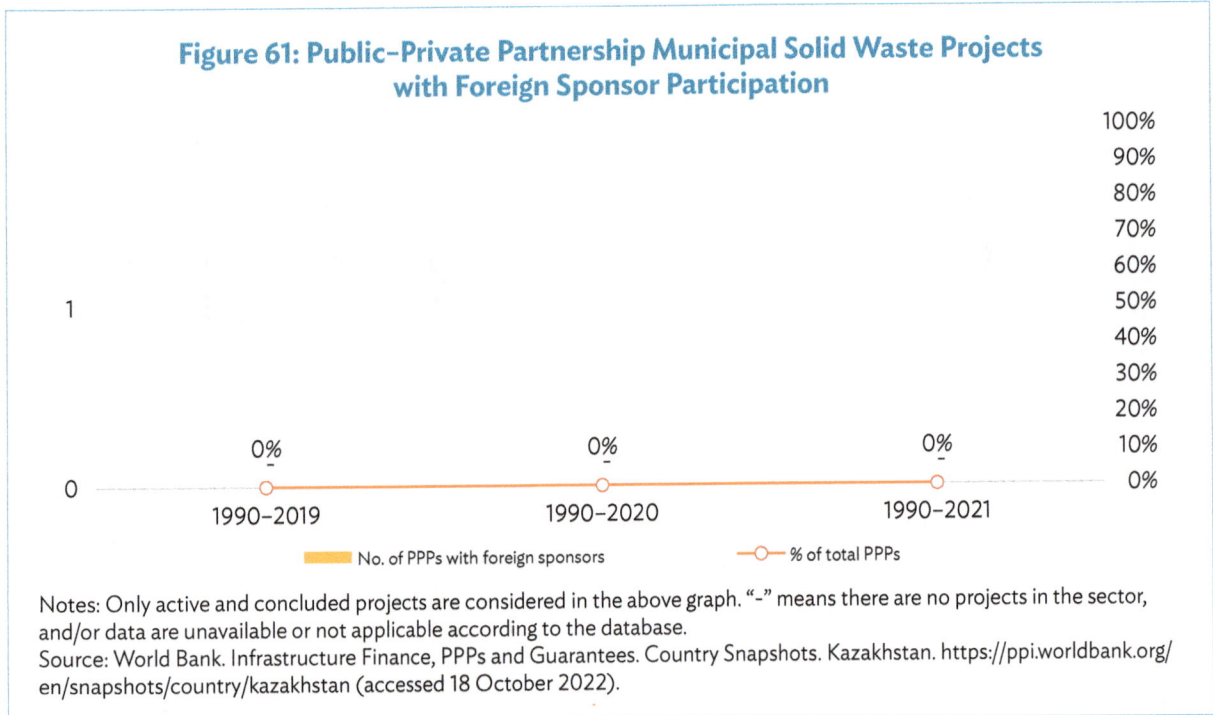

Notes: Only active and concluded projects are considered in the above graph. "-" means there are no projects in the sector, and/or data are unavailable or not applicable according to the database.
Source: World Bank. Infrastructure Finance, PPPs and Guarantees. Country Snapshots. Kazakhstan. https://ppi.worldbank.org/en/snapshots/country/kazakhstan (accessed 18 October 2022).

The number of PPP projects that have received government support, including VGF mechanism, government guarantees, and availability or performance payment in the municipal solid waste sector of Kazakhstan is shown in Figure 62.

Figure 62: Government Support to Public–Private Partnership Municipal Solid Waste Projects

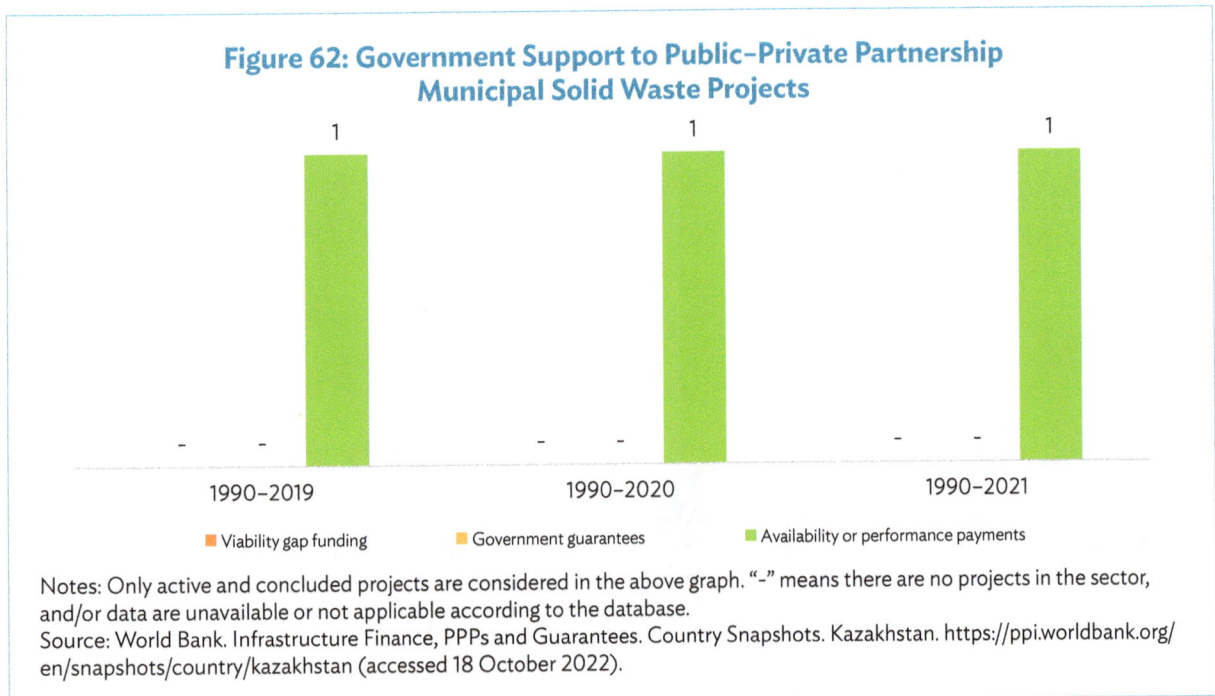

Notes: Only active and concluded projects are considered in the above graph. "-" means there are no projects in the sector, and/or data are unavailable or not applicable according to the database.
Source: World Bank. Infrastructure Finance, PPPs and Guarantees. Country Snapshots. Kazakhstan. https://ppi.worldbank.org/en/snapshots/country/kazakhstan (accessed 18 October 2022).

Figure 63 shows the number of PPP projects that have received payment in the form of user charges and government pay (offtake) in the municipal solid waste sector of Kazakhstan.

Figure 63: Payment Mechanisms for Public–Private Partnership Municipal Solid Waste Projects

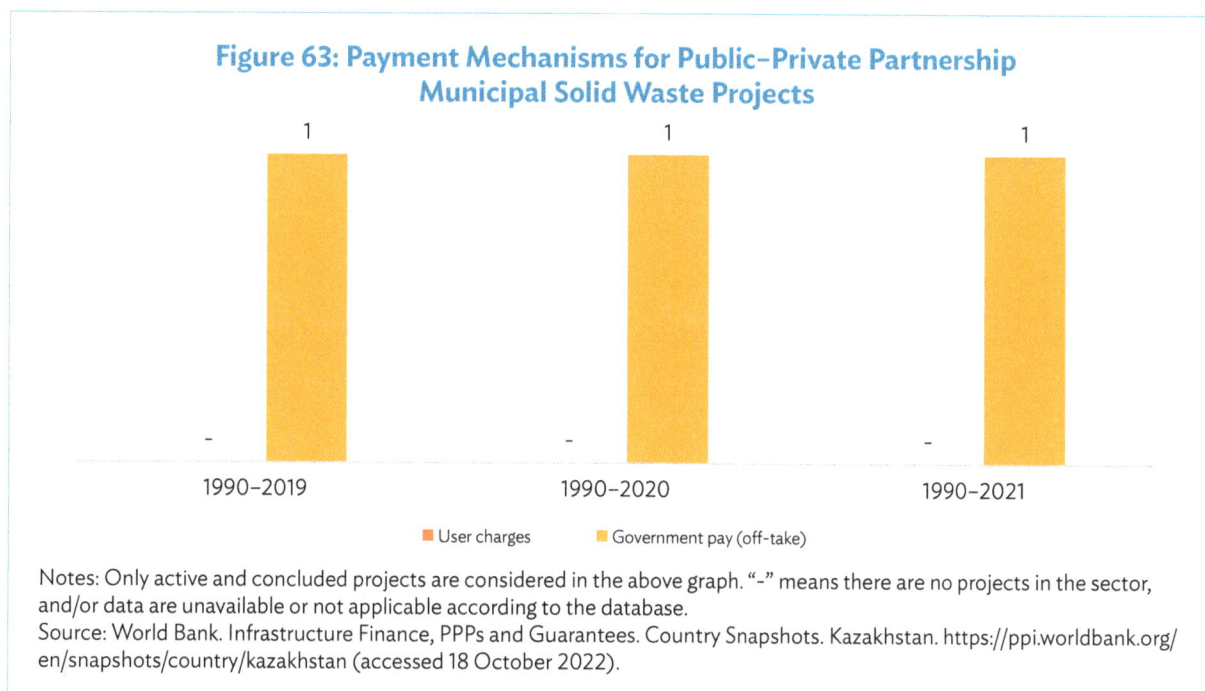

Notes: Only active and concluded projects are considered in the above graph. "–" means there are no projects in the sector, and/or data are unavailable or not applicable according to the database.
Source: World Bank. Infrastructure Finance, PPPs and Guarantees. Country Snapshots. Kazakhstan. https://ppi.worldbank.org/en/snapshots/country/kazakhstan (accessed 18 October 2022).

The past PPP projects in the municipal solid waste sector according to the PPP Center's database, classified based on the jurisdiction, is provided in Table 22.

Table 22: Summary of Projects Across Public–Private Partnerships in the Municipal Solid Waste Sector

Sector	Number of Projects	Total Cost (T million)	Total Cost ($ million)
Local level	3	6,118	13
Republican level	0	0	0
Grand total	3	6,118	13

Note: Currency equivalent is as of 1 September 2022.
Sources: Kazakhstan Public–Private Partnership Center. PPP Project Database. http://www.kzppp.kz/projects (accessed 18 October 2022); Unicase Law LLP.

4.1 Tariffs in the Municipal Solid Waste Sector

Tariffs in the municipal solid waste sector are set by the *akimats* for each regional center and city of national status in accordance with the Ecological Code and the Order of the Minister of Ecology, Geology and Natural Resources No. 377 dated 14 September 2021. Tariffs calculated are finally approved by local representative bodies (*maslikhats*).

For instance, the following tariffs are set for Almaty City (Table 23).

Table 23: Tariffs in the Municipal Solid Waste Sector for Almaty City

Name	Unit	Price, T (including VAT)	Price, $ (including VAT)
Collection, transportation, utilization, recycling, and disposal of solid waste – population	One inhabitant per month	553.04	1.17
Collection, transportation, utilization, recycling, and disposal of solid waste – population – commercial entities	1 cubic meter	2,288.46	4.87

Source: https://adilet.zan.kz/rus/docs/V17R0001405 (in Russian).

4.2 Typical Risk Allocation for Past Public–Private Partnership Projects

Information on typical risk allocation arrangements in municipal solid waste PPP contracts is unavailable.

4.3 Financing Details on Past Public–Private Partnership Projects

Parameter	1990–2019	1990–2020	1990–2021
PPP projects with foreign lending participation	NA	NA	NA
PPP projects that received export credit agency/international financing institution support	NA	NA	NA
Typical debt to equity ratio		NA	
Time for financial close		NA	
Typical concession period		25 years	
Typical financial internal rate of return		NA	

NA = not applicable, PPP = public–private partnership.
Source: World Bank. Infrastructure Finance, PPPs and Guarantees. Country Snapshots. Kazakhstan. https://ppi.worldbank.org/en/snapshots/country/kazakhstan (accessed 18 October 2022).

5. Challenges in the Solid Waste Management Sector

The main challenges in the solid waste management sector are as follows:

- Slow reforms in the solid waste management sector and low waste separation and recycling culture result in 80%–90% of waste being landfilled.

- Low tariffs for collection and disposal make investments and operations of modern garbage trucks and landfills commercially unattractive.

- Low demand for recycled products against high logistics costs affects profit margins.

IV. Local Government Public–Private Partnership Landscape

Parameter	Value	Unit
Number of subnational governments (SNGs)[a]		
– Municipal level	2,345	Number
– Intermediate level	220	Number
– Regional or state level	17	Number
Total number of SNGs	2,582	Number
SNG expenditure profile[b]		
Total SNG expenditure as % of GDP	9.40	%
– SNG current expenditure as % of GDP	6.80	%
– SNG staff expenditure as % of GDP	2.00	%
– SNG investment as % of GDP	2.60	%
Total SNG expenditure as % of the total general government expenditure (% of total public expenditure)	46.30	%
– SNG current expenditure as a % of total current expenditure of the general government	–	%
– SNG staff expenditure as a % of total staff expenditure of the general government	61.90	%
– SNG investment as a % of total investment of the general government	63.70	%
Current expenditure of SNG as a % of total SNG expenditure	UA	%
Staff expenditure of SNG as a % of total SNG expenditure	UA	%
Investments of SNG as a % of total SNG expenditure	UA	%
SNG expenditure by function[b]		
– General public services	10.80	%
– Defense	0.50	%
– Security and public order	3.70	%
– Economic affairs	15.60	%
– Environmental protection	0.40	%
– Housing and community amenities	14.70	%
– Health	16.40	%
– Recreation, culture, and religion	5.40	%
– Education	29.00	%
– Social protection	3.60	%

continued on next page

continued from previous page

Parameter	Value	Unit
SNG revenue profile[b]		
Total SNG revenue as a % of GDP	9.50	%
– SNG tax revenue as a % of GDP	3.70	%
– SNG grants and subsidies as a % of GDP	5.60	%
– SNG other revenues as a % of GDP	0.20	%
Total SNG revenue as % of total general government revenue	37.2	%
– SNG tax revenue as a % of total general government tax revenue	17.8	%
– SNG grants and subsidies as a % of total general government grants and subsidies	–	%
– SNG other revenues as a % of total other revenues	–	%
SNG tax revenue as a % of total SNG revenue	38.70	%
SNG grants and subsidies as a % of total SNG revenue	59.40	%
SNG other revenues as a % of total SNG revenue	1.90	%
SNG debt profile[b]		
Outstanding SNG debt as % of GDP	0.5	%
Outstanding SNG debt as % of total outstanding debt of general government	4.10	%
Parameters for transfers to the subnational governments from the national government[c]		
Score on transfers to subnational governments	C	
– Score on system for allocating transfers	C	
– Score on timeliness of information on transfers	C	
– Score on extent of collection and reporting of consolidated fiscal data for general government	A	
Value of central government transfers to subnational governments	UA	% of GDP
Value of actual budgetary allocation to subnational governments from national government	UA	% of total expenditure
Value of deviation of actual against the budgeted transfers to subnational governments	8.7	% of budgeted transfers

GDP = gross domestic product, UA = unavailable.

a   Data is as of December 2021. In March 2022, Kazakhstan created three more regions by splitting the Almaty region to (Almaty and Zhetsu), the East Kazakhstan region (to East Kazakhstan and Abay) and Karaganda (to Karaganda and Ulytau) The number of subnational governments will increase to 20 (17 regions and 3 cities of regional importance).

b   Organisation for Economic Co-operation and Development (OECD), United Cities and Local Governments (UCLG), Agence Française de Développement (AFD). 2016. *Subnational Governments Around the World: Structure and Finance.* Paris and Barcelona (Part III – Country Profiles). http://www.uclg-localfinance.org/observatory.

c   World Bank. 2018. *Kazakhstan Public Expenditure and Financial Accountability (PEFA): Assessment Report 2017.* Jakarta and Washington, DC. https://www.pefa.org/sites/pefa/files/2019-11/KZ-Dec18-PFMPR-Public%20with%20PEFA%20check_ENG_0.pdf.

Local Governance System in Kazakhstan

Law No. 148 on "Local Government and Self-Government," dated 23 January 2001 (Self-Governance Law), is the presiding legal framework for subnational governments in Kazakhstan, which was last amended in December 2021. The law regulates social relations in the field of local government and self–government, and determines the powers, organization, and procedures for local executives (*akimats*) and representative bodies (*maslikhats*).

The Self-Governance Law established a three-tier system of subnational governments:

- At the upper level, there are 17 regions (*oblasts*) and three cities of republican significance (Almaty, Astana, and Shymkent) which have a status equivalent to the regions. They are headed by regional/city governors (*akims*) appointed by the President, and have also regional/city councils elected by universal suffrage (*maslikhats*).

- At the intermediate level, there are 37 towns of regional significance and 161 districts (*audans*), of which 16 are city districts and the rest are rural.[71] Their executives (*akims*) are appointed by the regional/city *akims* and they have a directly elected council (town or district *maslikhats*).

- The third tier has 47 "towns of district significance" and 2,298 villages and rural communities recognized as local self-governments (*auls*). It also comprises around 4,325 rural settlements.

- The Self-Governance Law, as amended in 2013, introduced some elements of decentralization, such as election of local *akims* through indirect suffrage by local level councils. The Concept for Development of Self-Governance until 2025, adopted in August 2021, calls for direct election of third-tier *akims* by citizens and for a decentralization of certain budget and financial functions.[72]

The regional budgets; the budgets of the cities of republican significance and of the capital city; the district (city of regional significance) budgets; the budgets of the towns of district significance; and the budgets of villages, townships, and rural districts all form the local budgets.[73] The budgets are formed and executed at the following levels:

- Oblast, city of republican status, capital
- Districts (towns of regional significance)

Infrastructure Development Plan of Local Governments

The local governments are responsible for a variety of development activities in their respective jurisdictions:

- management of community property at the district or city level, as applicable
- primary, basic secondary, and general secondary education
- social assistance and social security, including housing assistance
- housing and utilities infrastructure, including housing stock improvements, organization of the maintenance of public housing area, construction of the communal housing stock, provision of sanitation for the settlements, maintenance of burial places, street lighting in the settlements, and landscaping of settlements
- culture and sports
- transport and communication, including construction, reconstruction, and repair and maintenance of roads; technical means of traffic control on roads; passenger transportation on socially important urban/rural areas; and suburban and inter-district communications, except for railroads
- organization of water supply and waste of settlements

---

[71] In March 2022, Kazakhstan created three more regions by splitting the Almaty region to (Almaty and Zhetsu), the East Kazakhstan region (to East Kazakhstan and Abay) and Karaganda (to Karaganda and Ulytau) The number of subnational governments will increase to 20.

[72] "Concept for the Development of Local Self-Government in the Republic of Kazakhstan until 2025" adopted by Order of the President of the Republic of Kazakhstan No. 639 dated 18 August 2021.

[73] Budget Code of Republic of Kazakhstan of December 25, 2017, No. 120-VI ZRK. https://adilet.zan.kz/eng/docs/K080000095_#:~:text=121-V (in Russian).

The exact detail and nature of the activities and the extent of expenditure differs to a minor extent depending on the entity—the city of republican significance and the capital city; the district (city of regional significance); the city of district significance; or a village, township, or rural district.

Sectors for Potential Public–Private Partnerships with Local Government Projects

The local governments have actively been undertaking PPP projects across various sectors. However, education and healthcare have been sectors of prime importance. A snapshot of the key sectors in which the local governments have been implementing PPPs and the number of projects are shown in Table 24.

Table 24: Public–Private Partnership Projects at the Local Government Level

Sector	No. of Projects (cumulative)	Total Commitments (T billion)	Total Commitments ($ million)
Agriculture, forestry, and fisheries	10	1.3	2.85
Culture and sports	95	1,127.1	2,400.13
Education	764	312.6	665.67
Energy, housing, and utilities sector	167	646.3	1,376.28
Financial and insurance activities	6	1.1	2.34
Healthcare and social services	229	187.6	399.49
Information and communication	2	11.1	23.64
Manufacturing industry	2	3.7	7.88
Transport and communications	30	183.5	390.76
Other	13	80.0	170.36
Total	**1,318**	**2,554.34**	**5,439.40**

Note: The list includes projects that are under implementation, those with expired agreement, and those that have been terminated. Currency equivalent is as of 1 September 2022.
Source: Government of Kazakhstan, Kazakhstan Public–Private Partnership Center. PPP Project Database (accessed 18 October 2022), http://www.kzppp.kz/projects.

Despite the significant number of regional projects, many of these are small and short-term, which makes their classification as PPPs arguable.

Revenues for Subnational Governments

According to the *Budget Code*, subnational governments' local budgets can draw revenues from 7 taxes,[74] 7 excise duties,[75] 5 environmental payments,[76] and 9 different non-tax revenues[77]. As most state revenues come from

---

[74]   Taxes on land, property, advertisement, transport vehicle (individuals), transport vehicle (firms), land lease, and social security contributions.
[75]   Spirits and alcohol (locally produced and exported), beer, tobacco, cars, and petrol.
[76]   Water use, forestry use, emissions, land use, and use of specially protected territory.
[77]   Payments for licensing and registration of property, pledges, rights, advertisement, etc.

corporate taxes and National Fund[78] transfers—and accumulate centrally—subnational governments depend on upper-tier budget transfers. Only a few of the 20 regions generate surplus revenues as donors to the republican budget (e.g., Almaty and Astana cities, Atyrau and Mangistau regions).

Apart from the republican transfers, the most prominent sources of local budget revenues, as established by the statutory income distribution of local *maslikhats,* are individual income tax, social tax, and environmental and emissions fees. Other revenues of varying importance are advertisement fees, fees for use of water resources and forestry, and fees for use of specially protected natural territories of local significance.

In Kazakhstan, the law stipulates the independent formation of local budgets, which have legislatively assigned tax and non-tax revenues that form their profits. However, the formation of local budgets is highly influenced by the transfers, the provision of which is determined by the central authorities, which makes the local government budgets depend on the budgetary allocations of higher governments.

The local governments, in aggregate, derive about 40% of their revenue from the taxes and non-tax revenues whose yield is allocated to them by the Budget Code. The rest is transfers from the upper-level budgets (e.g., republican budget transfers to regional authorities). Total revenues of local governments in 2021 were T8,742.6 billion (about $20 billion); of these T3,666.4 billion (about $8 billion) had been accrued through taxes, and T4,754.9 billion (about $10.7 billion) are total transfers received from the central /republican budget. Of the total transfers received by regional budgets, T2,120.9 billion (almost $5 billion) were received as subsidy/dotation, and T2,463.0 billion (about $5.7 billion) as targeted transfers for current expenditure and development.[79]

Borrowings by Local Governments

The Budget Code and its rules legally allow any subnational government to raise external debt in the form of bonds or bank loans, provided that total annual repayments would not exceed 10% of their revenues. The annual borrowing limits are approved for the regions and republican cities on an annual basis, as part of the state budget approval process. All subnational governments submit budget execution statements, together with the reports of the Audit Commissions established to review them, within 9 months of the end of each fiscal year. Subnational government total borrowing amounts to only about 0.5% of total state debt; amounts are published quarterly together with other state debt statistics.

Based on the statistics published by the Ministry of Finance, Government of Kazakhstan, the total debt of the local governments as of 1 April 2022 is as follows:

- to the Government of the Republic of Kazakhstan—$1.6 billion

- to other creditors—$2.4 billion.[80]

---

[78]   The Kazakhstan National Fund was established in 2000, primarily to act as a stabilization fund to lessen the impact that volatility in oil, gas, and mineral prices have on the Republic of Kazakhstan. It is financed from surplus revenues gained from taxes on the development of oil, gas, and mineral reserves. The National Bank of Kazakhstan lists assets for the fund at $52.4 billion as of October 2022. About $2.1 billion of that total was in gold (the limit is set at up to 5% of the portfolio).

[79]   Ministry of Finance. 2022. Statistical Bulletin for 2021. Astana

[80]   Ministry of Finance. 2022. Statistical Bulletin. 1 April. https://www.gov.kz/memleket/entities/minfin/documents/details/260596?lang=ru (in Russian).

Budgetary Allocation to Local Governments

In addition to revenues from their own taxes and other sources, there are also budgetary transfers between each level. Transfers between republican and regional budgets are regulated by transfers and budgetary credits while those between regions and districts are regulated by transfers, budgetary credits, and norms of income distribution. Transfers are divided into two types: transfers of a general character (subsidy/dotation) and targeted transfers.

- Transfers of general character include budget subsidies and budget withdrawals, depending on the deficit or surplus at the lower budget and the principles set out in the Budget Code. The volume of transfers of a general character changes every 3 years. These transfers aim to level the budgets of regions and provide equal fiscal capacities for services guaranteed by the state.

- Targeted transfers are categorized into targeted current transfers and targeted transfers on development. The targeted current transfers are transfers provided during a 3-year period of the transfers of a general character. They are provided from a higher budget to a lower budget to compensate for losses of the lower budget due to the adoption of legislative acts, entailing an increase in costs and/or a reduction of local incomes. They are also provided from a lower budget to a higher budget to compensate for losses of the higher budget due to the adoption of legislative acts, entailing increased costs in the higher budget, or due to a redistribution of government functions in public administration. The targeted transfers on development are transfers provided by a higher budget to a lower budget to implement local investment programs, limited to the amounts approved in the republican or in regional budgets.[81]

Credit Rating of Local Governments

Almaty City is the only subnational government with an active credit rating (BBB, stable outlook by Fitch Ratings). The affirmation reflects Fitch's expectations that the city's credit quality will remain sound over the 2021–2025 rating horizon. Fitch expects that despite the increased 2020 debt burden, which was partly triggered by the coronavirus pandemic, the city's debt sustainability will remain strong under Fitch's rating case scenario and commensurate with a Standalone Credit Profile (SCP) of *BBB+,* above Kazakhstan's sovereign international depository receipts (BBB/Stable).[82]

Case Study

Despite the abundance of small, regional PPP projects, reliable information is lacking on their sponsors, costs, finance structures, and key contract features.

---

[81]   Budget Code of Republic of Kazakhstan of December 25, 2017., No. 120-VI ZRK. https://adilet.zan.kz/eng/docs/K080000095_#:~:text=121-V (in Russian). Chapter 7. Articles 45 and 46.
[82]   Fitch Ratings. 2022. City of Almaty. https://www.fitchratings.com/entity/almaty-city-of-80613022.

Appendix

Critical Macroeconomic and Infrastructure Sector Indicators for Kazakhstan

Parameter	Value	Unit
Total population (2021)	19.0	million
Average annual population growth rate	1.4	%
Population density	7	persons per square kilometer (km²) of surface area
Urban population (2021)	59.2	% of total population
Surface area	2,724.90	'000 km²
Unemployment rate (2021)	4.90	%
Proportion of population below $5.5 purchasing power parity (PPP) a day	0.4	%
Nominal gross domestic product (GDP, 2021)	193.0	$ billion
	4.5	%
Annual growth rate of GDP (2019)	4.5	%
Annual growth rate of GDP (2020)	–2.5	%
Annual growth rate of GDP (2021)	4.3	%
GDP at purchasing power parity per capita (2020)	24,410.0	$
GDP at current market prices	152.70	$ billion
Gross fixed investment at current market prices (2021)	26.7	% of GDP
Per capita gross national income (GNI), Atlas Method (2020)	8,710	$
Inflation rate (2019)	5.30	%
Inflation rate (2020)	6.80	%
Inflation rate (2021)	8.0	%
Current account (2021)	–3.0	% of GDP
External trade, goods, value of imports, CIF (2016)	25.38	$ billion
External trade, goods, value of exports, FOB (2016)	36.73	$ billion

continued on next page

continued from previous page

Parameter	Value	Unit
CPI % change over 2019	UA	% of CPI in 2019
Real effective exchange rate	UA	
Investment in energy with private sector participation	28.20	Current $ million
Investment in transport with private sector participation	NA	Current $ million
Investment in water and sanitation with private sector participation	NA	Current $ million
Logistics Performance Index rank	44	Number
Logistics Performance Index score	3.18	Number
Customs rank	40	Number
Customs score	2.96	Number
Infrastructure rank	52	Number
Infrastructure score	2.91	Number
International shipments rank	44	Number
International shipments score	3.21	Number
Logistics competence rank	42	Number
Logistics competence score	3.13	Number
Tracking and tracing rank	38	Number
Tracking and tracing score	3.32	Number
Timeliness rank	52	Number
Timeliness score	3.50	Number
Structure of Output (% of GDP at current producer | basic prices, 2021)		
Agriculture	5.1	%
Industry	35.4	%
Services	53.6	%
Consumer price index (national)	5.30	% annual change
Producer price index	19.00	% annual change
Wholesale price index (national)	5.10	% annual change
Retail price index	6.90	% annual change
Exchange rates (end of period)	384.20	Local currency: $
ADB Portfolio		
Total number of loans	6,438.8	43
1. Sovereign	5,835.22 60.00	28 (OCR loans) 4 (ADF loans)
2. Non-sovereign	543.58	11
Net loan amount	1,135.50	$ million, cumulative
1. Sovereign	1,055.30	$ million, cumulative
2. Non-sovereign	80.20	$ million, cumulative

continued on next page

continued from previous page

Parameter	Value	Unit
Disbursed amount	125.20	$ million, cumulative
1. Sovereign	NA	$ million, cumulative
2. Non-sovereign	NA	$ million, cumulative
Net foreign direct investment (FDI) inflows	2.70	% of GDP
Sovereign debt risk rating	47.00	Letter rating
Central government debt	16.80	% of GDP
CPIA quality of budgetary and financial management rating	NA	1=low to 6=high
Ease of Doing Business		
Ease of doing business rank	25	Number
Starting a business (rank)	22	Number
Dealing with construction permits (rank)	37	Number
Getting electricity (rank)	67	Number
Registering property (rank)	24	Number
Getting credit (rank)	25	Number
Protecting minority investors (rank)	7	Number
Paying taxes (rank)	64	Number
Trading across borders (rank)	105	Number
Enforcing contracts (rank)	4	Number
Resolving insolvency (rank)	42	Number
Corruption and Sustainable Development Index		
Corruption Perceptions Index rank (out of 180)	113	Number
Corruption Perceptions Index score (out of 100)	34	Number
Sustainable Development Index rank	65.00	Number
Sustainable Development Index score	71.06	Number
Cumulative Lending, Grant, and Technical Assistance Commitments		
Number of projects	145	Number
Total lending	6,499.6	$ million
GCI infrastructure score	4.20	out of 7
EIU Infrascope Index Score		
PPP regulations score (out of 100)	54	Number
PPP regulations rank	42	Number
PPP institutions score (out of 100)	86	Number
PPP institutions rank	13	Number
PPP market maturity score (out of 100)	48	Number
PPP market maturity rank	55	Number

continued on next page

continued from previous page

Parameter	Value	Unit
PPP financing score (out of 100)	41	Number
PPP financing rank	35	Number
Investment and business climate score (out of 100)	72	Number
Investment and business climate rank	15	Number

CIF = cost, insurance, and freight; CPI = consumer price index; EIU = Economist Intelligence Unit; FOB = free on board; GCI = global competitive index; GDP = gross domestic product; GNI = gross national income; NA = not applicable; PPP = public–private partnership; UA = unavailable.

Note: EIU Infrascope ranks are at regional (Asia) level.

Sources: ADB. 2021. *Basic Statistics 2021*. Manila. https://www.adb.org/publications/basic-statistics-2021; ADB. 2020. *Key Indicators for Asia and Pacific 2020*. Manila. https://www.adb.org/publications/key-indicators-asia-and-pacific-2020; ADB. GDP Growth in Asia and the Pacific, Asian Development Outlook (ADO). https://data.adb.org/dataset/gdp-growth-asia-and-pacific-asian-development-outlook (accessed 18 October 2022); IMF. https://data.imf.org/?sk=85b51b5a-b74f-473a-be16-49f1786949b3 (accessed 18 October 2022); IMF. Exchange Rate Selected Indicators. https://data.imf.org/regular.aspx?key=61545850 (accessed 18 October 2022); World Bank. Logistics Performance Index Rankings 2018. https://lpi.worldbank.org/international/global?sort=asc&order=LPI%20 Score#datatable; ADB. 2017. *Kazakhstan: Country Partnership Strategy, 2017–2021*. https://www.adb.org/sites/default/files/institutional-document/357421/cps-kaz-2017-2021.pdf; World Bank Group. 2020. *Doing Business 2020. Ease of Doing Business in Kazakhstan*. https://www.doingbusiness.org/en/data/exploreeconomies/kazakhstan; Transparency International. Countries. https://www.transparency.org/en/countries/kazakhstan#; Sustainable Development Report. https://dashboards.sdgindex.org/rankings; ADB. Cumulative Lending, Grant, and Technical Assistance Commitments. https://data.adb.org/dataset/cumulative-lending-grant-and-technical-assistance-commitments (accessed 18 October 2022); PPP Legal Resource Center. Kazakhstan. https://ppp.worldbank.org/public-private-partnership/country-profile-kazakhstan; The Economist Intelligence Unit. Kazakhstan. https://infrascope.eiu.com/.

www.ingramcontent.com/pod-product-compliance
Lightning Source LLC
Chambersburg PA
CBHW050044220326
41599CB00045B/7276